"The U-boat Archive"

Countermeasures against U-boats
Monthly Reviews

Countermeasures against U-boats
Monthly Reviews

Reproduced from the secret
Anti - Submarine Reports
which were released by the
British Anti - Submarine Warfare Division of the Naval Staff
throughout the Second World War for limited distribution to selected officers.

Edited by
Jak P. Mallmann Showell

For the
International Submarine Archive (U-Boot-Archiv)
in Germany and produced in conjunction with
The Royal Navy Submarine Museum
in Gosport (England) and with
The Bletchley Park Trust
in Bletchley, Milton Keynes (England)

Reprinted with kind permission of
Her Majesty's Stationery Office

This volume is sent free to 'English Language'
Friends of Traditionsarchiv Unterseeboote (U-Boot-Archiv)
'German Language' members receive a different journal, also
containing extracts from documents in the Archive's collection.

Any members wishing to contribute further annotations for this volume with the
possibility of adding more pages at a later date please contact the editor
Jak P. Mallmann Showell,
3 Sandpiper Road, Hawkinge, Folkestone, Kent CT18 7TA, England
Telephone 01303 893606

Further information about the U-Boot-Archiv is also available.

Other publications in The U-boat Archive Series

The U-boat Archive   -   -   November 2002
Volume 3

Countermeasures
against U-boats
Monthly Reviews

Annotated extracts from
Secret British Wartime Anti - Submarine Reports

Edited by
Jak P. Mallmann Showell

For
U-boot-Archiv, 27478 Cuxhaven – Altenbruch, Germany
and produced in conjunction with
The Royal Navy Submarine Museum
and
The Bletchley Park Trust

Military Press

This edition of The U-boat Archive Series,
Countermeasures against U-boats (Monthly Reviews)
was first published by The Military Press in 2002

Military Press
1 Gallagher Close
Milton Keynes
Buckinghamshire MK80LQ England

This edition 2002

ISBN 0-85420-091-6 [Cased Edition]
ISBN 0-85420-301-X [Paper Edition]

U-Boot-Archiv
Bahnhofstrasse 57, 27478 Cuxhaven – Altenbruch, Germany
Telephone: 04722 322
(Lines open between 9-12 hours, German Time on Mondays, Tuesdays, Thursdays and Fridays.
The Archive is usually closed between Christmas and the end of February)

The Royal Navy Submarine Museum
Haslar Jetty Road, Gosport PO12 2AS, England
Telephone 023 925 10354 Extension 226
e-mail: archives@rnsubmus.co.uk

The Bletchley Park Trust
The Mansion, Bletchley Park, Bletchley, Milton Keynes MK3 6EF, England
Telephone: 01908 640404

The U-Boot-Archiv does not receive any form of official funding and relies entirely on visitors, friends and archive users for its income. There are no paid employees and helpers provide their services on a voluntary basis, often also paying their own expenses. Please bear this in mind when approaching the Archive and, if you find anything you don't like, please don't complain but volunteer to improve it.

The U-Boot-Archiv also produces a German language journal DAS ARCHIV containing extracts from documents in its collection.

The Monthly Anti - Submarine Reports

The Monthly Anti-Submarine Reports, circulated secretly to selected officers throughout the war, were a major weapon in the all important distribution of information for the Battle of the Atlantic.

Sadly, most of these reports vanished into obscurity once hostilities ceased and the surviving copies left in military libraries were eventually recalled for destruction, rather than being declassified for free access. However, the few remaining volumes in public archives are now a major primary resource for anyone studying U-boats and the Battle of the Atlantic.

Each month's Report included summaries of the latest developments in The U-boat Offensive and the Countermeasures taken to combat the threat.

This volume contains reprints of the majority of monthly Countermeasure Summaries while the next edition will deal with the U-boat Offensive.

Please bear in mind that these reports were written over a period of more than six years by a substantial number of contributors and both spellings and terms used varied considerably. It has been most tempting to standardise these for this reprint, but it is thought the information is more authentic if the original idiosyncrasies are left as they were first printed.

The original text is in the standard font and
post-war information has been added in italics.

CONTENTS
The Monthly Reviews have been organised chronologically by year and within the year by month

Additional information has come from the following sources:

Busch, Rainer and Röll, Hans-Joachim; **Die deutschen U-Boot-Kommandanten 1939-1945**, Verlag E.S.Mittler & Sohn, Hamburg, Berlin, Bonn 1996. Translated as **U-boat Commanders**, Greenhill Books, London. Sadly the translation was made from an uncorrected copy and the information in this volume was taken from a copy kept in the U-Boot-Archiv containing latest corrections.

Hessler, Günther and others, although published anonymously by HMSO, London,1989 as **The U-boat War in the Atlantic**. This work includes charts with details of wolf pack formation and details of which U-boats were at sea on any particular day.

Kemp, Paul; **U-boats Destroyed**, Arms and Armour, London 1997. Although some information in this book is superseded by more recent research by Axel Niestlé, it is based on the Secret Anti-Submarine Reports and contains interesting, explanatory comments.

McCartney, Innes; **Submarine Wrecks of the English Channel**, Periscope Publishing, 33 Barwis Terrace, Penzance TR18 8AW, 2002 with details of visited U-boats wrecks.

Niestlé, Axel; **German U-boat Losses during World War II**; Greenhill Books, London 1998.

Rohwer, Jürgen; **Axis Submarine Successes of World War Two**; Greenhill Books, London and US Naval Institute Press 1999.

Unpublished U-Boot-Archiv, files.

We are grateful to Richard Thwaites for helping with this production.

Attention is called to the penalties attaching to any
Infraction of the Official Secrets Acts.

Monthly
Anti-Submarine Reports

Anti-Submarine Warfare Division of the Naval Staff

British counter measures in general followed the lines that had been adopted in September. It is impracticable to trace the movements of A/S craft throughout the month, but tables showing the distribution of destroyers, patrol vessels, escort vessels and A/S trawlers are given for the 1st, 15th and 30th October.

Owing to the improved political relations with Italy, many anti-submarine vessels were moved towards British waters during the month.

There was a considerable increase in the number of A/S trawlers brought into service, 65 being in operation at the end of the month. Others are working up at their bases.

In addition to these trawlers, 31 yachts have been taken up for local A/S duties. These were fitted at first with depth charges only for use inside the protection of shore defences. It is the intention to carry out a full conversion of these ships in due course; this will entail the fitting of asdics and the mounting of a gun. Four are at present converted.

It is to be noted that the destroyers for convoy duties in the Western Approaches have been based at Plymouth, Milford Haven and Liverpool.

During the month under review, the number of collisions and mechanical breakdowns in A/S vessels was largely due to the severe strain on personnel and material in bad weather.

Distribution of A/S Forces on 1st October 1939

Command	Destroyers	Escort / Patrol vessels	A/S trawlers	Damaged, boiler cleaning & refitting
Home Fleet	16	-	-	1 destroyer
Humber Force	3	-	-	2 destroyers (collision)
Mediterranean	31	5	5	1 destroyer
North Atlantic	8	-	-	1 destroyer
China	6	7	-	-
South Atlantic	4	4	-	-
America & West Indies	-	2	-	-
East Indies	-	8	-	-
Australia	5	2	-	-
RCN E. Coast	4	-	-	-
RCN W. Coast	2	-	-	-
Portsmouth	12	-	5	2 destroyers
Dover	5	3*	-	3 destroyers
Western Approaches	46	-	3	-
Belfast	6	-	-	6
Rosyth	7	6	3	1 destroyer
Portland	-	-	11	-
Sheerness	-	-	1	-
Tynemouth	-	-	1	-
Ardrossan	-	-	4	-
Milford Haven	-	-	2	-

Note — This table does not show destroyers undergoing long refits nor those being converted to escort vessels.

Distribution of A/S Forces on 15th October 1939

Command	Destroyers	Escort / Patrol vessels	A/S trawlers	Damaged, boiler cleaning & refitting
Home Fleet	17	-	-	3
Humber Force	-	-	-	-
Mediterranean	16	4	5	1
North Atlantic	9	-	-	-
China	6	7	-	-
South Atlantic	9	4	-	-
America & West Indies	-	2	-	-
E. Indies	2	8	-	-
Australia	5	2	-	-
RCN E. Coast	4	-	-	-
RCN W. Coast	2	-	-	-
Portsmouth	9	-	5	-
Dover	6	2	6	1 escort 2 destroyers
Western Approaches	40	1	3	6
Belfast	-	7*	-	-
Rosyth	19	6	3	5
Portland	1	-	36	-
Sheerness	-	-	2	-
Tynemouth	-	-	3	-
Ardrossan	-	-	4	-
Milford Haven	-	-	1	-
Leith	-	-	1	-
Larne	-	-	4	-
Yarmouth	-	-	2	-
Harwich	-	-	-	-

Distribution of A/S Forces on 31st October 1939

Command	Destroyers	Escort / Patrol vessels	A/S trawlers	Damaged, boiler cleaning & refitting
Home Fleet	23	-	-	4
Humber Force	-	2*	-	-
Mediterranean	7	3	5	-
North Atlantic	9	-	-	-
China	10	8	-	-
South Atlantic	5	4	-	-
America & West Indies	4	2	-	-
E. Indies	2	8	-	-
Australia	-	2	-	-
RCN E. Coast	4	-	-	-
RCN W. Coast	2	-	-	-
Portsmouth	7	-	5	1 destroyer
Dover	1	-	18	1 patrol vessel
Western Approaches	39	-	3	11 destroyers
Belfast	-	-	-	2
Rosyth	19	6	3	5 destroyers
Portland	-	-	27	-
Sheerness	-	-	4	-
Tynemouth	-	-	9	-
Ardrossan	-	-	4	-
Milford Haven	-	-	4	-
Leith	-	-	5	5
Orkneys	-	-	6	-
Yarmouth	-	-	2	-
Harwich	17	-	7	-

Note — These tables do not show destroyers undergoing long refits nor those being converted to escort vessels.

2

There has been no radical departure from the principles adopted at the beginning of the war to combat the submarine menace. A new form of submarine control for the west coast of Ireland and Lewis has, however, been inaugurated with the object of attacking the submarines as they make their landfalls and departure's. From the tables of the distribution of the anti-submarine forces it can be seen that in November we continued to withdraw A/S vessels from distant stations and concentrate them nearer home.

The number of light craft and destroyers in particular, which appear on paper as being available at any given moment for escort and hunting duties is very deceptive. Small repairs due to collision, heavy weather, machinery defects and minor overhauls continually reduce the effective strength. An example of this was given in a signal by the Commander-in-Chief Home Fleet in the last days of November when he reported 45 per cent, of his destroyers as unfit for sea.

There has been a considerable decrease in the number of attacks on U-boats, since the mine-laying U-boat is much more difficult to locate; it does not give its position away like the U-boat that uses torpedoes or gunfire.

The completion and commissioning of A/S trawlers has been proceeding satisfactorily during the month, and on the 1st December 96 trawlers were at the operational base, and a further 23 were working up at Portland. In addition 15 of the 30 armed A/S yachts taken up are either being or have been fitted with Asdics. A new anti-submarine school is being started to assist with the training of operators.

January / February 1940

Summary of Allied Counter Measures

Allied counter measures fall under five headings:—
(a)   Convoys.
(b)   Striking forces.
(c)   Local defence forces.
(d)   Fixed defences.
(e)   Mined areas and barrages.
(f)   Building programme.

(a) Convoys escorted by A/S vessels. — At the moment the convoy system is probably the most effective anti-submarine measure, for in order to attack, the U-Boat must disclose itself within striking distance of the asdic-fitted escort vessels.

(b) Striking forces. — The duty of the striking forces is to take offensive action against U-Boats and search for all that are reported within their reach. When not actually hunting they are a source of anxiety to U-Boats in their vicinity.

(c) Local defence. — Experience gained in the last war, and up to date in this war, shows that this is the least profitable method of employing A/S vessels. It is an easy matter for the U-Boat to see the patrolling vessels before she is herself detected. On the other hand, although the U-Boat may not be sunk by these patrols, she may be deterred from achieving her object.

(d) Fixed defences. — The defence of harbours consists of booms, indicator loops, controlled minefields, and harbour defence asdics. A/S vessels are stationed behind indicator loops, to attack the U-Boat after it has crossed the loop. In order to reduce the number of attacking vessels required, the harbour defence asdic is used to supplement these vessels by locating the U-Boat and informing the attacking vessel of its position. Under-water defences are being designed and improved to resist the attack of very small U-Boats should these be used against us. Efforts are also being made to design fixed defences to detect U-Boats before they reach areas suitable for magnetic mine-laying.

(e) Mined areas and barrages. — On the outbreak of war, the Dover Mine-Barrage was commenced. The whole barrage is patrolled by destroyers and trawlers and is illuminated at night.

The East Coast barrage, extending from the Thames to the Moray Firth, is designed as a protection against U-Boats and surface raiders. Though not yet completely laid, it has up to date had the desired effect, in that submarines, except when mine-laying, have restricted their activities almost entirely to its northern entrance.

(f) Building programme. — The present building programme provides vessels suitable for convoy escort, striking forces, and local defence. It consists roughly of 67 A/S vessels of the destroyer type, 92 corvettes and sloops, 43 trawlers and 200 motor launches.

Brief Review of Anti-Submarine Operations in the first Six Months of the War

Convoy system. — The outstanding point in anti-submarine operations has been the success of the convoy system against direct attacks by U-Boats. This success was by no means unexpected, as experience in the last war proved the great value of the system. Out of 164 ships that have been sunk by U-Boats during these first six months, only seven were in convoys which were escorted by A/S vessels. An eighth convoyed ship was hit, but reached harbour.

These results have been achieved in spite of the fact that the A/S escort rarely consisted of more than two vessels, and frequently only one. It would appear, therefore, that the U-Boat has a marked antipathy against attacking convoys, preferring lone Neutrals, and stragglers from convoys. The reason for this is obvious when it is remembered that the convoy provides one of the best kinds of "bait," for if the attack on it is successful, the U-Boat reveals her presence within reach of one or more A/S vessels.

March / April 1940

The lull in the activities of the U-Boats has led naturally to a lull in anti-submarine operations during March.

The Orkneys and Shetlands area has been an exception. Here the U-Boats took advantage of the full moon between the 19th and the 25th March, to sink ten ships. Nine of these were unescorted neutrals; the one escorted ship to be sunk was the tanker "Daghestan," which was escorted by one A/S trawler. The U-Boat (*U57 : Kptlt. Claus Korth*) was not located.

On the 8th March, the armed trawler "Northern Reward," when 100 miles west of the Shetlands sighted and attacked in very heavy weather, and nearly collided with a U-Boat, steering an opposite course. The periscope being sighted only 30 feet distant on the starboard bow.

The same day two armed fishing trawlers, "Clayton Wyke" and "Chiltern," sighted the conning tower of a submarine, cut away their fishing gear and forced the U-Boat under by gunfire.

The Bomber Command carried out two successful attacks on U-Boats on the-surface; securing hits in each case.

In addition to the A/S forces, which consisted chiefly of trawlers, the Home Fleet destroyers were employed almost exclusively off Norway. One U-Boat was sunk and two more may have been either sunk or damaged.

The reason why our destroyers did not sink more U-Boats was probably because they were employed mainly on screening and escort duties, not for hunting. On only one occasion was a specific A/S search undertaken: this was carried out by four destroyers, a number insufficient to search a wide area. The 38 A/S trawlers employed on the Norwegian coast were limited to local defence and suffered intense air attack. Eleven were sunk and several damaged. The air menace was so great that A/S trawlers were often forced to take cover under the cliffs by day.

A/S Trawlers in Norwegian Waters

Eight A/S trawlers were sent to Narvik, 16 to Namsos, and 12 to Molde / Andalsnes. Intense day bombing resulted in the loss of seven trawlers at Molde / Andalsnes and four at Namsos, most of the remainder being damaged.The majority of the sinkings were caused by bombs dropping close alongside, which started leaks and also damaged the cast iron fittings in the engine room.

During the five days prior to the evacuation of southern Norway, overwhelming air attack was directed against any craft attempting to move by day. High level, low level, dive bombing and machine-gun fire was employed. The military situation was critical, wireless communication was bad and the trawlers were required to stand by for evacuation. The problem was therefore how to preserve the trawlers in order that they would be available to maintain communications, give A/S protection and carry out evacuation during the short hours of darkness. This was achieved by hiding them by day on the shady side of the fiord under the lee of steep hills and trees and thus making them the least inviting of the available bomber targets. Fires were banked and the crews removed to avoid any movement on deck being seen from the air.

The month of May opened very quietly and inactivity continued with few interruptions throughout the month, a natural result of the inactivity of the U-Boats.

Thirty-eight hunts by surface craft have been reported during the month, and in at least four of these a U-Boat was certainly present.

In one case the hunt resulted from a search by six A/S vessels which had been initiated as the result of a periscope sighting.

In another case, a destroyer sighted a U-Boat at night just as she was submerging, and immediately attacked. A third hunt followed the shelling of the "Dunster Grange." (*By U37 : Victor Oehrn*) Four A/S vessels were sent to search the area and one of them ("Rochester") was missed by a torpedo. She immediately gained contact and carried out three attacks.

The fourth hunt was the result of an asdic contact. In addition to the above, one definite success can be recorded. .On the 30th of May, H.M.S. "Weston," escorting an East Coast convoy, sighted "U13" (*Oblt.z.S. Max Schulte*) at 2209 hours and hunted her until she surrendered about three hours later.

Eleven aircraft attacks on U-Boats were made during the month, seven of which were made by the Coastal Command.

Coastal Command Operations

Total hours flown by Coastal Command	14,522
Total miles flown by Coastal Command	1,887,860
Hours on purely A/S patrols	2,576
Miles on purely A/S patrols	334,880
Hours on convoy duty	5,754
Miles on convoy duty	748,020
Number of convoys provided with escort	222
Total hours on other duty	6,190
Total miles on other duty	804,960
U-Boats sighted	19
U-Boats attacked	7

The greater number of U-Boat sightings have occurred in the southern North Sea, where the Coastal Command have been flying intensively in connection with the land operations, to guard against possible invasion and attacks on sea lines of communication.

A/S patrols have once again been flown mainly in the North. During the latter part of the month, however, these have been slightly reduced to allow of a greater concentration of aircraft in the South to meet requirements in that area. "Scarecrow" patrols, with the object of hampering U-Boats on passage, have been flown regularly.

A "Scarecrow" patrol is one undertaken with an aircraft of little military value with the object of reporting and hampering the movements of U-Boats.

Although U-Boat activity was intense during the month of June, particularly in the Western Approaches, there was not a corresponding intensity of A/S Operations. This was due to the lack of A/S Vessels. Military exigencies requiring small craft for evacuation duties left only the bare minimum of A/S Vessels for escort duties and practically none for use as striking or searching forces.

Throughout the month bolder attacks were made on British convoys, and eight ships were sunk: but these attacks occurred beyond the rendezvous where convoys are met by local escorts and in no case was an A/S Escort in company when the attack was made.

In the middle of June, with the object of using the small number of A/S Vessels available to the best advantage, two A/S patrols were temporarily established in the Western Approaches. Each consisted of two destroyers. One patrol was between Ushant and the Lizzard and the other between Ushant and the Loire, both areas in which U-Boats had been active. These patrols achieved no success and were discontinued after about ten days.

Twenty bombing attacks were made by aircraft during June and in four cases direct hits were reported.

Attacks on Italian U-Boats

A large number of A/S operations have been carried out against Italian U-Boats and the results have been most satisfactory, although poor asdic results were expected in the warm waters of the Mediterranean and Red Sea at this time of the year.

In many cases, energetic action has resulted in the U-Boats being surprised on the surface.

During June, six Italian U-Boats were destroyed in the Mediterranean and five in the Red Sea. Full accounts of these actions have not yet been received.

U-Boats are more easily sighted from the air in the clear waters of the Mediterranean, and a large number of attacks by aircraft have occurred.

German U-Boats sunk — proportion of total ascribed to various causes

	Known Sunk. per cent
Convoy Escorts	25
Independent Operations	29.17
Screening	8.33
On Patrol	8.33
Submarine	4.17
Aircraft	4.17
Mines	8.33
Marine Risk	4. 17
Cause of loss unknown	8.33

Upon the occupation of Northern France by the Germans, is was decided to route convoys through the North-Western Approaches instead of through the Western Approaches as heretofore.

Owing to a reduction of commitments elsewhere, it became possible to reinforce the escort forces in the Western Approaches Command.

However, although U-Boats were active and the number of ships sunk was high, few U-Boats were intercepted and only ten hunts, took place in which a U-Boat is believed to have been present; of these, two were known to be successful.

Eleven attacks were made on U-Boats by aircraft of the Coastal Command.

The East Coast Mine Barrier has considerably reduced U-Boat activity in the North Sea, and throughout July no ships were torpedoed in this area.

As a result of our successful A/S operations against their U-Boats in June, the Italians have become more wary. However, in two attacks off Malta one U-Boat was probably sunk and another seriously damaged. It is expected that Asdic conditions in the Mediterranean will improve considerably with the colder weather.

The curtailment of routine A/S patrols in favour of anti-invasion patrols was continued throughout July and the anti-invasion patrols accounted for the majority of U-Boat sightings.

The discrepancy between the number of U-Boats sighted and those attacked is explained by the fact that either there were surface craft in company which were attacked in preference to the U-Boats, or that the aircraft carried no antisubmarine bombs.

Previously only U-Boats seen at periscope depth or above were counted by Coastal Command for the purposes of their statistics: this month, however, there have been a number of occasions on which patrols have bombed oil streaks suspected as coming from U-Boats.

During this month Coastal Command have used the naval depth charge modified for air use, although so far without known success. Sunderland aircraft now carry both depth charges and bombs when patrolling.

The daily average of convoys escorted was 16.

August 1940

The intensive attacks on convoys continued during August and U-Boat activity was still concentrated in North-Western Approaches, but attacks on U-Boats were made in many areas.

In the North Sea Dutch submarines made three attacks on U-Boats which were leaving Germany.

A total of 32 attacks were made by surface vessels during August: in 9 cases a U-Boat was known to have been present.

The Fleet Air Arm operated successfully against Italian U-Boats in harbour, Swordfish aircraft using torpedoes.

The number of sightings by aircraft, which have been confirmed as U-Boats by other sources, has been considerable and Sunderland aircraft of the Coastal Command made their first successful depth charge attack on a U-Boat.

During the past few months, both Britain and Germany have made increasing use of aircraft as a counter to submarines. Though suffering from many limitations for A/S operations, the aeroplane possesses obvious advantages denied to many surface vessels, e.g., speed, cheapness, large field of vision and economy of personnel and material. Another asset of aircraft is their ability to take cover in clouds and emerge as frequently as necessary to scan the entire area they are patrolling.

A submarine on the surface can rely on the fact that she will, almost certainly, sight an enemy surface vessel before she herself is seen. The chief dangers which she has to fear are those beneath the surface or in the air. The "harrying" effect of aircraft on a patrolling submarine should not be underrated; reports from our own submarine officers, who have recently completed many arduous patrols off the Norwegian Coast, confirm this.

Coastal Command Operations

	July	August
Total hours flown by Coastal Command	15,212	13,676
Total miles flown by Coastal Command	1,977,560	1,777,880
Hours on purely A/S Patrol	2,020	1,363
Miles on purely A/S patrol	262,600	203,970
Hours on convoy duty	5,850	6,699
Number of convoys provided with escort	176	179
U-Boats sighted	22	32
U-Boats attacked	11	20

Since the transfer of shipping routes to North-Western Approaches, aircraft have escorted convoys further into the Atlantic; therefore, the time spent on this duty exceeds the previous month's return by 849 hours.

Of the 12 sightings made without attack, in six instances U-Boats dived before an attack could be delivered: on four occasions the aircraft sighting were on convoy A/S duty and reported to surface escort vessels who took action. One sighting was by an aircraft that was not suitably armed, and another failed to relocate the U-Boat, owing to low visibility.

Naval depth charges, modified for use in Sunderland aircraft, are believed to have obtained their first success on August 16th, when a U-Boat is thought to have been sunk by an aircraft of 210 Squadron in position 24° St. Kilda, 164 miles. A further possible sinking is recorded on the 29th August when a Sunderland of the same squadron delivered an attack in co-operation with H.M.S. "Mackay," in position 277° Oban 130 miles. In view of the initial successes obtained by Sunderlands, modifications are in progress to other Coastal Command aircraft which will enable them also to carry depth charges, when it is expected the lethal value of air attack against U-Boats will be considerably increased. (*No U-boats were lost this month, so both boats survived.*)

The main pre-occupation of our naval forces in Home Waters was the threat of sea-borne invasion. This necessarily confined large numbers of our destroyers to the East and South Coasts. As Enemy U-Boat activity was concentrated almost exclusively in the North Western Approaches, this reacted unfavourably on our Anti-Submarine operations.

In spite of this, however, the increase in the numbers of A/S vessels available for convoy escort duties in the North Western Approaches, which was recorded in August, was maintained. This was largely due to the number of new corvettes and new or converted A/S trawlers which came into service during the month. In the middle of the month these increases suffered a temporary set back due to the withdrawal, for anti-invasion duties, of a number of trawlers from the Belfast trawler force, however, the net increase at the end of the month was 11 ships.

The fitting of depth charges instead of bombs in aircraft engaged on operations is being continued as rapidly as possible.

Forty-nine attacks on U-Boats or supposed U-Boats were made; thirty-two being carried out by warships, nine by submarine, six by aircraft and two by merchant ships, who had previously been unsuccessfully attacked.

U-Boat attacks on convoys during the month were, in nearly every case, made at night. There is strong evidence that the attacks have been made on the surface, generally from a position broad on the bow of the convoy, and that the U-Boat has then withdrawn on the surface, at high speed, in the direction of her original approach.

The measures taken to counter these new tactics included re-disposition of the convoy escorts in positions down each wing, and at a greater distance from the convoy than heretofore, and the issuing of instructions to the escorts concerning their action in the event of attack. These instructions directed escorts to proceed outwards from the convoy at full speed, firing star shell to illuminate the area where the U-Boat might be, in an attempt to sight or force her to submerge and improve the chances of asdic detection.

Another change made during this month was the taking over by the Admiralty of responsibility for the routeing of all ocean-going convoys, thus enabling emergency changes to be made without delay, when, information was obtained of the presence of U-Boats near convoy routes.

In order that the efficacy of our counter-measures may be continually kept under review and improved without delay, a weekly meeting at the Admiralty, attended by Officers responsible for the organisation and administration of convoy escort forces in the North Western Approaches, was instituted. The first meeting was held on 1st October.

Thirty-five attacks on U-Boats or supposed U-Boats were made during the month. Eighteen of these by surface ships, four by submarines and thirteen by aircraft.

This month has been devoted to developing and improving measures taken to counter day and night U-Boat attacks on convoys. To this end changes have been made both in the dispositions of convoys and of their escorts.

Great efforts are being made to equip all convoy escorts with apparatus which will enable them to locate a U-Boat on the surface at night outside visibility distance. As more ships are fitted, dispositions will be changed so as to make the maximum use of this aid.

This new equipment has also been fitted into aircraft of Coastal Command and Fleet Air Arm. It will detect U-Boats on the surface up to a range of 15 miles, and will be especially valuable for detecting U-Boats on the surface at night.

It is hoped that depth charges will be carried by the aircraft, but in any event the enemy can be forced under and kept submerged until the arrival of asdic fitted ships, or until he is compelled to surface to re-charge batteries.

The transfer of all convoy routes to the North Western Approaches in July led to considerable difficulty in the provision of air escorts for convoys, owing to the lack of adequate landing ground facilities in that area; these difficulties are being surmounted and it is now becoming possible to operate aircraft at night for convoy escort work. It is intended to provide the maximum air escort for three hours before darkness falls, as this is the period in which U-Boats take up their shadowing positions, preparatory to night attack.

The high percentage of hits recently obtained by U-Boats in night attacks has made it necessary to increase the distance apart of convoy columns from three cables to five cables. This materially reduces the theoretical chances of more than one ship being hit by a salvo. (*One cable's length was originally 100 fathoms, which equalled 182 metres. However the British military tended measure one cable as being 608 feet or 185.3 metres, while the United States took one cable to be 720 feet or 219.5 metres*)

The following measures are employed by convoy escorts against the enemy tactics:—

By Day
On an attack being made, escorts on each side of the convoy form on line of bearing on the mean line of advance of the convoy, ships 2,500 yards apart, then move to a position three miles in rear of the convoy, turn outwards together 90° and sweep in line abreast for one hour. All ships drop depth charges on the initial turn and further depth charges every two miles of the sweep. If by this time no contact has been obtained, escorts re-join the convoy.

By Night
Escorts are disposed in line ahead 3,000 yards apart at visibility distance from the convoy. In the event of attack, all ships on the engaged side, or on both sides if the side of attack is in doubt, turn 90° outwards together and proceed at full speed for a distance of 10 miles from the convoy, firing star shell to illuminate the area. Destroyers are stationed in van and rear positions where possible.

Coastal Command Operations	September	October
Total hours flown by Coastal Command	13,787	11,858
Total miles flown by Coastal Command	1,792,310	1,541,540
Hours on purely Anti-Submarine Patrol	1,792	1,811
Miles on purely Anti-Submarine Patrol	224,770	235,430
Hours on Convoy duty	5,986	5,700
Number of convoys provided with escort	778,180	741,000
U-Boats sighted	18	18
U-Boats attacked	10	10

SEPTEMBER

The flying time during September was divided between Anti-Invasion Patrols, reconnaissance and offensive operations.

In six cases of submarine sightings the aircraft either carried no A/S bombs or was in the vicinity of a convoy and summoned surface hunters. In two cases the U-Boat dived too quickly for an attack to be made.

OCTOBER

The decrease in the total of hours flown in October is mainly attributed to longer hours of darkness.

Some promising attacks on U-Boats were made during this month by aircraft of the Command.

The Photographic Reconnaissance Unit have contributed valuable information concerning the location and activity of various enemy submarine bases and building yards. The ensuing bombing attacks may curtail enemy submarine.

November 1940

Twenty-six attacks on U-Boats or supposed U-Boats were made during November. Nineteen of these by surface ships, four by submarine and thirteen by aircraft. (*The number 26 has been corrected by pen to 36*)

Day

No great change has taken place or is envisaged in the tactics to be adopted against U-Boats by day.

Night

At night escorts are disposed in line ahead 3,000 yards apart at visibility distance from the convoy. Thus a U-Boat attempting an attack may well be sighted or heard by hydrophone effect before she reaches a firing position. If she gets through the escort unobserved and undetected, the first intimation that an attack has taken place, is generally the flash or noise of a torpedo explosion.

The effect of this explosion varies considerably, and cases have occurred in which escorts only a short distance away from a U-Boat victim, have not seen or heard anything, and also when men in torpedoed vessels have not been awakened by the explosion.

For this reason, the vital importance of the torpedoed ship firing a white rocket to announce that she has been struck, has been impressed on the captains of merchant vessels. Some merchant ships have been unable to determine on which side they have been hit, or even worse, have been convinced that they have been hit on the opposite side to the true one (the use of red and blue flares has, for this reason, been discontinued).

The action to be taken by escorts in the event of a night attack on a convoy remains as established. That is to say, all escorts on the engaged side, or on both sides if the side of attack is in doubt, turn 90° outwards together and proceed at full speed for a distance of ten miles from the convoy, firing starshell over the whole arc away from the convoy to illuminate the area.

These tactics have been carefully worked out as the best measures to overcome the present methods practised by the U-Boats, but it is obvious that immediate action and close co-operation by escorts and merchant vessels is essential in order to obtain full benefit from the counter procedure.

Lack of appreciation by ships in convoy, of the vital importance of immediate indication of attack, no doubt contributed to the confusion that appears to have occurred after some attacks on convoys, such as the attack on H.X.83, but since the responsibility for destroying the enemy rests entirely upon the escorts, too much reliance should not be placed upon information from merchant ships. The importance of efficient look-out particularly on bearings abaft the beam, cannot be over-emphasized. Good eyes and constant vigilance are the most likely qualifications to achieve success.

In order to improve the tactical efficiency of the destroyers, sloops, corvettes and trawlers which now form escorts for convoys, these ships are being formed into groups to work under their own senior officers. As far as possible, ships of one group will always work together.

In the night attacks by U-Boats on our convoys we are faced with a straightforward, if difficult tactical problem, but with adequate numbers, maximum training, quick wits in appreciating the situation, good team work and inspired leadership, we shall succeed in mastering the enemy.

December 1940

The main British counter-measure against attacks on our shipping has been the adoption of a far wider degree of dispersion of our convoy routeing, both before and after the longitude at which the A/S escort joins them.

We are, in fact, relying on the principal of evasion which played so important a part in reducing the U-Boat menace in 1914 - 18.

Owing to damage incurred in heavy weather, on an average over the past month, only 50 per cent of the destroyers allocated for service in the North-Western Approaches have been at sea, or in readiness for sea, at any time. It is hoped that this position will improve and that our numbers will at last increase.

There have been thirty-four attacks on enemy U-Boats or supposed U-Boats during the month. Twenty-five of these were carried out by surface ships, seven by aircraft, and two by submarine.

H.M.S. "St. Laurent" and H.M.S. "Viscount" counter-attacked one of the German U-Boats that torpedoed ships in H.X.90.

H.M.S. "Harvester" made an attack upon the Italian U-Boat *("Argo" : Alberto Crepas)* which sank the British S.S. "Silverpine," of 5,000 tons, on the 5th December. Although her attacks probably damaged the enemy, an Italian communique stated that the U-Boat reached her base.

There were no other very decisive attacks until 14th December, when H.M.S. "Hyperion" and H.M.S. "Hereward" attacked the Italian U-Boat "Naiade." Details of this sinking are not yet available.

The two submarine attacks on U-Boats were carried out by H.M.S. "Thunderbolt" and H.M.S. "Tuna."

INSTRUCTIONS FOR CONVOY ESCORTS

Pending experience gained with R.D/F fitted ships, the 'following instructions have been issued regarding the disposition of such escorts.

By day — R.D/F escorts on bow and quarter of convoy at approximately visibility distance, manoeuvring as considered best to prevent shadowing.

By night — one R.D/F escort on each beam of convoy, at least four miles from convoy and close escort. Beam escorts to steam on same and opposite courses as convoy, to cover approach between 70° and 120° on bow, zigzagging as requisite for self-protection.

R.D/F escorts in excess of two to carry out a broad zigzag ahead and astern of convoy.

The remainder of escorts to be disposed as before, bearing in mind that at night the rear wing positions are the most important.

Constant asdic listening watch maintained; asdic transmissions at the discretion of the Commanding Officer.

If the convoy is attacked, all escorts on the engaged side, or both sides if doubt exists, turn 90° outwards together, proceeding 10 miles at full speed, firing starshell away from the convoy.

If unsuccessful, all escorts rejoin on completion of the search. If search leads to contact, two escorts hunt, the remainder rejoin the convoy.

As the coloured signal used by merchant ships to indicate the side of the ship the torpedo has hit, has been abolished, the only way in which escort vessels will know on which side of the convoy the U-boat is attacking, will be by inference from the position of the ships torpedoed.

There seems no doubt that the reduction in our shipping losses is due to the thorough diversion of convoy routes, which has been the main counter-measure against U-Boat attack for the past two months.

Losses have emphasized the danger of straggling, for the Germans resorted to the much easier task of "picking off" lone ships, rather than face the counterattacks of convoy escorts.

Every effort is being made to reduce straggling. Masters are being impressed with the dangers involved in the hope of reducing avoidable straggling. Efforts are being made to improve the quality of coal for bunkering and to improve ballasting in outward-bound convoys. Steps are also being taken to order the return of chronic stragglers before reaching the danger area, but drastic action on these lines has obvious disadvantages in reducing imports.

It must be expected that the Germans, backed by the Italians, will put out a strong U-Boat effort in the spring months, and we must make preparations accordingly.

It is hoped that the lengthening daylight hours will be to our advantage, but it should be remembered that although short nights reduce the U-Boat's chances of successful night attack, long days increase their chances of locating our convoys and shipping. This point is of importance when considering the prospects of evasive routeing. Another point of importance is the prospect of Focke-Wulf aircraft operating in the near future from bases in Southern Norway, which are at present probably snowbound.

Inter-Communication in Escort Groups

All ships working in the North-Western Approaches are now fitted with R/T for inter-communication, and it is hoped that will ensure co-ordination of movements and efficient team work in counter-attacks.

A.S.V. in Escort Ships

There can be little doubt that, as an A/S device, A.S.V. has, up to the moment, been a disappointment. Used under favourable conditions, good results can be obtained from surface ships, from the land and from aircraft, but escort ships stationed on convoys have had considerable trouble owing to confusing "back echoes" from the convoy.

It is hoped that by reducing the A.S.V. scale from 10 miles to 5 miles this trouble can be alleviated, leaving a part of the A.S.V. screen on which the approaching U-Boat can be detected, untouched by either the near echoes from waves or the far " back echoes" from the convoy.

But this is a palliative and not a cure. A newly designed aerial, screened to cut out the "back echo" has been produced by the Signal School and has now been fitted in "Legion" for trials. If this aerial operates successfully a similar design will be provided for all destroyers fitted with A.S.V.

Work on the improvement of A.S.V. is being carried on at high pressure, and it is hoped that a design may soon be evolved suitable for operation in a corvette. Meanwhile, in order to maintain the closest touch between A/S operations and the Signal School, a Lieutenant A/S has been appointed to the staff of the Captain of the Signal School.

The evasive routeing of shipping was continued with success during February, and when the Germans intensified their efforts to find our convoys, the shadowing U-Boat became our main problem.

Having contacted a convoy, the enemy takes great care not to reveal his presence by attacking in daylight, but shadows at some distance. There is, therefore, small chance of the limited escorting surface vessels discovering these U-Boats, and the task must fall to the escorting aircraft. In view of this it was decided to reinforce the number of Coastal Command aircraft available for escort duty in the North Western Approaches, and it is hoped that this measure will enable a constant A/S patrol to be maintained round every convoy. This has not been possible in the past owing to the limited number of aircraft available and the bad weather prevalent at the aircraft bases.

Steps have also been taken to deal with the co-operating German long range aircraft. "Wair" class destroyers, with powerful A.A. armament, have been sent from East Coast Routes to reinforce convoy escorts in the area of main activity.

To meet the possibility of U-Boats dodging the starshell search by our escort ships, which develops abeam of the convoy, action has been taken to search astern of the convoy, and the Commander (D) of Escort Vessels free hand to modify the existing rules for starshell search to meet any situation.

Twenty-eight attacks on U-Boats or supposed U-Boats were made during the month, 22 of these by surface vessels and six by aircraft, but the damage to the enemy was below the average.

Coastal Command Operations

	February 1941
Total hours flown by Coastal Command	6,732
Total miles flown by Coastal Command	875,160
Hours on purely A/S Patrol	440
Miles on purely A/S Patrol	57,200
Hours on Convoy duty	3,670
Miles on Convoy duty	477,100
Convoys provided with air escort	314
U-Boats sighted	5
U-Boats attacked	4

The best attack of the month was on 10th by an A.S.V. fitted Whitley bomber.

Operations against U-Boats have been more successful in March 1941 than in any other month of the war.

There has been clear evidence of increased efficiency of A/S escorts and the U-Boats which attacked adequately escorted convoys were dealt with effectively.

Fifty attacks on U-Boats or supposed U-Boats were made during March, thirty-nine by surface vessels and eleven by aircraft.

The most interesting occurrence of the month followed the attack on Convoy H.X. 112. Two and possibly three U-Boats were sunk that night, one as the result of an A.S.V. contact.

After being depth charged by the escorting destroyers "U100" (*Kptlt. Joachim Schepke*) surfaced and might have escaped in the darkness had she not been detected by H.M.S. "Vanoc's" A.S.V. The destroyer rammed this U-Boat and while she was picking up survivors another escort obtained asdic contact in the vicinity. Although it was considered unlikely that another U-Boat would remain as close, the A/S Control Officer and operator were so convinced that their classification was correct that H.M.S. " Walker" fired six depth charges. This attack was extremely accurate and brought "U 99" (*Kptlt. Otto Kretschmer*) to the surface almost at once.

These successes resulted in the death and capture of two of Germany's star Commanders.

The effect of the loss of two of the enemy's most skilful U-Boat Captains was soon apparent; the U-Boats were once more forced westward. Thus the chief problem of the Navy has been that of extending A/S escort as far west as possible, and it is hoped that this will be simplified by the use of Hjalfiord in Iceland as a base for our escort vessels. At the moment escort further west can only be achieved at the expense of weaker escorts and all reinforcements that can be obtained will be used to reduce this weakening to a minimum. The lengthening hours of daylight in the Northern latitudes will allow a limited number of escorts to afford an increased degree of protection to convoys.

Depth Charges

Apparently some officers have a wrong impression of the cost of depth charges; a depth charge, complete with explosive and pistol, costs £37.

The supply position is very satisfactory and, at the present time, reserves at home and abroad exceed 24,000. The average monthly expenditure is 1,200 charges.

(As comparison: 5-8 depth-charges were needed to buy an 'average' house in London and 10 would have bought e very good one. In 1944 a Flight Lieutenant in the R.A.F. earned about £22 per month and a Flying Officer about £18 per month.)

COASTAL COMMAND OPERATIONS

	March 1941
Total hours flown by Coastal Command	11,850
Total miles flown by Coastal Command	1,540,500
Hours on purely A/S Patrol	658
Miles on purely A/S Patrol	85,540
Hours on Convoy duty	7,210
Miles on Convoy duty	937,300
U-Boats sighted	12
U-Boats attacked	10

Coastal Command have been able to increase their operational time for A/S measures during March, and ten attacks have been made against U-Boats, the highest number since the period of intense German activity last September and October.

April 1941

ICELAND ROUTEING

During April the Iceland routeing scheme was adopted to combat the U-Boats operating West of the point where convoys had been met by A/S escorts.

The 3rd, 6th and 12th Escort Groups were based on Iceland. By working one of these Groups in two divisions it was possible to meet convoys where the escort from United Kingdom had to leave, and accompany them out to about 35° West, the escort there picking up an incoming convoy and turning it over to a U.K. based escort group to the southward of Iceland.

Sunderland and Hudson aircraft have also been moved to Iceland and have been working with our convoys in waters which cannot be covered by aircraft flown from U.K. aerodromes.

The operation of the H.G. and O.G. and the S.L. and appropriate O.B. convoys has remained as before, the escort groups being based on the U.K.

Obviously this considerable increase in the distance over which our cross-Atlantic convoys are escorted was only achieved at the expense of weaker individual escorts with each convoy, but this was partly compensated by reinforcing the Western Approaches by ships of the 1st and 6th Minesweeping Flotillas ("Halcyon" class). The majority of these ships are now fitted with Asdics and the remainder will be so fitted at the first opportunity. On joining the Western Approaches Command they were fitted with R/T.

It is equally clear that the use of Iceland necessitated a certain rigidity of routeing and tended to make the location of our convoys by the U-Boats and aircraft a simpler business. Against this the daylight hours in these Northern latitudes are rapidly lengthening and the U-Boat danger in daylight is a lesser menace.

Although the British counter measures were not quite so successful as in March, the number of attacks, including Mediterranean reports, increased and there were in all 59 attacks on U-Boats or supposed U-Boats during April. Of these, fifty were made by surface vessels, and nine by aircraft.

After the attack on convoy S.C.6 "Wolverine" with "Scarborough" and "Arbutus" in company, carried out a search. "Wolverine" gained contact and carried out two single charge attacks, but her Asdic recorder was out of action and she called the other two ships to attack.

"Scarborough" carried out one attack with eight charges set to 150 and 300 ft. which brought U76 to the surface. This U-Boat sank after a spirited attempt by "Arbutus" to take her in tow.

Following the daylight attack by a U-Boat (*U76 : Kptlt. Friedrich von Hippel*) on the 28th a series of promising attacks were made by "Inglefield" and "Maori".

H.M.S. "Douglas" and H.M.S. "Gladiolus" also made good attacks upon the U-Boats which intercepted convoy H.X.121.

May 1941

The big attack by U-Boats on H.X.126, west of 410 West, before the escorts had joined, forced the adoption of complete trans-Atlantic escort. This is achieved by basing escort forces in St. Johns, Newfoundland, and escorting in stages from the United Kingdom, using the Iceland route, with Hjalfjord (*Iceland*) as a refuelling base.

This of course entails a considerable weakening of the escort force with a convoy at any one moment, but this must be accepted for the sake of some degree of protection throughout the voyage. During the long daylight hours of the summer months, particularly in the high latitudes, the smaller escorts should be sufficient to give the convoy considerable security.

The Royal Canadian Navy is co-operating in these measures whole-heartedly and all available R.C.N. corvettes (a large number are coming forward into service) are joining the Newfoundland force.

The remainder of the Newfoundland Escort Force will be constituted by the R.C.N. destroyers and destroyers of long endurance from the existing groups, and there will also be a Sloop Division. The total force operating from Newfoundland will be 31 destroyers, 9 sloops, 24 corvettes, in addition to the increasing number of R.C.N. corvettes.

A further reinforcement to our escort forces is now coming into service in the form of the 10 cutters turned over by the United States Navy. The first five of these ships have already arrived in this country and four have proceeded to Londonderry for a short work up before commencing escort duty. The fifth ship is to be fitted with various modifications, as a prototype, before passing into service. Three other cutters are on passage and two will sail shortly.

Four destroyers, ten corvettes and six A/S trawlers have been operating in the South Atlantic Command, and to meet the increased U-Boat activity off Freetown, measures have been taken to reinforce this area. Four more destroyers and ten corvettes have been sent to Freetown and at least six more A/S trawlers have been allocated.

Action has also been taken to divert all shipping from the Freetown area except those ships which must of necessity pass through those waters. This should effect a reduction of some 60 per cent, in the Freetown traffic and will also make a considerable reduction in the size of the S.L. convoys.

Attacks on U-Boats

There was a still greater increase in attacks on U-Boats or supposed U-Boats during May. In all 64 attacks were made, 47 of which were by surface vessels, 15 by aircraft and two by submarine.

The U-Boats which intercepted Convoy O.B.318 from 7th – 10th were located and very heavily attacked by the escorts. The first one which sank two ships on the 7th was dealt with by H.M. ships "Bulldog," "Amazon" and "Rochester."

Two U-Boats regained touch with the convoy and torpedoed four vessels on the 9th. H.M. ships "Broadway" and "Aubretia" immediately counter attacked and at least one U-Boat was known to have been sunk.

One of the U-Boats which took part in the attacks on H.X.126 before the escorts had joined was later hunted by the escorts and heavily depth-charged.

June 1941

Many more U-Boats were sent to sea in June than in May and the number of attacks on U-Boats or supposed U-Boats rose to 82. Of these 50 were made by surface vessel, 32 by aircraft and two by submarine.

There were more accurate attacks in June than in any other month, and the lack of successful U-Boat activity was entirely due to the increased efficiency of British counter measures.

Arrangements for escorting H.X. and S.C. Convoys between Iceland and Newfoundland were completed and a force of R.N. and R.C.N. destroyers, R.N. sloops and R.N. and R.C.N. trawlers assembled at St. John's, Newfoundland. The first escorts sailed with Convoy H.X.129 on 31st May and, similarly, Convoy O.B.331 was escorted from Iceland to the westward.

As a natural sequel to this development it was later decided to escort our convoys all the way from Halifax.

This large extension of the distance over which protection is provided has been greatly facilitated by the action of the Royal Canadian Navy in putting all their destroyers and a large force of corvettes into service with the escort forces of the Western Zone.

The Germans hunted in vain for our trans-Atlantic convoy routes until the 23rd of the month when H.X.133 was located. A large number of U-Boats moved to the reported position to deliver the much overdue concentrated attack.

However, early knowledge of the impending danger, and fortunate disposition of A/S vessels enabled the escorts of this convoy to be reinforced.

Following the first attack, when two ships were sunk, H.M. ships" Gladiolus" and "Nasturtium" attacked a U-Boat. After being depth charged, the enemy surfaced and "Gladiolus" claims to have sunk her by gun-fire at close range. (*The boats escaped. There are no records of any having been lost.*)

On 26th a second attack on the convoy was made, when two ships were sunk and one damaged.

The counter measures by the escorts "Nasturtium," "Gladiolus" and "Celandine" were known to be successful and 41 prisoners were taken from "U 556" (*Kptlt. Herbert Wohlfarth*) before she sank.

The Germans still followed and on 29th carried out an attack in daylight from a submerged position, sinking one ship. By now the convoy was under the protection of a strong escort force from the United Kingdom.

In spite of the difficulties of a number of non-sub echoes, the U-Boat was hunted relentlessly and eventually, after being heavily depth-charged, "U 651" (*Kptlt. Peter Lohmeyer*) surfaced and was scuttled as H.M.S. "Malcolm", the escort leader, closed.

The disappointment of the German Admiralty must have been very bitter, for, in addition to the comparative lack of success against the merchant vessels, they suffered the severe loss of certainly two and possibly three U-Boats. (*Boats sunk during 1941 were U138, U147, U556 and U651.*)

July 1941

If June was a good month, July, up to the twenty-sixth day of the month, was a better. Up to that date there had been no U-Boat attack on any convoy, though we had lost five ships after they had dispersed from convoy, and two ships sailing independently.

But, from another point of view, July compares unfavourably with the previous month, in that we had no case of a U-Boat surfacing and surrendering after being attacked. There have, however, been a number of promising attacks on U-Boats.

The first convoy to be attacked was O.S.1. It was in a position about 60 miles north-west of Bloody Foreland, when two ships were torpedoed apparently by a single U-Boat. (*U141 : Philipp Schüler*) One of these ships was sunk, but the other was able to make Lough Swilly, though drawing 43 feet forward. (*The 5106 GRT "Botley" was sunk in Convoy OS1 and the 5133 GRT "Atlantic City" was torpedoed, but reached port. A third ship was probably hit, but not damaged.*)

After this attack, which was delivered at night, two destroyers made contact. Though they hunted for about 7 hours and fired all their depth charges, there is no evidence to show that the U-boat suffered any damage.

The other convoy attacked was O.G.69. This was a long drawn out affair, and though the losses were considerable, they were scarcely commensurate with the enemy's efforts and still less with his claims.

This convoy began by successfully evading what was believed to be a concentration of U-Boats to the westward of Ireland, but it was less fortunate in avoiding location by a Focke-Wulf aircraft, which sighted it when in about latitude 50° 00' N.

It was expected that the enemy would make a great effort to redeem his long run of failure, but for 24 hours the U-Boats did not make contact.

The convoy was sighted again by a Focke-Wulf aircraft, and it became evident that a U-Boat had sighted it on the evening of the 26th July. By this time four of the nine escorting corvettes and one A/S trawler were due to leave O.G.69 to join an H.G. convoy, but only two corvettes were detached that night, and the other two were ordered to stay with the outward-bound convoy until the next morning, in preparation for the expected attack.

At 2100 on 26th July, the ships of the convoy which were bound for South Atlantic ports, 13 in number, were detached and ordered to proceed independently. It was hoped that their higher speed would enable them to win clear of the pursuit which was believed to be coming up astern.

This decision proved sound, for only two ships, the "Shahristan" and the Dutch "Sitoepondo," were caught and sunk in the early hours of the 30th July (*by U371 : Heinrich Driver*). Their combined tonnage was about 14,000 tons.

Three hours after the ships bound for the South Atlantic ports had left the main convoy, the attack began with the sinking of s.s. "Kellwyn." (*By U79 : Wolfgang Kaufmann*) This was followed 2 hours later by the loss of s.s. "Hawkinge." (*By U203 : Rolf Mützelburg*)

After the sinking of "Kellwyn," H.M.S. "Rhododendron" sighted a U-Boat on the surface and, gaining contact, delivered four attacks. Contact was lost at 0116, and though she searched for another 1.5 hours, it was not regained. While "Rhododendron" was thus engaged, H.M.S. "Sunflower" sighted another U-Boat on the surface, but when it dived she could not make contact.

She and H.M.S. "Pimpernel" had given up the search by 0255, the time at which "Hawkinge" was torpedoed. Corning up at full speed, at 0330 they sighted a U-Boat 400 yards away on the surface. An effort to ram failed, but a ten-charge pattern was dropped by eye, and after contact had been made two more attacks were carried out, possibly with some success.

During the afternoon and evening of 27th July, three U-Boats were sighted on the surface, astern of the convoy.

On the second night, the attack began about the same time with the sinking of s.s. "Erato" (Commodore's ship) and s.s. "Inga I." (*By U126 : Ernst Bauer.*) "Rhododendron" made contact and carried out four attacks and H.M.S. "Begonia" also attacked on making contact, but neither ship sighted the U-Boat which the Commodore had reported after the torpedoing of his ship.

A U-Boat was again sighted at about 0300, but it was not until 1.5 hours later that the last attack of the night was made and s.s. "Wrotham" was hit. (*By U561 : Robert Bartels*) Despite a search, nothing was sighted nor was contact made.

The Commodore, before his ship sank, had ordered the convoy to disperse, and by the evening of the 28th July, five ships, out of the 13 who had been in the convoy when it was first attacked, were proceeding in company with five corvettes.

The events of the night began with a report that a Catalina aircraft had attacked a U-Boat 12 miles astern. H.M. Ships "Pimpernel" and "Larkspur" were ordered to sweep astern and rejoin in 2 hours' time.

About an hour after they had left, a periscope was reported astern and almost immediately afterwards s.s. "Lapland" and s.s. "Norita" were torpedoed — both on the port side. (*By U203 : Rolf Mützelburg*) Half a minute after these merchantmen had been struck, "Rhododendron" observed three torpedoes approaching, her from her port quarter. Taking violent avoiding action, she turned into the tracks, and one torpedo passed ahead, and another astern, of her. The third went underneath her. It is recorded that no hydrophone effect from the torpedoes was heard.

H.M.S. "Fleur de Lys" made contact within 3 minutes of the torpedoing of the merchantmen and "Rhododendron" also picked up contact at long range. The two ships attacked and went on attacking until they only had three depth charges left between them. Eventually, contact faded out and was not regained; there was no conclusive evidence of success.

These three nights of attack had cost us seven ships, of a total tonnage of 11,303, making, with the "Shahristan" and "Sitoepondo," a grand total of 15,288 tons. The very extravagance of the enemy's claim — 140,000 tons, a destroyer and a corvette — may well be accepted as a measure of his embarrassment over the failure of his U-Boat campaign in the month of July.

As regards A/S escort, the "Iceland" route, with a change-over of escorts to the southward of Iceland and the use of Hjalfjord (*Iceland*) as a refuelling base, has worked smoothly and, so far, effectively.

The main development has been with our convoys to Gibraltar and Freetown, and the degree of success achieved may be shown by the reduction in the tonnage sunk in the Freetown area from 186,000 tons in May to 13,000 tons in July. It is possible, however, that the enemy shifted his operations during the month to an area further north, closer to the Azores.

End to end A/S escorts for both Gibraltar and Sierra Leone convoys have been adopted in place of the arrangements whereby the Gibraltar convoys had only the protection of a single sloop in the middle passage; with full escort at either end, and the ships in the Sierra Leone convoys had to make a great part of their voyage either unescorted or independently after dispersing.

The Gibraltar convoys will be escorted the whole way by groups of five corvettes, led by a sloop, this force being strengthened by local escorts at either end. Convoy O.G.69 was the second convoy to have this end-to-end escort, but the sloop to lead the corvettes was not available at the time of sailing. A corvette, with her inadequate communication facilities, is unsuitable for the work of leading an escort group.

With regard to Sierra Leone convoys, questions of endurance make it impossible to give complete end-to-end escort. Sloops and cutters will, however, escort these convoys from the United Kingdom to approximately the latitude of Bathurst (*Gambia in West Africa*), where a Freetown escort will meet them. The cutters and sloops will go into Bathurst to fuel and, having done so, will take over northbound convoys from a Freetown escort, approximately in the position in which they leave the southbound convoys. During the passage of the Western Approaches, north and southbound convoys will be protected by an escort from the United Kingdom in addition to the sloops and cutters.

Our primary object was more or less achieved during the month of July; our ships went upon their ways and the enemy, despite his efforts, could only destroy a score of them.

Improvements have been made in defensive arrangements. Every effort is being made to press on with offensive weapons, which will ensure that a U-Boat, once located, has only a slight chance of survival.

It can never be too strongly emphasised that, with our present asdic methods and weapons, the destruction of a U-Boat is not a simple matter and can only be achieved by a well-handled ship with a well-trained team formed by the Captain, his A/S control officers and his crew. Every opportunity for practice must be seized and then such a ship, given her chance, will not have to rely on good luck to bring about the desired result.

COASTAL COMMAND ACTIVITIES

	July 1941
Total hours flown by Coastal Command	13,505
Total miles flown by Coastal Command	1,620,600
Hours on purely A/S patrol	2,166
Miles on purely A/S patrol	259,920
Hours on convoy duty	4,303
Miles on convoy duty	516,360

During the month of July aircraft reported the sighting of U-Boats on eleven occasions and the sighting of oil patches or streaks on twelve. This total of twenty-three sightings is a large reduction as compared with June, when forty-three were reported.

Aircraft were particularly active in the southern area of the Western Approaches, no less than thirteen sightings occurring in positions west or south-west of Ushant, west of Land's End (*Cornwall, south-west England*) or south-west of Slyne Head (*Galway, Ireland*). Five sightings were made in the area to the north-west of Bloody Foreland (*Donegal, Ireland*). Apart from one sighting off Spurn Point (*Humber Estuary to the east of Hull*), the other incidents recorded took place to the north-westward of the British Isles.

As regards the aircraft engaged, Wellingtons made the largest number of sightings (seven), Hudson and Beauforts each making four, and Whitleys three. Catalinas, Sunderlands and one Anson also made reports.

The offensive importance of Coastal Command aircraft in the anti-Submarine campaign is shown by the fact that on only four occasions were the aircraft engaged in escorting convoys. In all other cases their duty was either cross-over patrol or A/S search.

Although on six out of the twenty-three occasions, attacks were either not made, or, if made, were not reported, a considerable weight of explosive was dropped in the other seventeen cases. Twenty-three 450-lb. and eighteen 250-lb. depth charges were dropped as well as three 500-lb., four 250-lb. and two 100-lb. A/S bombs.

In the last week of the month a large number of ships passed safely through an exceptionally heavy U-Boat concentration in the North Atlantic; the vigilance, ingenuity and flexibility, which made this possible, won praise from the highest quarters.

Taken as a whole, August was a satisfactory month. Although the increase in U-Boat construction, begun at the outbreak of war, is now being translated into a steady increase in the numbers of U-Boats operating, our losses are still being kept down to comparatively low figures.

This is due partly to the greater efficiency of our A/S escort forces and aircraft against enemy units, the latter reduced in efficiency by a combination of past losses in personnel and the dilution inevitable in a heavy programme of expansion.

Good management has earned good luck and fortune has smiled on us.

On 11th August it became evident that Convoys O.N.4 and O.N.5 had been sighted by the enemy. Neither convoy was attacked, but it is believed that a U-Boat (*U568 : Joachim Preuss*) followed up the ships of O.N.5 which left the convoy for Iceland under escort of H.M. Ships "Picotee" and "Ayrshire," and torpedoed and sank the former.

On the same day, 11th August, Convoy H.G.70 was sighted and reported by U-Boats not long after it had left Gibraltar. The large number of U-Boats believed to be operating against the convoy were kept at bay by the attacks of the escorting ships and aircraft, and the convoy, turning to the northward considerably east of the usual position, shook off the enemy and came safely to port.

In the following week another Gibraltar convoy, O.G.71, was located first by Focke-Wulf aircraft and then by U-Boats, when in a position south-west of Ireland. The first attack developed a little after midnight on the night of 18th/19th August with the sinking of H.M. Ship "Bath," (*By U204 : Walter Kell*) who was returning from a sweep and was at the time about 2.5 miles astern of the convoy. Five minutes later s.s. "Alva" was struck by a torpedo (*from U559 : Hans Heidtmann*) on her starboard side. The convoy proceeded on its course, but two hours later the Commodore's and Vice-Commodore's ships were sunk.

In the course of the day H.M. Ships "Gurkha" and "Lance" left Convoy W.S.10X, joining O.G.71 at about 0320/20, but though they suspected the presence of U-Boats while approaching astern, they could not obtain contact. A Focke-Wulf aircraft hovered round the convoy during the following day, but it was prevented by gunfire from attacking; apparently it did not then "home" any U-Boats on to the convoy for no attack developed during the night.

During the afternoon of the next day a Focke-Wulf aircraft again appeared and was again kept away from the convoy by gunfire. In the evening it became evident that there were about half a dozen U-Boats spread on a rough line of bearing parallel to the convoy about fifteen miles away.

Evasive measures were successful and, apart from a fierce action fought by H.M. Ship "Bluebell" for ten minutes against an imaginary foe (a "ruse de guerre" which may have succeeded), the night was quiet.

On 22nd August a Catalina aircraft joined and later Focke-Wulf aircraft put in an appearance for the third day running. The two enemy aircraft did not endeavour to attack the convoy, but they probably "homed on" the U-Boats, which were in the sector opposite to that in which they were flying. "Lance" was therefore ordered five miles to the eastward (the convoy's course had been altered from 140° to 190° on the appearance of the enemy aircraft) with the idea of keeping them as far from the convoy as possible, and thereby reducing the strength of the signals to the U-Boats.

About noon the Catalina reported a U-Boat ahead, but though "Lance" and H.M. Ship "Boreas" hunted for it, they could not make contact. By the afternoon it was estimated that there were at least eight, and possibly nine, U-Boats in the area (most of them to the westward), some of which were either not far below the horizon, or had sighted the destroyers on the extended screen.

The Senior Officer of the escort did not spoil the success of his previous night's "ruse de guerre" by attempting to repeat it.

He ordered the convoy to alter course to 120° at 2300 and back to 150° at 0400, before which time it was hoped that a vigorous A/S sweep might have driven the U-Boats back to the westward to a depth of fifteen miles.

If the convoy was attacked, the corvettes were told to remain near the convoy and fire Snowflake; the destroyers were to sweep outwards with starshell, at the same time sweeping across the sides of the convoy with searchlights. Unfortunately, it turned out that only one corvette had Snowflakes and these ideas did not work out according to plan.

At 2100 the destroyers began their A/S sweep in excellent Asdic conditions, but obtained no contacts.

Less than an hour later the U-boats (*U564 : Teddy Suhren*) attacked, sinking s.s. "Empire Oak" (*a small tug of 484 GRT*) and s.s. "Clontara." "Gurkha" came up and searched, but only obtained a non-sub contact. At 0115, two more merchantmen were torpedoed, one of them bursting into flames and lighting up the scene for miles around. An attack on s.s. "Cervantes" at about 0250 was unsuccessful, two torpedoes missing. (*In Axis Submarine Successes of World War Two, Prof. Rohwer has identified three more sunk ships: "Stork," "Aldergrove" and "Spind."*)

At 0400 the convoy turned to 150°, and as some time had passed without an attack, "Gurkha" decided to create a diversion. Turning to 000° at 27 knots, she fired a depth charge and a rocket at 0428 and afterwards red and white Verey lights. After carrying out a starshell search to the north and north-west, she set course to rejoin the convoy.

At 0430, H.M. Ship "Zinnia," stationed on the port beam, was torpedoed (*by U564 : Teddy Suhren*) while turning and sank in fifteen seconds; the rest of the salvo must have passed astern of the convoy.

The last casualty was s.s. "Spind" which had become separated from the convoy during the night. About 0600 this ship was attacked by a U-boat with gunfire (*from U552 : Erich Topp*). "Boreas" went to her assistance, but "Spind" was so badly damaged that she had to be sunk at about 0900.

The rest of the convoy arrived safely in the Tagus (*Lisbon – Portugal*).

In the last week of the month there were nine convoys at sea at a time when the enemy had concentrated an exceptionally large number of U-Boats in the North Atlantic. On 24th August the most westerly of these was H.X.145, which was in a position between 30° W. and 35° W.; H.X.144, followed closely by S.C.40, was some two hundred miles to the eastward, the three convoys being between 58° and 59° N.; O.N.9, proceeding on a south-westerly course, was in position 56°00'N. 16°00'W. at midnight on the 24th and dispersed on the following day; S.L.83, homeward bound, passed through 53°00'N. 20°00'W. in the course of the 24th August; O.G.73 was some hundred miles to the southeastward of S.L.83; O.S.4 was leaving the North Channel. Later in the week convoys H.G.71 and S.D.10 came into the danger area.

All the homeward convoys came safely into port.

Shortly after midnight on the night of 26th/27th August, O.S.4, which had probably been sighted by a U-Boat in the early evening, was attacked in a gale and heavy sea, despite an alteration of course. Another attack was made at 0330 and five ships in all were lost. Three destroyers, one sloop, two cutters and two A/S trawlers were escorting the convoy, but they had no luck in sighting or counter-attacking any U-boats. In the bad weather prevailing, there was apparently a general failure in the convoy to make any signals or to fire any rockets to indicate an attack. The destroyers of the outer screen were further hampered by the absence of reports from the A/S escort of the inner screen.

H.X. 145, which, on the 27th, was approaching the position in which O.S.4 had been attacked, may have been sighted by a U-Boat about noon on that day, but it passed through the area without incident.

During the night of 27th/28th, two U-Boats were sighted on the surface closing Convoy O.S.4, then steering into a south-westerly wind and sea. Thanks to action taken by H.M. Ships "Walker" and "Bideford," no attack developed. S.S. "Otaio" was, however, torpedoed and sunk in the afternoon of the 28th (*by U558 : Günther Krech*), shortly after she had left the convoy, which may itself have been sighted by a U-Boat a little later. There were probably several U-Boats in the area, but they did not attack again.

Great as was the success achieved in the last week of the month, it was not perhaps so great, or so encouraging, as the record of Convoy H.G.70; this convoy, beset by several U-Boats, beat off the attack and won through unscathed.

The day may come when we have sufficient strength in A/S escorts to invite attack and to fight our way through the U-Boats. But that day is still distant.

September 1941

After two months of good luck, the tide of fortune set against us in September, and our losses rose sharply.

The enemy, reaping the fruits of his 1939 programme of U-Boat construction, was able to maintain in operation perhaps five times as many U-Boats as were at sea a year ago. Yet his achievements were by no means equal to his exertions. (*The daily average number of U-boats at sea during the last six months of 1940 was 11.6 and this had risen to 33 for the last six month of 1941.*)

In September, 1940, with an average of seven U-Boats at sea, the enemy secured the destruction of 265,000 tons of our shipping; a year later his far greater efforts were rewarded with a tonnage smaller by 50,000 tons.

A year ago the U-Boats were attacking our convoys with impunity. Rarely was a U-Boat sighted during her attack, even more rarely was the enemy counter-attacked. To-day it is a matter for the keenest disappointment if a convoy is attacked and the enemy escapes unpunished.

The first convoy attacked during the month was S.C.42, which was sighted by U-Boats when it was proceeding to the eastward of Greenland. Protected by a slender escort consisting of H.M.C.S. "Skeena" and three R.C.N. corvettes, later reinforced by H.M.C. ships "Chambly" and "Moosejaw," who were carrying out a "shake-down" cruise in the neighbourhood, it was heavily attacked on the night of 9th/10th September, twice in daylight on the following day and again on the second night, fifteen out of sixty-seven ships being torpedoed. The enemy paid a fair price, for this success, since " Chambly" and "Moosejaw" celebrated their first appearance with a convoy by sinking a U-Boat ("U501" : *Korvkpt. Hugo Förster*) as they were closing S.C.42.

On 11th September, the escort was strongly reinforced by the arrival of the United Kingdom escort group; aircraft from Iceland also joined. An encouraging feature of the episode was that, although the U-Boats are believed to have been present in some force, the attacks carried out by the Canadian escort on the 9th and 10th, and by H.M. ships "Veteran" and "Leamington" and the aircraft, after their joining on the 11th, were enough to discourage them from further efforts until the night of 16th/17th, when another ship was torpedoed (*by U74 Eitel-Friedrich Kentrat*).

In mid-September, S.C.44, escorted by one destroyer and four R.C.N. corvettes, suffered a night attack, in the course of which H.M.C.S. "Levis" was torpedoed (*by U74 : Eitel-Friedrich Kentrat*); though taken in tow she sank during the following evening. The U-Boats must have followed up the convoy for, in a second night attack, four merchantmen were torpedoed and sunk. No counter-attacks were made and, indeed, it does not appear that any ship of the escort sighted a U-Boat. By making drastic emergency turns in the darkness (which caused some of the ships to lose the convoy) the pursuit was shaken off and no more attacks developed.

Later in the month the enemy turned his attention again to the Gibraltar convoys, which had suffered at his hands during August. O.G.74, which had been located by Focke-Wulf aircraft, was attacked by U-Boats on two successive nights (20th and 21st) and lost three ships. In this case again the escort (a sloop, five corvettes and an A/S trawler) were not able to make any counter-attacks. Nevertheless the U-Boats were forced to relinquish their contact with the convoy, which proceeded without further loss.

Three out of four ships which had failed to hear an emergency turn signal and had lost contact with the main body on the night of the 20th were, however, torpedoed and sunk on the following night when some 25 miles astern of the convoy.

H.M.S. "Audacity," an auxiliary aircraft carrier, started her career in good style; one of her fighter aircraft shot down a Focke-Wulf aircraft which was attacking the rescue ship.

In the last week of the month another Gibraltar convoy, H.G.73, was attacked on three successive nights. First sighted by a Focke-Wulf aircraft when off Cape St. Vincent, the strong escort (one destroyer, one sloop and eight corvettes for twenty-five ships) was too much for an Italian U-Boat, which was fairly soon shaken off. H.M.S. "Springbank" catapulted her fighter aircraft, but the Focke-Wulf lived to fly another day and the convoy ran into a concentration of German U-Boats, which attacked three nights running. One ship was sunk on the first night, five ships on the second night and three on the third. We also lost "Springbank." H.M.S. "Larkspur" made a strong counter-attack during the action on the second night.

A three-night attack was also made between 21st and 24th September on a Sierra Leone convoy of twelve ships, escorted by two cutters, a British sloop and a Free French sloop. Eight ships were torpedoed, four on the last night; two or more U-Boats attacked, but it seems that no U-Boat was sighted nor was any counter-attack made.

Five independently routed ships were sunk and five ships, dispersed or straggled from convoys, were also lost.

Though the U-Boat packs have shown persistence in their shadowing methods, no convoy has been attacked for more than three consecutive nights. With S.L.87 the losses on the last night were the most severe, while H.G.73 suffered most heavily on the second of the three nights. S.C.42 was probably saved from a third night attack by the arrival of the United Kingdom escort group, and even if S.C.44 did lose touch with some of its ships by making drastic emergency turns during the second night, it also lost contact with the enemy. The U-Boats failed to keep in touch with O.G.74 after the second night — possibly the loss of their guiding Focke-Wulf hampered them.

Although there was an unsatisfactory absence of sightings and counter-attacks at the time of the torpedoings, yet there is evidence of the ability of escorts, taking the offensive at times of their own choosing, to drive the enemy off the scent.

A powerful concentration of U-Boats was discouraged by attacks made by "Veteran" and "Leamington," assisted by aircraft, from following up two nights of successful attacks on S.C.42.

It is possible that, just as the summer of 1940 saw a change in anti-submarine warfare and in U-Boat tactics, so also has the summer of 1941 seen a change, this time in our favour.

It is to be hoped that it is not extravagant to say that the offensive is passing from the enemy to ourselves. Last autumn an experienced U-Boat captain could pick his victims — a large tanker here, a 7,000-ton freighter there. By March of this year U-Boat "aces" had started to pay the price of over-confidence, and within a few months the enemy had lost a number of his star performers. Now, though still hard to combat due to the increase in the number of U-Boats at sea, attacks seem to have lost some of their finesse, and our larger escorts and better A/S measures have started to compensate for this increase.

It is impossible to dogmatise on the subject of U-Boat tactics. The evidence of prisoners confirms that, whatever degree of efficiency may exist in the remainder of the crew, the success or failure bf a U-Boat depends on the personality of one individual — the Captain.

Although the asdic set has shown that it can be successfully operated under conditions much worse than was generally believed, it has been found extremely difficult to make contact even though a U-Boat has torpedoed a ship only a few miles away; upon this difficulty turns the whole question of escorts acting as striking forces away from convoys.

The original A/S striking forces had no success, even though they operated in restricted coastal areas. How much more difficult would be the task of an ocean A/S striking force?

In this connection it is important to remember that, although in normal visibility a U-Boat on the surface should have the advantage of first sighting, yet there was recently a case where two U-Boats were sighted on the surface; in one case the sighting was mutual, in the other the surface craft apparently sighted the U-boat before she herself was sighted.

In the early part of this month the enemy operated rather fewer U-Boat than in September but the numbers at sea appeared to rise progressively until, towards the end of the month, there were nearly as many in the Atlantic as the previous peak period in August. Tonnage sunk totalled about three-quarters of the September figure.

It became clear that a few German U-Boats had entered the Mediterranean and were working off the coast of Libya.

In the South Atlantic the scale of effort declined in the first week of October and several U-Boats began to return, including U111 (*Kptlt. Wilhelm Kleinschmidt*) which was sunk so gallantly by H.M.S. "Lady Shirley" near the Canaries. Since the latter part of September there has been no activity in the Brazil area but, on 22nd October, a U-Boat (*U68 : Karl-Friedrich Merten*) visited St. Helena and torpedoed a ship (*8145 GRT Darkdale*) in the harbour. It is probable that it then move towards Walvis Bay. Another was off the coast between Takoradi and Lagos and an American ship was sunk off Freetown.

The Western area of the North Atlantic was an active one and several ships were lost in longitudes 25°W. to 35°W., the majority in the only heavy convoy attack during the month, made upon S.C.48 during the 15th and the three subsequent days. In all nine ships were sunk from the convoy as well as two British escorts; one American escort was torpedoed but reached port.

A convoy from Gibraltar was attacked early in its voyage and shadowed for several days. Owing to excellent work by the escorts who counter-attacked and hunted almost to exhaustion of fuel and depth charges, only four ships were sunk. The convoy consisted of seventeen ships and the enemy claimed in one broadcast to have sunk fourteen, in another seventeen.

A Sierra Leone convoy, heavily beset on 21st, lost two ships when, west of Ireland and an outward-bound convoy was so effectively protected in the same area that only one ship was sunk and the shadower was driven off.

A convoy bound for America was apparently shadowed for several clays a the end of the month but, so far as is known, the only ship hit (*by U106 : Hermann Rasch*) was the American tanker "Salinas" which reached St. John's.

Air attacks in Bay of Biscay in particular increased in frequency and still more in efficiency and there was again ground for gratification in the fact that s large a force of U-Boats did not achieve greater success.

November 1941

In the middle of the month the Berlin correspondent of a Swedish newspaper reported that the recent reduction in the sinkings of merchantmen in the Battle of the Atlantic was ascribed by German "semi-official" quarters to the use by the British of new weapons for counter-attacking, whereby they had gained a temporary alleviation of their losses. Naturally the report went on to say that Germany also had new surprise weapons and a new building programme for U-Boats, and concluded with the statement that the Todt organisation had found a new method of protecting building yards against air attack.

There is at least one true statement in this report: our losses have fallen. Despite an effort by the enemy which, though starting at a high peak and gradually decreasing as the month passed, was always considerable, the figures of merchant tonnage lost in the Battle of the Atlantic are the best for 18 months. It is also heartening to record the certain sinking of two German U-Boats one by H.M.N. Submarine O21 (*Lt.Cdr. J.F. van Dulm*) — in the Mediterranean, into which sea a number of German U-Boats have passed and the possible destruction or damaging of several others. (*One U-boat, U95 : Kptlt. Gerd Schreiber, was sunk.*)

At the beginning of the month the enemy, pursuing his policy of attacking escort vessels, attempted to sink H.M.S. "Buxton." This destroyer, which was escorting Convoy H.X.156, was missed by several torpedoes. She carried out counter-attacks, but without visible results. In the event the convoy arrived intact without further incident.

On the same day H.M. ships "Gorleston" and "Verbena," who were escorting Convoy O.S.10, delivered attacks on a U-Boat, which, it is claimed, was sunk. At present, however, no details of the incident are available. On the following day U-Boats were twice sighted and chased; no attack on the convoy developed. (*The boat got away. There are no records of any having been lost.*)

On the 2nd and 3rd November occurred the heaviest losses of the month. Convoy S.C.52 was attacked by a number of U-Boats close to the eastward of Newfoundland, and four ships in all were sunk. Fog made concerted action by the escorts difficult, but it is reported that H.M.C.S. "Buctouche" carried out a counter-attack, which produced a quantity of oil.

After these events there was a lull in U-Boat activity until nearly the end of the month. On the 28th H.M.T. "Lady Madeleine," one of the escorts of Convoy O.N.40, sighted the periscope of a U-Boat and made an attack; her conning tower was then observed and another attack was delivered, after which contact was not regained.

On the next day Convoy O.S.12 lost one ship, the torpedoing being followed by a promising counter-attack by H.M.S. "Totland." On the 30th another ship of the escort of the convoy, H.M.S. "Wellington," whose asdics were out of action, sighted two U-Boats on the surface and by gunfire forced them to dive. The last casualty of the month was a ship torpedoed south of the Azores (*was the 5569 GRT "Thornliebank," which was sunk by U43 : Wolfganf Lüth*). It had sailed in O.S.12.

Two ships sailing independently were sunk during November, one of them being on her maiden voyage.

The month closed with the suspension of the sailing- of the homeward-bound convoy from Gibraltar and the use of every available ship in an endeavour to close the Straits of Gibraltar to the passage of U-Boats and to destroy U-Boats attempting the passage.

The heavy gales which raged in the North Atlantic during the month and were especially felt by the O.N. convoys, must have prevented the U-Boats from taking advantage of the inevitable straggling that they caused. To some extent, therefore, the weather contributed to the reduction in losses, but our success was mainly due to skilful evasive routeing.

Successful evasion means fewer chances of contacts between escort vessels and U-Boats, and therefore less chance of the destruction of the enemy. We cannot at present, have it both ways. We cannot risk heavy loss to our merchant shipping and neither our strength in escort vessels nor the effectiveness of our A/S measures have yet reached the point at which we can invite attack. Finally, we cannot put enough faith in our ability to evade the enemy to effect a compromise under which we can evade with some weakly escorted convoys whilst we fight our way through with other convoys heavily escorted.

In last month's Report reference was made to the range of German torpedoes. It seems probable that the U-Boat (*U81 : Friedrich Guggenberger*) which torpedoed H.M.S. "Ark Royal" fired from long range, possibly just outside the asdic range of the destroyer screen and from a bearing between the starboard bow and beam, since the rear destroyer on the starboard side of the screen heard hydrophone effect on her starboard bow shortly before the torpedo hit; this, though attributed to the next destroyer ahead of her, was probably from the torpedo. If it is the fact that the U-Boat fired outside the water effectively swept by the asdic screen, she must have fired from a range of 4,500 yards or more, which is near the extreme range of a 5,400 yards torpedo.

The enormous expansion of the U-boat arm, the full consequences of which we have still to face, has probably compelled the enemy to shorten training and he has endeavoured to disguise the gaps by the artificial bolster of propaganda. German seamen, thus prepared for submarine warfare, set out full of self-confidence and high spirits, which might carry them to some degree of success; but should they meet skilful and well-trained opponents, then, in the heat of action, these supports will fail them and they will pay the penalty of insufficient training.

But these facts also emphasise the necessity of putting up our maximum A/S effort now, at a time when so many "green" U-Boat crews are at sea and. before they have the chance to shake down and acquire genuine self-confidence, inspired by sea-service, as opposed to propaganda. Despite our policy of evasion opportunities do arise and contacts between surface ships and U-Boats do occur. Only by constant drill, by seizing every chance of training and by welding all hands into an efficient team, will ships be able to put their opportunities to good account.

No one will deny that good luck is required to convert a good attack on a U-Boat into a "kill," but it is impossible to compare the reports on successful attacks with those on unsuccessful attacks, without realising that the good luck comes to the Commanding Officer who, by dint of hard work and quick wits, has earned it.

December 1941

December was a memorable month. Many effective attacks were made; seven U-Boats are known to have been destroyed; for the first time aircraft successfully carried out night attacks on U-Boats; most important of all, the naval and air escort of a convoy combined together to form a particularly successful anti-submarine striking force.

On the other side of the account, we lost H.M. Ships "Stanley" and "Audacity" during the passage of Convoy H.G.76 and enemy U-Boats also sank H.M. Ships "Galatea," "Lady Shirley," "Salvia" and "Rosabelle." Our merchant shipping losses were again low, though they increased as compared with the very low November figures. For the time being the scene has changed and, apart from an attack on Convoy S.C.57 in a position to the westward of the Hebrides, almost all the activity has been in the Mediterranean and, in the Atlantic, to the southward of Cape Finisterre. At the end of the month, however, there were signs that the enemy was preparing to resume the main battle against our Atlantic trade.

There was considerable activity in the Eastern Mediterranean. We lost three ships sailing on the supply route off Libya, but the price exacted for this success was high. In the second week of the month, H.M.S. "Farndale" sank an Italian U-Boat off the Libyan coast. Twelve days later H.M. Ships "Hasty" and "Hotspur" destroyed one German U-Boat (*U79 : Kptlt. Wolfgang Kaufmann*), and on the 28th H.M.S. "Kipling" sank another (*U75 : Kptlt. Helmuth*

Ringelmann). The 18th December saw two promising attacks off Alexandria, one by H.M.S. "Jervis" and the other by H.M.T. "Kingston Cyanite." "Jervis" attack is considered by the Commander-in-Chief, Mediterranean, to have destroyed the U-Boat.

These successes are indeed notable, but even they must give pride of place to the passage of Convoy H.G.76. Its sailing, originally arranged for last month, was delayed for about a fortnight and, while it lay waiting in harbour, there was great activity in, and to the westward of, the Straits of Gibraltar. U-Boats were frequently sighted in the Western Approaches to the Straits, and our forces made a strong effort to close the Straits themselves. The aircraft establishment at Gibraltar was strengthened by the arrival of Hudson aircraft of 233 Squadron and by Swordfish aircraft of the Fleet Air Arm; the latter carried out some markedly successful night patrols over the area close westward of Cape Spartel (*North Africa*). In the second week of December the patrol of the Straits was temporarily lifted and the escort group thus released was sent out to reinforce the group escorting an approaching outward-bound Gibraltar convoy. Hopes of offensive action inspired this decision but they were in vain; it was perhaps unfortunate for the campaign on U-Boats that the enemy failed to locate this very strongly escorted convoy, which arrived safely in harbour on 13th December.

On 14th December a German U-Boat was sunk by H.M.S. "Nestor," in a position to the westward of the Straits. (*U127 : Kptlt. Bruno Hansmann*)

H.G.76 sailed during the afternoon of 14th December. It consisted of 32 ships and had, for the first two days a double escort, and thereafter two sloops, three destroyers and seven corvettes, with the auxiliary aircraft carrier "Audacity" in company. Of the destroyers, two left the convoy to return to Gibraltar on the morning of the 18th and the third (H.M.S. "Stanley") was sunk (*by U574: Dietrich Gengelbach*) in the early hours of the 19th, when stationed right astern of the convoy on the outer screen "Audacity" was sunk (*by U751 : Gerhard Bigalk*) during the evening of 21st December in a position about ten miles from the convoy, which she was leaving in the hopes of obtaining greater safety from her speed whilst acting independently at some 30 miles range.

During the 22nd, Liberator aircraft, which had flown out some 750 miles, gave the convoy air cover; the aircraft escort during the afternoon attacked one U-Boat with depth charges and sighted and put down two others. Thanks to this effective air cover, combined with drastic evasive action and a dummy starshell battle staged to take place in. the position in which the convoy should have been, the U-Boats were shaken off and the convoy, passing south of Ireland, came safely into harbour.

This convoy had to fight its way through the enemy. The casualties on our side were two merchant ships out of 32 leaving Gibraltar, "Stanley" and "Audacity"; the enemy lost three U-Boats for certain and two Focke-Wulfs, a third being damaged. It provided a good example of the effective combination of aircraft with surface anti-submarine striking forces. The new auxiliary aircraft carriers will carry T.S.R. aircraft, capable of detecting U-Boats by A.S.V. and attacking with depth charges. It is hoped that these ships will commission at the rate of one a month during 1942.

Another form of our offensive is the initiation of night anti-submarine patrols by aircraft. Swordfish aircraft of the Fleet Air Arm have maintained a night patrol over an area close westward of Cape Spartel (*North Africa*) and A.S.V.fitted Whitley aircraft over the Bay of Biscay. Seven attacks have been made by night, as well as one by day. Some of them have inflicted damage of varying degrees of severity. At 0320 on 21st December a Swordfish completely surprised a U-Boat off Cape Spartel. She dropped three depth charges, one of which is thought to have exploded beneath her; at all events a patrolling corvette later picked up one survivor who proved to be the First Lieutenant of a German U-Boat. (*U451 : Kptlt. Eberhard Hoffmann*) A Whitley aircraft also made one good attack in the Bay of Biscay.

U-Boats have hitherto regarded the darkness as their best friend. Prisoners have spoken with feeling of Coastal Command's daylight sweeps, which have forced them continually to dive; at night they have been able to feel reasonably safe on the surface, relaxing strained nerves as well as charging batteries. Now, if night detection and night attacks by aircraft prove successful, U-Boat crews may come, instead, to dread nightfall. Attacks by day and attacks by night should have a cumulative effect upon their morale.

Though we know that we destroyed seven U-Boats during the month, the enemy is building them faster than we can sink them. (*Ten U-boats were lost to all causes*) Every new U-Boat at sea proportionately reduces the value of evasive routeing, which, though it has been carried out with success, is essentially defensive. The German Navy is again maintaining a large number of U-Boats in the North Atlantic, and is also carrying out an offensive against us in the Mediterranean. It may be thought that the enemy will have difficulty in manning the U-Boats now coming from the yards, but the problem is not beyond his solution, as long as he can find a keen and experienced officer to act as Captain and half a dozen officers and petty officers of average efficiency. As for the rest of the crew, a little training and a good deal of propaganda will provide him with a number of obedient ratings. This is the stuff of which successful U-Boat crews can be made.

Propaganda may be found a poor substitute for thorough training when it comes to action with a well drilled team like the 36th Escort Group, or a resolute crew like that of H.M.T. "Lady Shirley," but it may well succeed when a U-Boat crew realize that they have escaped from an awkward position because the attacking ship has been unready or inefficient. Thus the failure to set a pattern of depth charges correctly, the loss of Asdic contact when it should have been maintained, or some other mistake that give just that boost to the morale of propaganda-fed and inadequately trained Germans necessary to transform them into a confident and dangerous crew. The proof of the above fact can be found in the high percentage of U-Boats that are sunk on their maiden war cruise. Furthermore, though we have sunk a satisfactory number of U-Boats in the past few months we have mostly destroyed those commanded by the less distinguished captains. Too many "aces" still remain at large.

The month has seen a successful offensive against the U-Boats; more important, it has shown the great possibilities which exist for anti-submarine striking forces when a convoy is provided with a large escort assisted by carrier-borne aircraft. There are likewise great possibilities in night attacks by aircraft.

January 1942

An extraordinary change in the Battle of the Atlantic has occurred in the latter part of January. The enemy suddenly increased his effort and concentrated his forces in the West Atlantic area. With one exception, the convoys in this area have passed unassailed through waters in which many unescorted ships have been sunk. This policy of avoiding possibly expensive contact with our escort vessels has paid the enemy well. He has taken a very heavy toll of shipping in North American waters.

Unfortunately only scanty information is at present available of the Allied counter-measures in this area. It is, however, known that the Royal Canadian Navy, the Royal Canadian Air Force and the United States Navy have taken all possible counter measures with the forces at their disposal. United States aircraft are making use of a 350-lb. anti-submarine bomb. A Catalina aircraft of 116 Squadron of the R.C.A.F. made a promising attack off Sydney, Cape Breton, on the 21st January, and the United States Naval Authorities announce that there is credible evidence of the sinking, or severely damaging, of a number of U-Boats.

On the 26th January, the Free French corvette "Roselys" lightly rammed a U-Boat, which was also attacked with depth charges, but unfortunately these were set to 100ft. and not to 50ft.; it is probable that the U-Boat reached home. s.s. "Aagtekerk" is also reported to have made a promising attack.

Only four conveys, in addition to the one attacked in West Atlantic area, were in contact with the enemy. In two cases, escort vessels were sunk — H.M.S. "Culver" (*by U105 : Heinrich Schuch*) to the westward of Ushant, and H.M.S. "Belmont" (*by U82 : Siegfried Rollmann*) in a position 300 miles to the southward of Newfoundland — without attacks being made on merchant ships. Convoy S.L.97G. was passing through the area in which "U93" was sunk and, although prisoners from her stated that there were other U-Boats in the vicinity, the convoy was not attacked.

"U93" (*Oblt.z.S. Horst Elfe*) was sunk on the 15th January by H.M.S. "Hesperus," who was acting as a striking force with H.M.S. "Laforey," in a position 300 miles west of Cape St. Vincent. She was the only U-Boat known to have been lost by the enemy in the Atlantic during the month.

In the Mediterranean H.M. Submarines "Unbeaten," "Upholder"and "Thorn" torpedoed and sank one German (*U374 : Oblt.z.S. Unno von Fischel*) and two Italian U-Boats. Promising attacks were made by Swordfish aircraft of 815 Squadron, Hudson aircraft of 230 Squadron and a Sunderland. Some sinkings are claimed and in other cases it seems fairly certain that serious damage was caused; full reports,however, of the attacks have not yet come in.

H.M.S. "Gurkha" was torpedoed and sunk (*by U133 : Hermann Hesse*).

Japanese U-Boats have been active as far as the Bay of Bengal and off the coast of Ceylon. Two have been sunk in the South-West Pacific area, one by H.M.S. "Jupiter," after a spirited gun action, and the other by an Allied Force composed of Royal Australian Navy and United States Navy units. In the Pacific Ocean, U.S. Submarine "Gudgeon" claims to have sunk another Japanese U-Boat near Midway Island on 26th January. Before these three attacks, the
Japanese had announced the loss of one U-Boat.

The night anti-submarine patrols initiated last month have been continued with some measure of success by the A.S.V-fitted Swordfish operating in the Mediterranean, but in the Bay of Biscay there were no night attacks during January.

December saw the costly attacks on Convoy H.G.76. In January the activities of Focke-Wulf aircraft were greatly diminished and Convoy O.G.78 was able to take particularly short course, apparently making the passage without being sighted by the enemy.

The events in the West Atlantic are not only serious by reason of the loss of tonnage. Of even greater importance is the fact that the U-Boat crews are gaining not only successes against shipping but also experience and confidence. Some of the ratings who return from these operations will form a valuable nucleus for the manning of the U-Boats now coming from the yards in such numbers. Although there are a few new weapons with which to help defeat the U-Boats, our main business is to perfect our tactics, training and tools, and to visualise beforehand opportunities which may arise, so that when they come and excitement is high, drill is perfect and nothing left to chance.

February 1942

(Germany introduced the new four wheel Enigma Machine on 1st February 1942.
This was known as "Shark" at Bletchley Park.)

During February the Germans reverted to their previous tactics and, while still taking advantage of the acute shortage of anti-submarine vessels in Central and North American waters, delivered a comparatively heavy and protracted attack, upon a North Atlantic convoy to the westward of 380 W. This convoy — O.N.67 — was escorted by the United States destroyers "Bemadou," "Edison," "Lea" and "Nicholson" and H.M.C.S. "Algoma." The attacks began on night of 21st/22nd February, when two ships were lost and the convoy was again beset on the night of 23rd/24th. On this occasion the U-Boats made five attacks and sank two ships, two others being damaged.

A drastic alteration of route was ordered on the 24th. The Escort Commander then employed offensive tactics and assigned ships from the escort to patrol areas distant about 15 miles on each flank throughout daylight. At night escorts freely used for sweeping to about six miles in the direction of D.F. bearings. During the day and night following the mass attack of the 23rd/24th February escorts reported "five submarine sight contacts on the surface" but, notwithstanding this, the convoy made the remainder of its passage unmolested.

The Escort Commander thus successfully took advantage of the high speed possessed by his destroyer escort. With slower craft carrying out night sweeps the convoy is liable to be left unprotected for considerable periods; moreover if most of the escort are fitted with R.D.F. and ships are rejoining after a night sweep, the advantage is lost of being able to assume the probable presence of the enemy for all R.D.F. contacts outside the screen.

On 5th February a U-boat was D/F'd in the vicinity of Convoy O.N.63 and H.M. Ships "Arbutus" and "Chelsea" were ordered to search for it on the starboard quarter. At 1952 "Arbutus" (fitted with R.D.F., Type 271) reported that she had made R.D.F. contact at a range of 3000 yards and a little later reported that she had sighted a U-boat and that she had attacked it with depth charges after it had dived. "Chelsea" turned towards the U-boat's most probable position and, 15 minutes after the torpedoing, sighted it on the starboard bow. She opened fire on the U-boat as it passed down the starboard side at a range of 300 yards and possibly obtained a hit. The U-boat was seen submerging as it passed astern. Asdic contact was obtained at 2157 and four attacks were made with depth charges, but there was no evidence of any damage to the U-boat.

March 1942

During March the greatest successes of our counter-measures were achieved by our submarines. In the Mediterranean the "Admiral Millo" was sunk by H.M. Submarine "P 34" on the 16th March and H.M. Submarine "Unbeaten" reported the sinking of another Italian U-Boat on the 17th; both actions took place to the southward of the Straits of Messina. On the 18th H.M. Submarine "Upholder" also reported that she had sunk an Italian U-Boat, while patrolling off Brindisi, so achieving her "hat trick" and a record. (In the last war, H.M. Submarine "E54" sank two U-boats.)

There are also reports of successes by our submarines in northern waters. Full information is not yet available but H.M. Submarine "Seawolf" claims to have secured one hit on a U-Boat in a position West-North-West of Aalesund; towards the end of the month the Soviet Submarine "Azeodki 171" reported that she had sunk another in Varanger Fjord. (*No U-boats were lost*)

In addition to these sinkings by Allied submarines, a ship of the First Minesweeping Flotilla, H.M.S. "Sharpshooter," while escorting a convoy in the Arctic, sighted a surfaced U-Boat fine on the bow and one cable distant in a snow storm. She rammed the enemy at 13 knots and is reported to have rolled the U-Boat right over; there were no survivors *from U655 : Kptlt. Otto Dumrese.*

The general policy of the enemy remained the same in March as it had been in February and it continued to pay him a handsome dividend. He inflicted severe losses on British and Allied shipping in North and Central American waters, to say nothing of an occasional attack on a genuine South American neutral. During the latter half of the month an increasing number of attacks were carried out by the forces of the United Nations operating in these waters. The United States Naval Authorities report two attacks by surface craft and three by aircraft, all of which may have destroyed or damaged a U-Boat, and there has been some surface evidence that damage was caused by an attack by a ship of the Royal Canadian Navy and by two attacks by aircraft of the Royal Canadian Air Force. Detailed accounts of these attacks by units of the Canadian and United States Forces are not available. (*There is an interesting twist in the English language in this paragraph, which may not be appreciated by readers who do not have English as their first language: "a genuine South American neutral" suggests some neutral ships were not genuine. This implies that Britain was disguising some of her ships to look like neutrals.*)

Plans have been prepared for the establishment of Caribbean convoys and of convoys for coastwise Atlantic shipping. They will be put into force as soon as adequate escorts are available.

The month has also seen a renewal of U-Boat activity in the North Western Approaches and in the Rockall area. Up to the present date this renewal of activity has been a great encouragement to us and, it must be presumed, a great disappointment to Admiral Dönitz. It has produced no attack on any of our convoys but has resulted in several attacks by our surface forces on the U-Boats. Unhappily in no case has the attack given the ship the deep satisfaction of seeing a U-Boat come to the surface, with her crew tumbling on deck to surrender, but the evidence shows that several attacks were extremely promising and it is to be hoped that some resulted in "clean kills." Attacks carried out in this area included a hunt by United States Ships "Babbit" and "Badger," who were escorting Convoy S.C.L.71, on 6th March in a position 59°00'N. 25°53'W.

The anticipated attack upon our convoys between Iceland and Russia has come to pass. There were indications that U-Boats were in the neighbourhood of the homeward bound Convoy Q.P.9, but no attack developed; in the case of the outward Convoy P.Q.13, however, U-Boats were sighted and several signals, evidently U-Boat transmissions, were made in the area.

P.Q.13 sailed on Friday the 13th March. With the exception of bad luck in meeting with heavy weather, which appears to have partially scattered the Convoy, it seems to have survived ill omens in a remarkable way, considering the scale of the effort made by the enemy. Not only did the convoy meet a heavy concentration of U-Boats, but it was attacked by aircraft and destroyers into the bargain. Nevertheless, out of the nineteen ships which sailed, fourteen reached harbour; four are known to have been sunk, and one is still missing and is presumed lost. There was at least one promising attack on a U-Boat in the course of the convoy's passage.

There is little information of U-Boat warfare in the Indian Ocean, but the Commander-in-Chief, East Indies, reports that the "Aetos," a destroyer of the Royal Hellenic Navy, made an "apparently successful" attack on a U-Boat in the Colombo area. (*There is no record of a U-boat having been lost.*)

Our casualties in the course of March included H.M. Ships "Naiad," (*sunk by U565 : Johann Jebsen*) "Jaguar" (sunk by *U652 : Georg Werner Fraatz*) and "Heythrop," (*also sunk by U652*) all sunk in the Eastern Mediterranean, and H.M. Trawler "Notts County," (*sunk by U701 : Horst Degen*) lost either by torpedo or mine, while escorting a convoy to the south-eastward of Iceland.

It is interesting to note that the U-Boats operating in the Rockall — North Western Approaches area appear to have been working more often as single units, rather than in "wolf-pack" formation. It may be that this is more apparent than real, and has been due to the quick action of surface forces in locating and counter-attacking the first U-Boat to make contact.

A feature of the month was the unusual number of sightings by surface craft of U-Boats on the surface; cruisers and destroyers sighted ten, and corvettes and trawlers three. The U-Boat, at one time regarded as an almost entirely underwater craft, has tended, during this war, to become more arid more a surface craft endowed with the power of submerging but, nevertheless, no specific reason can be given to account for this large number of sightings. It may be due to a better look-out kept by our ships; alternatively, it may indicate that U-Boat crews are less highly-trained and more careless than they used to be. If this is so, there should be some good opportunities for successful attacks.

May 1942

During April two U-Boats are known to have been sunk. On the 14th U.S.S. "Roper" sank "U85" (*Kptlt. Eberhard Greger*) off Cape Hatteras and about midnight on the same day H.M. Ships "Vetch" and "Stork," escorting Convoy O.G.82, sank another, whose number is not known. (*This was U252 : Kptlt. Kai Lerchen*)

A full report of "Roper's" success has not yet been received but it is believed that she detected the U-Boat by R.D.F. and attacked it first with gunfire and then with depth charges. No survivors were picked up but 29 bodies were recovered.

The action with the other U-Boat also began with an R.D.F. contact, obtained by "Vetch," who was some five miles ahead of the convoy.

The enemy has continued to make his main effort in the Western Atlantic and our losses have again been heavy, though there has been a slight reduction as compared with March. It is also satisfactory to record that ships have escaped attack, in some cases after opening fire. It is hoped that the coming month will see the introduction of convoy and escort in United States coastal waters, but it appears that more time must elapse before convoy can be instituted in the Caribbean Sea. With the coming of convoy and the commissioning of newly-built anti-submarine craft, we can look for an improvement in the situation and a reduction in the serious losses which have occurred in the early months of the year.

Aircraft of the Royal Canadian Air Force have made an increased number of attacks: in some of them, at least, it can be said with assurance that damage must have been inflicted.

The reappearance of U-Boat activity in the North-Western Approaches and in the Rockall area, mentioned in the last Report, has not been continued, perhaps as a result of the rough handling which the enemy then received. An occasional U-Boat was sighted from the air and attacked but these were probably boats on passage; no attempts to make contact with our convoys seem to have been made.

Outside the Western Atlantic and the Caribbean Sea, the main U-Boat operations of the month have been in Arctic waters, where a considerable force of U-Boats has co-operated with both air and surface craft to interfere with our convoys to and from Russia.

Confined to a comparatively narrow sea-lane off the coast by the ice and within easy distance of enemy air bases, there has been no possibility of evasion and the Russian convoys have had to fight their way through.

In the event we have suffered losses both by U-Boat and air attack, but considering the scale of the effort made by the enemy, these losses cannot be considered heavy. We have been able to reinforce our anti-submarine escorts and have given the convoys generous anti-submarine, protection, judged by Atlantic standards. As a result, there have been several encounters between our anti-submarine forces and the U-Boats and, although no definite case of a "Known Sunk" can be claimed, there can be little doubt that some U-Boats have been damaged in varying degree and that a large number have been thoroughly well shaken up, to the detriment, it is hoped, of their morale.

June 1942

The enemy's main strategy has remained substantially the same and he has found it worth his while to continue to concentrate his primary effort off the American coast and. in the Caribbean Sea, accepting the long distance on passage thus involved. There is no conclusive evidence that U-Boats are being fuelled or given fresh torpedoes except when they return to French ports.

There has been a great increase in anti-submarine attacks, particularly to the westward of 40° W. On some days up to four, or even more, aircraft attacks have been made. An interesting attack was made at night by a United States aircraft on a surfaced U-Boat which was caught in the process of striking down torpedoes from its upper deck stowage. In the West Atlantic area an aircraft of the Royal Canadian Air Force carried out a promising depth charge attack, which resulted in an oil patch three-quarters of a mile square, the aircraft being also able to fire five hundred rounds into the U-Boat before it submerged.

We continue to be unlucky with prisoners and with other positive proofs of sinkings, but there have been several cases of circumstantial evidence of success. Off Key West, United States surface craft and aircraft attacked a U-Boat with the result that deck gratings and two pairs of leather trousers came to the surface. The depth of water was, about 400 fathoms. In the same category can be placed attacks carried out by H.M. Submarine "Turbulent," and a Catalina aircraft in the Mediterranean, though of the first no details have so far become available. The classification of the aircraft attack depends on the fact that about forty-five men were seen in the water. (*There are no records of a U-boat having been lost.*)

It has also been reported from the Mediterranean that a reconnaissance aircraft sighted two U-Boats close together, one apparently damaged transferring stores and crew to the other. An aircraft attack had been made in the vicinity some hours earlier.

We have obviously harried the U-Boats in the Mediterranean to a considerable extent, but they in their turn have caused us considerable damage. During the hot weather asdic conditions will deteriorate in this area.

There is no doubt that the most striking development of the month has been the great increase in effective air attacks on U-Boats. In addition to the attacks on U-Boats mentioned above, one German and one Italian were forced to take refuge in Spanish ports as a result of damage caused by Torpex depth-charges. The episode of the Italian U-Boat, which is of particular interest in that the first damaging attack was made by a Wellington aircraft fitted with a Leigh searchlight.

(U573 : Kptlt. Heinrich Heinsohn was damaged and then surrendered to an aircraft which was running low on fuel and left the scene. The men in U573 took advantage of the situation, repaired the damage and successfully put into Cartagena, where the boat was taken over by the Spanish Navy as G7. This gave rise to the Admiralty issuing an order to kill survivors, even if they were surrendering. Details of this are given on pages 36 & 37 of Volume 2 – "Weapons used against U-boats during World War Two".)

The attack which caused the German U-Boat to seek shelter in Spain was made in daylight and is typical of the attacks which are being made with increasing frequency by aircraft of Coastal Command. There have been five other attacks which sound most promising but of which we have no corroborative details; one of these was the first to be carried out by a Lancaster, the aircraft being on passage to escort Convoy H.G.84.

Some minor attacks have been made on North and Central American coastal convoys. The effect of' the institution of convoys in the Caribbean Sea remains to be seen. It can be confidently forecast that it will cause an immediate reduction of the heavy losses that have been inflicted in those waters; it may well bring about a change in the area of the main U-Boat attack. It seems likely that the attack on Convoy H.G.84 will be the forerunner of other heavy-scale attacks on convoys in the Eastern Atlantic and it may be that increasing anti-submarine defence in the Western Atlantic may encourage attack on cross-Atlantic convoys.

In fact, we now face a possible change in U-Boat strategy. A renewal at the present time of the attacks on the convoys in mid-Atlantic and Eastern Atlantic waters would come at a time when the strength of our escorts with individual convoys has been reduced by the transfer of some of our anti-submarine forces to meet the danger in the Western Atlantic and to reinforce our convoys to and from Russia in fighting their way through U-Boat and aircraft attack.

The weakness of our escorts cannot be denied, but against this there are some solid advantages. There is a steadily growing feeling of confidence amongst our escort groups that they can compete with and defeat the U-Boat attacking at night; many of them have worked together for some time now and have acquired a team spirit and mutual self-confidence. Moreover, there is the steadily increasing efficiency of R.D.F. which brings with it an ever-growing confidence in this method of U-Boat detection; very good results have also been recently achieved by intelligent and efficient use of H.F./D.F. and M.F./D.F.

It is to be hoped that we may be able to add to these advantages an increase in the deadliness of our anti-submarine attack resulting from the advent of the ahead-thrown weapon. The Hedgehog, however, still awaits adequate opportunities to prove itself and remains an untried development; perhaps the Mark X (one ton) depth-charge may yet be the first new weapon to claim a U-Boat victim.

Whatever the outcome, we can confidently expect that, if the onslaught on our Atlantic convoys is renewed, the U-Boats will find themselves given a far more difficult task than they had in the past. We shall, inevitably, suffer losses, but we should also be able to inflict heavy losses on the enemy.

40

Last month a possible change in U-Boat strategy was forecast and there are many indications that this change is imminent, if, indeed, it has not already taken place.

The establishment of the convoy system in the Western Atlantic and the immense increase in the counter-measures against U-Boats taken in those waters were the basis on which it was forecast that the U-Boats would shift the main thrust of their attack and would start to probe for another "weak spot."

It is significant that U-Boats have been sighted or D/F'd in the vicinity of our convoys and that there have been a certain number of attacks on convoys in mid-ocean; perhaps of even greater-significance is the re-appearance of German U-Boats in the Freetown area. Finally, we are in the unusual position of having been given a tip straight from the horse's mouth; Admiral Dönitz has given one of his rare interviews to the German Press and has broadcast to the German nation. (*Details of this broadcast are given in Volume , pages 62-63 – "What Britain knew and wanted to know about U-boats."*)

Again we have to record an unfortunate lack of German prisoners, though an aircraft of the United States Navy obtained a few, including the Captain, when she sank "U701." (*Kptlt. Horst Degen*)

Although no prisoners were taken, it is believed that another three, or perhaps four, German U-Boats have been destroyed. On 17th July, aircraft of Coastal Command sank a U-Boat (*U751 Gerhard Bigalk*) in the Bay of Biscay, leaving her crew to swim the 300 miles to the nearest land. On 24th July an attack by H.M.C.S. "St. Croix" and, on 31st an attack by H.M.C. Ships "Skeena" and "Wetaskiwin," produced human remains and wreckage, pointing in each case to the destruction of a U-Boat. (*U90 : Kptlt. Hans Oldörp and U588 : Kptlt. Viktor Vogel*) Also on 31st July, H.M.S. "Rochester" sighted and attacked a U-Boat ahead of Convoy O.S.35, then in a position to the north-eastward of the Azores and reported that wreckage of German origin appeared on the surface. (*U213 : Amelung von Varendorff was sunk*)

Against the shortage of German prisoners we can set a fresh supply of Italians. In the Atlantic on 14th July, H.M.S. "Lulworth," escorting Convoy S.L.115, attacked and sank the Italian U-Boat "Pietro Calvi," thirty survivors being picked up. In the Eastern Mediterranean, on 9th. and 11th July respectively, H.M.S. "Hyacinth" accounted for the Italian "Perla" and H.M. Ships " Protea" and "Southern Maid," which are manned by members of the South African Naval Forces, sank the "Ondina" with some assistance from a Walrus aircraft. Prisoners were captured from both U-Boats.

In addition to these known results, there have been several other promising attacks and it is hoped that these successes are the forerunners of the increased rate of destruction of U-Boats, which is vitally necessary if the enemy is to be mastered.

August was expected to show a large increase in the number of attacks on escorted convoys and the re-Opening of large scale operations in the Freetown area. The attacks on convoys occurred but in the Freetown area the scale of attack was not as heavy as expected.

Four night attacks and seven day attacks on Atlantic convoys took place and in these nine ships were torpedoed by night and sixteen by day.

Admiral Dönitz has also shown himself to be a good prophet and, although this comparatively large number of ships has been sunk in convoy, the lot of the German U-Boat has undoubtedly been hard. Four out of the six German U-Boats known to have been destroyed were sunk while attacking a convoy and many other U-Boats were very severely harassed and probably damaged.

Numerically our escorts are weak, but there is little doubt that technical improvements, leading to a greater reliability in such aids as H/F D/F and R.D.F., combined with lack of experience on the part of the U-Boats, are telling, heavily in our favour; the numbers, range and anti-submarine weapons of our aircraft are also considerably more formidable than they were. There can, however, be no time for complacency. During the last two months, very large numbers of U-Boats are thought to have come into operational service, and in the same period the number of U-Boats operating in the Atlantic is estimated to have increased by fifty per cent.

Eleven U-Boats — seven German, two Italian — one of them being a "human torpedo carrier" — and two Japanese, were sunk during the month.

The number of sinkings by ramming was remarkable. By this means H.M.C.S. "Assiniboine" and H.M.S. "Dianthus" each destroyed a U-Boat while escorting Convoy S.C.94, and H.M.S. "Ithuriel" accounted for the Italian "Cobalto" and H.M.S. "Wolverine" for another Italian U-Boat during the passage of the Malta Convoy; in the last week of the month H.M.C.S. "Oakville" finished off a fifth by the same means to the eastward of Jamaica. (*The sinkings were as follows: "Assiniboine" U210 : Kptlt. Rudolf Lemcke; "Dianthus" U379 : Kptlt. Paul Hugo Kettner and "Oakville" U94 : Kptlt. Otto Ites.*)

Although it is only natural that ship's company should like to feel the scrunch of their bows smashing through a U-Boat and have the satisfaction of knowing that one of these pests is definitely destroyed, a certain amount of discretion is necessary before using this means of destruction.

In most cases it will mean that the attacking ship is herself put out of action as far as her immediate duties are concerned and that the number of escorts with the convoy or fleet will thus be reduced. Furthermore, in all probability it will entail a period in dock necessitating the employment of labour and materials that could be put to more fruitful use.

Before deliberately ramming, the Commanding Officer should consider whether the U-Boat is not already sufficiently damaged to ensure that her destruction or surrender can be achieved by other means.

Two German U-Boats were sunk in northern waters, H.M. Submarine "P.247" torpedoing "U335" (*Kptlt. Hans-Hermann Pelkner*) to the north-eastward of the Shetlands on the 3rd August, and "U464" (*Kptlt. Otto Harms*) being depth-charged and sunk by a United States P.B.Y. aircraft from Iceland; H.M.S. "Castleton" was fortunately close at hand to take prisoners from the latter U-Boat.

Off Haifa two U-Boats were destroyed. On the 4th August H.M. Ships "Sikh," "Zulu," "Croome" and "Tetcott" sent "U.372" (*Kptlt. Hans-Joachim Neumann*) to the bottom after a hunt which lasted fourteen hours — this example of holding contact is a credit to anti-submarine teams and materiel — and, during the same week, H.M. Trawler "Islay" found and sank an Italian "human torpedo carrier" at the entrance to the swept channel.

The Japanese lost a U-Boat to U.S.S. "Cummings" in the New Hebrides on 6th August. On the last day of the month U.S. aircraft and U.S.S. "Reid" sank the Japanese U-Boat "Ro.61" off Atka in the Aleutian Islands.

In addition to these "known sinkings," there are many attacks yet to be assessed, and preliminary reports give reason to hope that some 25 may have caused damage; of these 14 appear particularly promising. Excluding those which resulted in certain kills, 39 attacks were by surface vessels and 56 by aircraft under British control. During the month United States aircraft and surface craft averaged together about seven attacks a day.

It is noteworthy that the U-Boat commander who attacked Convoy S.C.94 at 1325 on 8th August showed a skill which was much in excess of that displayed by the commanders of the other U-Boats engaged. The efficient handling of certain U-Boats was likewise noticed by the escorts of Convoy O.N.115. (*U660 : Götz Baur heard torpedoes hit, but there were no detonations. U552 : Erich Topp also attacked the convoy.*)

When the ships are so fitted for reception, the first indications of the presence of U-Boats have been in every case H/F D/F bearings, and these have also been of great assistance to Escort Commanders in appreciating the subsequent situations. Type 271 R.D.F. has proved a most efficient detector by night and the quick action taken by escort vessels has, in many cases, thwarted the night attack.

This has apparently forced the U-Boats to abandon their usual tactics and to attack submerged in daylight, accepting lack of mobility and a low speed against an escort weakened by members searching on D/F bearings. These day attacks have resulted in as many as five ships being torpedoed by one salvo; to lessen the chance of such success recurring, instructions were issued in the third week of August to open out the distance between the columns of a convoy to five cables by day as Well as by night. (*Records in Jürgen Rohwer's Axis Submarine Successes of World War Two suggest the maximum number sunk with one salvo was 4, in the case of U214 : Günther Reeder, but several boats achieved three sinkings with one salvo.*)

Escort Group No. 42, escorting Convoy S.L.118, is worthy of special mention. The H/F D/F fitted in H.M. Ships "Gorleston," "Wellington" and "Folkestone," enabled the Senior Officer to deduce the movements and indications of the U-Boat with considerable accuracy, the correctness of his deductions being proved on several occasions by subsequent sightings and attacks. He was unfortunately, unable to obtain decisive results in his engagement with the enemy, owing to the number of escorts available and their slow speed. Again and again, encounters which might otherwise have been pursued to a successful conclusion had to be prematurely broken off in order to maintain safe minimum escort with the convoy.

With the incidence of day attacks on convoys, some discretion is necessary in coming to a decision as to whether it is profitable to search for the enemy on an H/F D/F bearing. What certainly is worth while is to take every possible step to attack the first U-Boat to report a convoy, as this may at least cause her to lose touch and cease making shadowing reports.

On the night of 16th August "Folkestone" obtained an R.D.F. contact ahead of Convoy S.L.118 at 6,000 yards range and moving rapidly away towards the port bow. This U-Boat was forced to dive by starshell and six attacks were carried out on it. Within an hour of making contact, "Folkestone" and "Gorleston" chased an R.D.F. contact away to the northward, but it is not clear whether this was the same U-Boat resurfaced, or another.

H/F D/F bearings continued to show that the convoy was still being shadowed by about three U-Boats and at 0706 "Gorleston" sighted two of them 12 miles on the port quarter. One dived but the other may have followed the cutter back to the convoy when she rejoined later in the day, since one U-Boat carried out a daylight attack on the convoy when only three escorts were in company. One merchant ship was hit and sunk.

After dark on the 17th H.M. Ships "Pentstemon" and "Wellington" chased a U-Boat away to the westward, and an hour later "Folkestone" intercepted a U-Boat with the aid of R.D.F. and attacked it four times, repeating the success on another U-Boat early in the morning on the 18th when she carried out two depth-charge attacks.

During the morning of the 18th the persistence of the enemy was revealed by H/F D/F bearings, which indicated the presence of about three U-Boats. Searches by "Wellington," "Pentstemon," "Folkestone" and "Gorleston" were, however, unsuccessful, and in the afternoon a U-Boat carried out another daylight attack and obtained hits on two merchant ships, one of which was sunk, and on H.M.S. "Cheshire." (*This was U214 : Günther Reeder*)

That at night "Folkestone" intercepted a U-Boat broad on the port bow of the convoy and by gunfire forced it to dive. Nevertheless, the H/F D/F bearings continued to tell the same tale of about three shadowing U-Boats, and a Liberator aircraft attacked one of them on the port beam of the convoy at daylight on the 19th. That afternoon the final attack was made and one ship was torpedoed and sunk. The U-Boats then ceased action, having followed the convoy for three days.

Convoy O.N.115 was attacked on the night of lst/2nd August and had three ships torpedoed. The escort, which already had the sinking of a German U-Boat to its credit, drove off U-Boats on the 2nd and 3rd August and brought the convoy into harbour without further loss.

Convoy O.N.122 was attacked by a pack of U-Boats from the night of 23rd August to the night of the 25th. The escort, making full use of H/F D/F and R.D.F. — 14 contacts were obtained between 2215 on 23rd August and 1231 on the 25th, and there was only one occasion when the sighting of a U-Boat was not preceded by a contact — carried out a number of most persistent and spirited attacks. A Hedgehog attack was made by H.M.S. "Viscount," who reported that within two seconds of the charges hitting the water there was a tremendous rippling explosion, followed three seconds later by a small explosion. (*Has anyone identified the source of these detonations?*)

Excellent work was done by the other ships of the escort, H.No.M. Ships "Potentilla," "Eglantine," "Acanthus" and "Montbretia." "Potentilla" specially distinguished herself, using all her depth charges in a number of well-delivered attacks, and at one time holding off two U-Boats simultaneously. The convoy had three ships sunk but on only one occasion was the escort forced by superior numbers to yield the initiative and the enemy did not gain his objectives cheaply. It was thought that the U-Boats attacked all endeavoured to surface as soon as they considered that they had the smallest chance of escaping.

On the 3rd September H.M. Ships "Pathfinder," "Quentin" and "Vimy " sank "U162" (*Fregkpt. Jürgen Wattenberg*) off Trinidad and took 45 prisoners. In the middle of the month a Sunderland aircraft from Gibraltar sank a German U-Boat off Algiers, being able to take photographs of men in the water; 36 were counted. (*This must have been an Italian, since no German U-boats were lost to a Sunderland during this month.*) Off Ascension Island, about the same time in the month, an aircraft of the United States Army Air Corps sank a German U-Boat; she reported that survivors from it were seen getting into lifeboats from the torpedoed liner "Laconia." (*Again it has proved difficult to identify this boat as German.*) H.M.C.S. "Georgian" has reported that she sank a U-Boat in the Gulf of St. Lawrence, where the enemy has been decidedly active. (*There were no sinkings to match this report.*)

U-Boats have continued to pay considerable attention to convoys and O.N.127 suffered particularly heavily, losing seven merchant ships and one of the escort, H.M.C.S. "Ottawa." It is thought that at least three U-boats were sunk during the passage of convoys P.Q.18 and Q.P.14 and others were certainly damaged. Unfortunately none of the escort were fitted with H/F D/F. The first attack took place during the afternoon of the 10th September, another daylight attack was delivered that evening and a third attack was made during the night; three more night attacks were carried out twenty-four hours later. "Ottawa" was sunk in the early hours of the 14th, (*by U91 : Heinz Walkerling*). In the first daylight attack, ships in positions 12, 22 and 32 were torpedoed and in the second the ship in position 84 — there were nine columns — suggesting that the attacks were made from outside the convoy. Reports of the attacks made by the escorts have not yet been received.

In the attacks on Convoy R.B.1, H.M.S. "Veteran" is presumed to have been torpedoed and sunk.

It was noticeable that the main weight of attack on Atlantic convoys was delivered in the areas outside full shore-based air cover. An example of what can be achieved by intelligent disposition of the surface escort — now largely a matter of correct use of information derived from H/F D/F — and by sound co-operation with aircraft, is given by Convoy H.X.206, which without loss reached the United Kingdom on 16th September. The surface escort was able to deal with those U-Boats which were not put down by the air escort.

The two North Russian convoys had to fight their way through incessant U-Boat and aircraft attacks, losing sixteen merchantmen in all. Six very promising attacks were carried out by the escorts, who were assisted by Swordfish aircraft from H.M.S. "Avenger." This was the first operation in which this type of auxiliary aircraft carrier has taken part. Unfortunately H.M. Ships "Somali" and "Leda" were torpedoed and sunk during the passage of the westbound convoy. (*The first mentioned by U703 : Heinz Bielfeld and the second by U435 : Siegfried Strehlow.*)

The first attack was made by H.M.S. "Faulknor" on the 12th September, a short time after a U-Boat had been reported diving four miles ahead of Convoy P.Q.18. An emergency turn of 40° to port was made and "Faulknor," reinforcing the starboard side of the screen, obtained an echo ahead at 2,100 yards range. The target was classified as "submarine" and was very probably with the U-Boat which had been sighted. Two attacks were carried out, bringing up diesel oil in some quantity but after a short search the contact was abandoned. (*U88 : Kptlt. Heino Bohmann was sunk.*)

Next day the first U-Boat attack developed and two merchant ships were torpedoed and sunk. H.M. Ships "Onslaught" and "Tartar" made a number of attacks in the course of the day.

At dawn on the 14th September H.M.S. "Impulsive," who was returning up the port side of the convoy after investigating a report of torpedo tracks, obtained a "submarine" echo near the convoy. As she ran in to attack, torpedo hydrophone effect was heard and a ship on the far side of the convoy was seen to be hit; it is considered that this U-Boat did not get away scot-free. Later in the day, as a result of a sighting by a Swordfish aircraft, H.M.S. "Onslow" carried out a series of attacks. These first produced a quantity of diesel oil and later, after an unexplained explosion, a variety of wreckage which included green vegetables and pieces of a U-Boat's wooden casing, *from U589 : Kptlt. Hans-Joachim Horrer.*

H.M. Ships "Impulsive" and "Opportune" carried out attacks on the 15th and 16th. One of "Impulsive's" attacks brought up oil and wreckage *from U457 : Korvkpt. Karl Brandenburg.*

A new development in our counter-measures has been the establishment in mid-Atlantic of a temporary reinforcing group, whose primary object was the destruction of U-Boats rather than the immediate defence of trade. H.M.S. "Stork" was Senior Officer of the group, which was designated the 20th Escort Group, and other ships taking part in its operations were H.M. Ships "Deptford," "Spey," "Rother," "Exe," "Tay," "Sabre," "Sardonyx," "Saladin" and "Scimitar." The oiler "Laurelwood" was sailed in Convoy O.N.S.132 with 1,500 tons of furnace oil and a supply of depth charges but unfortunately the inexperience of her crew made refuelling at sea extremely difficult.

The operations, which began on the 22nd September with the sailing from Londonderry of "Stork," "Deptford," "Spey," "Rother" and "Exe" with orders to reinforce the escort of Convoy O.N.S.132, were hampered by bad weather and by the fact that, owing to vessels having to be detached for a variety of reasons, the ships of the Escort Group were never all in company. The operations lasted until the 3rd October.

At 1730 on the 24th the ships were ordered to support Convoy S.C.100 which had been attacked on the two preceding days but it was not met as expected and they were only in company for a few hours on the 25th. The escort of O.N.S.132 was reinforced from the 26th to the 29th September and that of S.C.102 from the 1st to 3rd October. Shortage of fuel made it necessary for "Scimitar" and "Saladin" to leave O.N.S.132 at 1800 on the 25th September and for the same reason "Sabre" had to part company at 1000 on the 27th. These destroyers were, however, instructed to give support to Convoy R.B.1 which was being attacked.

A case of acute appendicitis on board "Exe" made it necessary for her to proceed to Iceland on the 25th and from there she was sent to search for survivors from "Veteran," *which had been sunk by U404 : Otto von Bülow.*

The weather, too, was unfavourable for the first week but nevertheless the Group achieved its essential purpose, that of catching U-Boats unawares between the convoy's close escort and the Reinforcing Group. At 1331 on the 26th an R/T report from H.No.M.S. "Eglantine" to H.M.S. "Fame," Senior Officer of the close escort of O.N.132 was intercepted; this stated that a U-Boat was believed to have dived four miles ahead of the convoy. About half an hour later "Fame" was heard reporting that a U-Boat was passing between the fifth and sixth columns of the convoy. The Group, which had been disposed with ships in line abreast eight miles apart, thereupon closed in to form an anti-submarine sweep. At 1520 the convoy was sighted ten miles ahead.

Twenty minutes later a U-Boat — probably that referred to by "Eglantine" and "Fame" — surfaced a mile ahead of "Stork." The discovery of the latter must have been an unpleasant surprise for the U-Boat captain, intent on the convoy which he was following, and he dived in fifty seconds. Contact was at once gained and held almost continuously for an hour and twenty minutes under most difficult asdic conditions. A counter-attack and four deliberate attacks were made by "Stork" between 1548 and 1702 and "Spey" also made a depth-charge and a hedgehog attack. A large quantity of oil was seen and it is thought that the U-Boat was at least severely damaged. After the attacks the ships of the Group took up positions on the outer screen of the convoy. (*There were no sinkings to match this report.*)

At 1443 on the following day "Rother" reported a U-Boat surfacing 1,000 yards on her beam — that is to say seven miles on the starboard bow of the convoy. It was blowing a full gale but "Rother" attacked, possibly with some success; "Stork" closed her but in the prevailing conditions did not endeavour to hunt. It is thought that this U-Boat had dived well ahead of the convoy in order to obtain some respite from the unpleasant weather and had surfaced in a good shadowing position, quite unaware of the reinforcement of the escort. (*There were no sinkings to match this report.*)

On the 28th, after an aircraft had reported attacking a U-Boat thirty miles astern of the convoy, "Stork" and "Rother" in company with H.M.S. "Viscount" made a sweep astern but without result.

At 1800 on the 29th, after the abortive effort to refuel from "Laurelwood," the Group left the convoy in position 49°15'N. 34°52'W. "Spey" and "Rother" were detached to Iceland to refuel but in the event "Rother" returned direct to Londonderry and "Spey" joined Convoy S.C.102 during the following night, "Stork," "Deptford" and "Tay" joining at 1400 on the 1st October. After two days devoid of incident the Group parted company from the convoy in position 56°50'N. 15°38'W. and returned to their bases.

The Group's operations may have resulted in at least severely damaging two U-Boats, and Convoy O.NS.132, which the enemy had had time to reconnoitre, was probably saved from attack. An indication of the value of a free-lance Escort Group may be gauged from the fact that the U-Boats which surfaced so imprudently more or less alongside "Stork" and "Rother" were, in fact, reconnoitring the convoy in the safest position normally available to them.

Admiral Dönitz found his new "soft spot" off the Cape of Good Hope and, though the blow had been anticipated, his U-Boats sank 14 independently routed ships within four days. Fortunately losses did not continue at this rate and, though more attacks were made in an area which extended to Durban, the sinkings after the first outbreak were not heavy. A number of aircraft attacks were made on these U-Boats and on the 3rd October H.M.S. "Active" gave one of them the full benefit of a ten-charge pattern, which resulted in an oil patch three miles long and half a mile wide. (*U179 : Fregkpt. Ernst Sobe was sunk on 8ᵗʰ October.*)

On the Transatlantic trade routes, although the Germans may claim successful attacks on four convoys, it is significant that 16 others were shadowed without any visible signs of attacks on the merchantmen in convoy. Another 18 evaded the U-Boats altogether. The four convoys attacked were S.C.104, O.N.139, S.L.125 and H.X.212, which lost a total of 28 ships in the course of 15 attacks.

In selecting convoy routes the advantage of the northerly route within the range of air cover from Iceland has to be balanced against the increased time on voyage, due to greater distance and worse weather, and the advantage which is restored to the U-Boat at night when Type 271 (Radar) in the escorts is not functioning at full efficiency.

This month the U-Boats made all their assaults by night and most of them in rough weather. It is probably safe to assume that the enemy still prefers to attack by night but that competent U-Boat commanders, if frustrated night after night by well-handled escorts taking full advantage of their R.D.F., Type 271, will occasionally manage to gain bearing on the convoy sufficient for a submerged attack by day. The rough weather during the month, by reducing the efficiency of R.D.F., was, to that extent at least, in favour of U-Boats attacking by night, but it may interest the escort vessels to know that, according to broadcast reports, the weather has also been a severe strain on the Germans.

U-Boats have been sighted or attacked off the United States eastern seaboard and in the Gulf of Mexico but, thanks to the effectiveness of the United States Navy's counter measures, there have been no losses in North or Central American waters, except in the busy Trinidad area. Thus, in just over nine months from their entry into the war, the United States, by the institution of escorted convoys and the provision of air cover and air patrols, have achieved a high degree of immunity from U-Boat attack.

Two reinforcing groups, similar to the 20th Escort Group, have been operating in the Western Approaches but both had to be diverted to rescue work.

During the attacks on Convoy S.C.104 H.M. Ships "Viscount" and "Fame" each rammed a U-Boat. "Fame" got prisoners from "U353" — the captain (*Oblt.z.S. Wolfgang Romer*) was caught asleep in his bunk — but her boarding party had to withdraw quickly from the sinking U-Boat.

On 6th October H.M.S. "Crocus," who was stationed at Freetown, attacked a U-Boat with depth-charges and gunfire, also ramming it twice, and it is considered that it was sunk. During the following week, H.M.S. "Celandine" and H.No.M.S. "Potentila," escorting Convoy O.N.137, reported attacks "believed successful" and "producing oil" respectively. (*There are no records of U-boats having been lost.*)

On the 21st of the month H.M. Submarine "Graph," on Bay of Biscay patrol, fired torpedoes "at a sister ship," (*probably U333 : Kptlt. Peter Cremer.*) Explosions were heard at the correct time and the enemy's hydrophone effect disappeared but "Graph" could not collect exhibits. On the 30th October a U-Boat was sunk after a series of attacks had been made by Sunderland aircraft and five destroyers; the action lasted 17 hours. (*This was U559 : Kptlt. Hans Heidtmann, which was sunk by H.M. Ships "Petard," "Packenham," "Dulverton," "Hunworth" and "Hero." Men from "Petard" managed to get on board to capture the new four wheel Enigma machine, which had been introduced in February 1942 and thus enabled Bletchley Park to break the code they called "Shark.")*

Two Hudson aircraft from West Africa achieved some measure of success against U-Boats. On 1st October a depth charge was dropped within 20 feet of an Italian U-Boat; blue smoke was seen coming from the conning-tower and a seaman fell overboard. From the amount of W/T traffic which ensued, it seems likely that the U-Boat was damaged. On the 28th, in an attack on a German U-Boat, one depth-charge bounced off the hull but two exploded very near. Photographs show 15 ft. of the U-Boat's stern at a steep angle and a large oil patch was observed.

A number of promising attacks by United States and R.C.A.F. aircraft have been reported from such widely separated places as the French Guiana coast, the St. Lawrence, Kiska and Guadalcanal. The first-mentioned attack was made on 2nd October by a United States Army aircraft, which reported the sighting of large quantities of oil and, five minutes later, a single survivor surfacing; eventually the oil slick stretched for six miles. (*One of these was U512 : Kptlt. Wolfgang Schultze.)*

New U-Boats continue to make the passage north or south of the Faeroes, and it is probable that between 20 and 30 passed into the Atlantic during the month. Aircraft patrols are now being reinforced by three destroyers working from Sullum Voe under the orders of Commander-in-Chief, Rosyth.

November 1942

For the first time for many months it can be said with fair certainty that the number of operational U-Boats has decreased. Apparently only about 12 U-Boats made the westerly passage north of Scotland. Our best estimate is a decrease of 10 during the month. In connection with the North African operations there is certain evidence of the killing of seven U-Boats and, as far as can be judged from preliminary reports from surface craft, another dozen attacks will eventually be assessed as "Sunk" or "Probably Sunk"; aircraft made 110 sightings and carried out 64 attacks, some 20 of which resulted in claims for the destruction or serious damaging of U-Boats.

It seems incredible that no U-Boat success was achieved against the convoys of the expeditionary force until after the assault troops had landed, for they appeared to pass through concentrations aggregating 30 to 40 U-Boats before reaching Gibraltar. Even after the 8th November, our losses were not severe though, despite casualties, the number of U-Boats operating in the Western Mediterranean rose from about 10 on the 8th to about 20 on the 11th.

H.M. Ships "Hecla," "Martin," "Broke" and "Avenger," H.Ne.M.S. "Isaac Sweers" and U.S. Transport "Rutledge" were sunk by U-Boats in the course of the operations. (*In the same order: U515 : Werner Henke, U431 : Wilhelm Dommes, U155 : Adolf Cornelius Piening and U431. U515 also hit the destroyer "Marne," mentioned below.)*

A verbal account of the sinking of "Hecla" has been given by a survivor. The ship was apparently hit by six torpedoes, the first two, at 2316 on the 11th November, stopping the ship.

H.M. Ships "Venomous" and "Marne," in company, were ordered to carry out a patrol round "Hecla" at 3,000 yards, but details of their movements are not yet known except that "Venomous" carried out a depth-charge attack. About an hour and a half later "Marne" closed "Hecla" to pick up survivors and was herself hit by a torpedo, which blew her stem off, when lying stopped off "Hecla's" starboard quarter. The U-Boat was seen momentarily after this attack. "Marne" was able to get into Gibraltar, being probably saved by the U-Boat running out of torpedoes.

The North African operations have not interrupted the Battle of the Atlantic, which has continued in much the same fashion as before. Between 70 and 80 U-Boats were operating against the 16 regular convoys which were at sea in the course of the month. U-Boats were in contact with 12 of these 16 but only five of them suffered loss. The main attack was on Convoy S.C.107; an analysis of the U-Boat operations has not yet been completed, but a track chart showing the main events appears in this Report.

Convoy O.N.138 was shadowed but not attacked. Its passage provides a good example of the effective use of H/F D/F, which, combined with a large alteration of course, succeeded in throwing the U-Boat pack off the scent.

On the evening of the 23rd October, the first transmission was D/F'd close astern of the convoy, the speed of which was seven knots. Thereafter a very large number of signals were intercepted and the Senior Officer (H.M.S. "Hesperus") was able to plot the movements of the three or four U-Boats involved with some accuracy. High speed sweeps were made during the night, which, though they did not result in contacts, evidently delayed the U-Boats in their attempts to get ahead and attack. They could not, however, entirely stop them and by the next morning two had succeeded in their endeavours to work round. One of these was sighted and attacked by "Hesperus" and the other was probably responsible for an attempt at 2000, which H.M.S. "Gentian" nipped in the bud. The corvette obtained an asdic contact and, after sighting a periscope, attacked the U-Boat, which probably escaped through the convoy.

Shortly after this, the convoy altered to the westward with a turn of 60° to starboard. "Hesperus" was then seventeen miles to port of the convoy, looking, for a U-Boat which was working ahead on that side. During the night the H/F D/F signals became weaker and it became evident that the pack had lost the convoy. The weather was clear.

This "kink" of 60° in the route given to the convoy was made at nightfall. A big alteration of course made and maintained by a convoy gives good evasive possibilities but, unfortunately, the necessity for fairly direct routeing, to allow a margin of endurance for the escorts, and the traffic control in the Atlantic, essential if awkward encounters between convoys are to be avoided, seldom allows of such routeing and timing with nightfall.

Reference was made last month to the attacks on Convoy S.L.125, which lasted for four days. The escort, of which H.M.S. "Petunia" was Senior Officer, were all fitted with R.D.F., Type 271; a number of break-downs were, however, reported by "Petunia" and H.M.S. "Crocus."

After each of the first three attacks Operation "Raspberry" was reported to have been carried out but without success. On the fourth night, that of 30th/31st October, "Petunia" suspecting the U-Boat of having made its escape between the fourth arid fifth columns in previous attacks, shaped a course at dusk to pass through the convoy with the intention of waiting for the U-Boat close astern, should it attempt the manoeuvre again. (*Details of "Operation Raspberry" are given in Volume 1.*)

Her appreciation was correct but the execution too late. When she was at the entrance to the columns the leading ship of the fourth column blew up; by the light of the fire and later by snowflakes the U-Boat was clearly seen on the surface about 500 yards ahead of the corvette.

In the chase which followed no hits were obtained by gunfire, owing to the rough weather and to merchant ships getting into the line of fire. Once clear of the convoy the U-Boat rapidly increased the range and disappeared beyond the area of illumination. The corvette astern, which had been ordered by R/T to intercept, failed to do so and the U-Boat got away with this bold manoeuvre unscathed.

Owing to bad weather and the reduction of the German Air Force in Northern Norway, Convoy Q.P.15 was not shadowed and so avoided a heavy concentration of U-Boats. The convoy was, however, badly scattered by gales and one ship was sunk by a U-Boat. The others arrived safely, except for one which went aground.

A Western Support Force, which will consist of approximately three destroyers based on St. John's, Newfoundland, has been organised. It will be sailed to support each regular east-bound mid-ocean group, leaving it in 35° W. and joining the appropriate west-bound group. It is hoped that this force will do much to bridge the gap where no air cover is provided.

Such trawlers as can be made available from Western Approaches are also being formed into mid-ocean support groups. They would be especially valuable in reinforcing the escorts of attacked convoys, screening damaged ships and helping in rescue work.

During November United States bombers and Bomber Command assisted our other countermeasures, the former by daylight precision bombing of the French U-Boat bases and the latter by frequent mining sorties in Bay of Biscay.

It has been a month of many opportunities offered and taken in anti-submarine operations and quite "a pain in the neck" for Admiral U-Boats.

Recently there have been some excellent results from quick counter-attacks with full patterns of depth-charges. It is, of course, a question for each individual Commanding Officer to decide whether he can afford to expend the depth-charges, but in every case it is essential that the pattern be ready and that the Commanding Officer is not restricted in his decision by the state of readiness or unreadiness of his depth-charge crew.

Every Escort Group, which is not fully equipped and which is not a well-trained team, must be converted into one and maintained as one by the utmost efforts of each member.

December 1942

Until the last few days of the month it looked as though our shipping losses were going to be very substantially reduced as compared with recent months, but in the last week an outward bound convoy was very roughly handled when out of reach of air cover. The enemy attributed the smaller sinkings to the bad weather; from enemy broadcasts it seems that fog is, in fact, a much greater hindrance to U-Boats than storm. Fortunately, gales seldom entail the grounding of aircraft and in such conditions as prevailed last month air cover becomes of cardinal importance.

Of the 15 transatlantic convoys which sailed during the month, only three — H.X.217, O.N.153 and O.N.154 — suffered loss. Their respective passages give a clear illustration of the necessity for an escort of both air and surface craft in these days of increase in the size of U-Boat "packs" to 15 or more. H.X.217 followed a northern route and was first sighted by, U-Boats in extreme visibility and good weather when about 500 miles from Newfoundland. On the day following an aircraft met it but obtained no sightings. That night, U-Boats delivered a series of attacks on the convoy, but the escort drove them off and only one ship was hit, the torpedo being fired from outside the screen.

By the third day the convoy was within 600 miles of Iceland and the three aircraft which provided air cover were rewarded with thirteen sightings and eleven attacks; they thereby prevented most of the U-Boats from working round and the attacks during the hours of darkness were considerably less heavy than they had been on the previous night.

The Iceland aircraft were grounded next day and a natural consequence was the intensification of the night attacks; the surface escorts, however, drove off the U-Boats in fine style and the renewal of air cover on the following morning brought their operations against the convoy to an end.

Convoy O.N.153 was just outside the 600-mile line when the attack developed on the 16th, resulting in the loss of two ships. It was attacked again that night and lost another merchantman and, a few hours later, the Senior Officer of the Escort. It was, however, possible to provide air cover and thus protected the convoy made a large alteration of course in bad weather and shook off the U-Boat pack.

The demonstration of the immense importance of efficiently combining surface and air escort was completed by the attacks on Convoy O.N.154, which was given a southerly route. Caught by a large pack of U-Boats as it was drawing away from the 600-mile circle, it lost three ships in an attack at 0415 on the 27th and had another two torpedoed at 2037 that night. When the U-Boats attacked about 2200 on the night of 28th, no less than 10 ships, aggregating 54,000 tons, were torpedoed, all but one of them being sunk.

Only one convoy running between the United Kingdom and North African ports was attacked, the 23,700 ton liner "Strathallan" being torpedoed in the Mediterranean (*by U562 : Horst Hamm*) while in KMF5. By fine seamanship more than 5,000 personnel — drawn from no less than 83 units — were taken off from the liner and H.M.S. "Laforey" got her in tow. Casualties were less than a score. Weather conditions were good and it seemed likely that she would be got in but, about twelve hours after being torpedoed, she burst into flames and had to be abandoned. Nothing was seen of the U-Boat, which had probably fired at extreme range.

Three destroyers were sunk by U-Boats during the month, H.M. Ships "Blean" (*by U443 : Konstatin von Puttkamer*) and "Partridge" (*by U565 : Wilhelm Franken*) in the Mediterranean and H.M.S. "Firedrake," (*U211 : Karl Hause*) who was the Senior Officer of the escort of Convoy O.N.153. "Firedrake's" casualty list was heavy and included three Anti-Submarine officers.

On 26th December H.M. Ships "Hesperus" and "Vanessa," who were escorting Convoy H.X.219, rather unexpectedly found "U 357" (*Adolf Kellner*) as far eastward as the Rockall area. The U-Boat, sixteen days out from Kiel on her first patrol, was attacked with five fourteen-charge patterns and a Mark X depth-charge. Shortage of high-pressure air and run-down batteries forced her to surface. She tried to escape but was rammed by both destroyers and only eight ratings were saved.

Searchlight-fitted Wellingtons operating from Gibraltar have made three attacks which may possibly have resulted in kills, and in the Atlantic 120 Squadron achieved two very successful attacks and 84 Squadron (U.S.N.) a third.

The escort of Convoy H.X.220 included H.M.S. "Battler"; Martlet aircraft were carried, as Swordfish and Albacores were not available in the United States when she sailed. As the convoy was not attacked, flying was not considered advisable in the rough weather experienced on passage.

In November we probably reduced the number of operational U-Boats for the first time for many months and in December we had the lowest merchant shipping losses since the first month of the year.

Two U-Boat packs, each about fifteen in number, are now operating in the Atlantic and there will soon be a third. The best opportunity for destruction exists in the vicinity of shadowed convoys, but so far the escorts which it has been possible to provide have been barely sufficient for fighting the convoy through, even when air cover has been provided for a proportion of the voyage.

The U-Boat that lives after attempting to attack a convoy lives to fight another day with the benefit of the experience gained and the enemy seems almost to be basing his training of U-Boat crews on this fact. An article in the Sixth Section of this Report shows that, while morale is still high, training has been shortened and efficiency, to some extent, reduced. Such crews are obviously easier to destroy whilst inexperienced.

The provision of new weapons and methods and the development of those at present in use are being pressed on, but in the last resort the battle is peculiarly one between teams and between individuals.

January 1943

As regards merchant shipping losses, which were lower than in any month of 1942, the new year started well, but it also saw the Germans for the first time operating a hundred U-Boats in the Atlantic. In spite of this large concentration on our northern trade routes it is astonishing that the U-Boats did not succeed in massing and attacking any of our convoys, though they did manage to pick off a few stragglers. Unfortunately no U-Boats were sunk in this area. (*The daily average number of U-boats at sea were as follows: Months for 1942 - J 42, F 50, M 48, A 61, J 59, J 70, A 86, S 100, O 105, N 95, D 97; Months for 1943 – J 92, F 116, M 116, A 111, M 118, J 86, J 84, A 59, S 60, O 86, N 78, D 67.*)

In the southern part of the North Atlantic they had considerable success in their attacks on Convoy T.M.1, bound from the Dutch West Indies to Gibraltar, and sank seven out of nine tankers. (*Prof. Jürgen Rohwer lists 17 ships in Axis Submarine Successes.*) The first attack was made at 2145 on the 3rd January when the convoy was about 1,100 miles north-east of Trinidad and may well have been the result of a chance encounter but, once sighted, the identity and probable destination of the convoy was evidently correctly appreciated. For five nights the tankers proceeded unmolested but on the night of the 9th/10th, when they were about 600 miles west of the Canary Islands, a series of heavy attacks resulted in the loss of five ships. At least one of these might have been able to reach harbour but the size of the escort — one destroyer and three corvettes — was insufficient to permit leaving anyone behind to stand by the damaged ships, nor were the escort able to hunt the U-Boats to destruction. There were indications that U-Boats were damaged by the escorts but no proofs of kills.

Twenty-four hours after this attack, one of the three ships then remaining was torpedoed and burst into flames, revealing four U-Boats between the convoy and its escorts.

All four escort vessels were fitted with R.D.F., Type 271, and the destroyer had H/F D/F, but during the critical period the R.D.F. in two out of the three corvettes was broken down. Some of the U-Boats were probably able to reach favourable positions and then to get past the escort — the protection that is afforded to the normal trade convoy cannot rightly be called "a screen" — submerged and undetected. All the attacks on the convoy took place well out of range of shore-based aircraft.

The only other convoy to suffer serious loss was T.B.1 (Trinidad to Baja), which had four out of twelve ships torpedoed and sunk. The U-Boats, operating in comparatively shallow water to the northward of Guiana, took advantage of a gap in the air cover to make their attacks.

A daylight attack was made on Convoy H.X.222 when it was about 450 miles south-west of Iceland. An aircraft sighted a U-Boat thirty miles ahead of the convoy some time during the forenoon of 17th January but unfortunately no direct report relative to the convoy was received by the escort. At about 1245 the 14,000 ton whale-oil factory "Vestfold" (64) was torpedoed (*by U268 : Günther Heydemann*) on her starboard side. "Artichoke" was ordered but three of the escort did not receive the signal. H.M.S. "Chesterfield" hauled out to starboard and obtained a contact which she attacked at 1254. Her asdic was thereby put out of order and H.M.C.S. "St. Croix" took up the hunt. She obtained a doubtful contact at 1330 and dropped two charges and then, influenced by the firing of tracer, hunted on a southerly course — the convoy's course was 060° — with "Chesterfield" and "Battleford" in company, but without success.

It is thought likely that the torpedo was fired at comparatively long range. "Chesterfield" probably made contact with the U-Boat but lost it by cutting left on the wake. A point of interest is that the sighting of torpedoes "near the surface and travelling very slowly" was reported; these may in reality have been submarine bubble targets, which the operator followed away from the U-Boat.

Although no U-Boats were destroyed in the North Atlantic no less than five fell to us in the Mediterranean. Corvettes of the Royal Canadian Navy, "Yule de Quebec" and "Port Arthur," accounted for a German and an Italian, Beaufort aircraft operating from Malta seriously damaged the Italian "Narvalo," which was easily finished off by destroyers in the vicinity, and five M.T.B.s caught another Italian U-Boat as it was being towed away from Tripoli on the advance of the Eighth Army. H.M. Submarine "Sahib" sank the fifth — "U301." (*Willy-Roderich Körner*)

United States aircraft attacked "U164" (*Korvkpt. Otto Fechner*) in a position north of Fortaleza (*Uruguay*) on the 6th January and reported the sighting of several mangled bodies and much miscellaneous wreckage. A week later two survivors from the U-Boat landed in Brazil and on interrogation said that they had been in the conning tower at the time of the attack, but they could not say for certain whether the U-Boat had been destroyed.

On the night of the 29th/30th H.M.N.Z. Trawlers "Kiwi" and "Moa" sighted a Japanese troop-carrying U-Boat on the surface off Guadalcanal. After she had been engaged with gunfire "Kiwi" rammed her and drove her ashore, where she was burnt out. One Japanese officer was captured.

To meet to some extent the need for shore-based air cover for transatlantic convoys, Coastal Command should, by the end of February, have forty V.L.R. aircraft, with an endurance of

2,000 to 2,500 miles. Action has been taken to increase considerably the number of V.L.R. aircraft on both sides of the Atlantic. Four Hudson aircraft of Coastal Command have operated as an experiment from Bluie West I Airfield in Greenland; it is hoped that soon there will be long-range aircraft at this airfield but their operations will be restricted by weather and other conditions.

It is now possible to provide continuous shore-based air cover on the coastal route between Gibraltar and Freetown.

Now that Grand-Admiral Dönitz is supreme Commander of the German Navy we may expect all units to operate in support of the U-Boat warfare and we shall be on the look-out for any indication of a change in policy. It is certainly going to be a grim fight in 1943 and, though we are not as ready for it as we should like to be, there have been plenty of examples in 1942 to demonstrate that, even with our present inadequate scale of air and surface escort, with good training and team work, it is possible to fight a convoy through a pack of U-Boats and give as good as we get.

February 1943

Team work of escort craft, both surface and air, has borne good fruit and it is believed that more than a dozen German U-Boats have been sunk in the Atlantic and two German and four Italian in the Mediterranean. In the Atlantic, U-Boat packs, being a collection of individual boats which are comparative strangers to each other and are working on a fairly rigid system of orders, have been deterred and disconcerted by escort teams which have been able to take the initiative and, with resolute action, to deliver early and telling blows. The chagrin of the enemy at the way the battle is going, for the time being, at least, continues to show itself in exaggerated claims.

It is evident that the U-Boats are trying hard to get ahead of convoys and to attack submerged in order to avoid detection by R.D.F. or visual sighting. With broad fronted convoys it is not possible for the few escort vessels available to give much of a screen against such a manoeuvre, and, where the defence has been successful, the U-Boats have almost invariably been detected on the surface while trying to get into an attacking position.

On the whole it is considered that the U-Boats are willing to get inside the convoy by day or on moonlight nights but that they are unlikely to accept such a situation voluntarily on a dark night.

Elsewhere in this section is an account of the nine-hour hunt which ended in the destruction of U 559 (*Hans Heidtmann*) on 30th October, 1942. Even more perseverance was shown in a hunt in the neighbourhood of Algiers, which began with an R.D.F. fix at 2125 on 20th February and ended over 60 hours later with depth-charge attacks by four destroyers. (*Probably U443 : Oblt.z.S. Konstatin von Puttkamer.*)

It is estimated that over twenty U-Boats made contact with Convoy S.C.118 which lost its rescue ship and eight merchantmen, one of these being a straggler. The convoy was first sighted on 4th February hut it was not until the night of the 6th/7th that the U-Boats really developed their attack and sank seven ships. An attack made on the following night cost the convoy only one ship "U 187," (*Kptlt. Ralph Münnich*) who probably made the first sighting, was sunk on the 4th by H.M.S. "Vimy" after a sweep along an H/F D/F bearing ahead of the convoy. (The

U-boat probably first sighted a snowflake, fired by mistake at about dawn on 4 February.

The escort on the night of the 6th/7th consisted of 12 ships, three being United State's destroyers. Air cover was provided on and after 6th February, despite the fact that the Iceland aircraft were grounded on the 7th. Co-operation between the air and surface escort was good — the "Air Patrol Table" worked well — and there were a number of promising attacks by both ships and aircraft, resulting, it is thought, in two U-Boats being sunk, in addition to "U 187," and seven or eight being damaged. (*The two U-boats were U609 : Kptlt. Klaus Rudloff and U624 : Kptlt. Ulrich Graf von Soden-Frauenhofen.*)

A meeting was held at Liverpool after the arrival of the convoy and the following points were brought out. First, the Escort Commander, who was ahead of the convoy, was not fully apprised of the situation and would undoubtedly have been better placed astern — the nights were dark and the wind quarterly, force 5; secondly, escorts must keep their Senior Officer fully informed of important (incidents and of any deviation from his last instructions; thirdly, it is most necessary to take prompt offensive action when a convoy is attacked and fourthly, it is extremely important for the Senior Officer to control firmly the number of escort vessels engaged in rescue work or screening other ships engaged in rescue work.

The only other eastbound convoy to be attacked was H.X.224. After proceeding uneventfully for five days, it was attacked on the 2nd and 3rd February; on both nights the time chosen was during the middle watch and the rear ship of a column was hit. Another attack was attempted and frustrated at 2037 on the 2nd. The U-Boats remained in contact until the convoy was within 36 hours of Barra Head (*Outer Hebrides*) but made no more attacks.

The convoy was a big one, consisting of 58 ships in 14 columns, and it was estimated that at one time during its passage it covered an area of no less than 52 square miles. Weather conditions were bad and on the night of 30th/31st January, the wind, which was blowing from the south-west, increased from Force 6-7 to 8, causing a dozen ships on the port wing of the convoy to heave to and eventually to leave the convoy. Presumably the U-Boats also found these conditions difficult.

The escort consisted of H.M.S. "Highlander" as Senior Officer, H.M.C. Ships "Restigouche," "Collingwood," "Amherst" and "Sherbrooke" and H.M.S. "Asphodel," who were reinforced by H.M. Ships "Clare" and "Londonderry" on 2nd February. It was unfortunate that circumstances made it necessary to deprive "Highlander" of the ships to which six months group training and preparation had been devoted. Loyal and intelligent as was the co-operation shown by the ships allotted to her, it could not make up for the group training and mutual understanding which had been achieved and which lie at the very root of successful convoy escort. Despite these difficulties, operations which lasted from about noon on 1st February to about midnight on the 3rd were carried out with a minimum of loss and possibly resulted in the sinking of a U-Boat. At 1452 on 1st February, "Amherst," on the port quarter, reported sighting a suspicious object bearing 234° distant 7 miles but, though "Amherst" and "Sherbrooke" investigated, they found nothing, nor was a Fortress aircraft any more successful.

At 2000 "Highlander's" appreciation was that there were two U-Boats in the vicinity but there was nothing to show that either of them was actually in contact with the convoy, though the stragglers might have been reported. It was a moonless night with a high sea and the wind blowing strongly from the convoy's port quarter, and "Highlander" did not anticipate attack that night. It developed, none the less, at about 0115/2, the U-Boat firing from the port quarter to sink the rear ship of the port wing column. No white rockets were fired — the convoy was at the time enveloped in a heavy sleet shower — and there was unfortunately a delay of about five minutes in reporting the attack to "Highlander." She at once ordered "Half Raspberry" (*further details in Volume 1.*) and then directed "Sherbrooke" and "Amherst" to carry out "Observant" round the wreck, but nothing was sighted. It is thought that the U-Boat escaped to leeward in the rain.

From then onwards H/F D/F bearings indicated that the convoy was being shadowed and that other U-Boats were closing it. Two fixes were obtained about noon but, though "Amherst," "Asphodel" and "Restigouche" were sent off to sweep, neither U-Boat could be located. At 2000 it was considered that the convoy was being shadowed from the starboard quarter, with a U-Boat on each bow, one on the port quarter and possibly two more in the neighbourhood. The U-Boat on the starboard bow apparently closed for an attack — there was a light horizon in the north-west and the convoy's course was 086° — but her enterprise was foiled by "Restigouche," who returned from her sweep just in time to force her to dive, and perhaps also by "Collingwood," who carried out an attack on a doubtful contact at 2037.

At 2200/2 the H/F D/F plot indicated that the procedure of the enemy was to shadow from the windward quarter but to close in astern at frequent intervals to check the convoy's course. Having done this and made a report, the U-Boat would quickly move out to the quarter again. "Highlander" determined to take advantage of this deduction and, calculating that the U-Boat would make its next dart in astern at 2300, despatched "Clare" and "Londonderry," who had joined during the afternoon, together with "Asphodel," on an R.D.F. sweep to a depth of 5 miles astern of the convoy. They started at 2239 and punctually at 2300 the shadower was heard making her report but, owing to a misunderstanding, the ships did not find her.

Two hours later, at 0102 on the 3rd, the enemy attacked again. As before, the attack coincided with a heavy shower and caught the rear ship of a column — this time the centre. On this occasion a rocket was sighted and "Half Raspberry" was carried out, but there was a delay of 10 minutes in the firing of snowflake by the merchantmen; the U-Boat apparently passed close to the wreck about 10 minutes after the torpedoing and then made off at high speed on a westerly course to leeward, as in the first attack.

A fine batch of H/F D/F bearings showed that the illumination of the convoy had not been wasted upon the U-Boats in contact and enabled "Highlander" to place one on the port bow, one on the port quarter and a third on the starboard quarter, at ranges estimated to be between 20 and 25 miles. There appeared to be no U-Boats ahead or on the starboard bow. To forestall the attack which, it was thought, might be made at about 0300, a starshell search was carried out a quarter of an hour before that time. Nothing was sighted and no attack developed.

The enemy was still in contact on the afternoon of the 3rd and "Highlander" devised a mild stratagem, which both secured the convoy's safety and possibly destroyed the industrious shadower astern. The Commodore was requested to alter course from 080° to 100° at 1700 — the time at which the air escort were due to leave — as if making for Malin Head, (*County Donegal – Ireland*) and to alter back at 2200. "Clare" and "Londonderry" were ordered to make a R.D.F. sweep astern, starting at 2145, so as to prevent the shadower from observing the alteration back. "Restigouche" was to go six miles ahead to put down the U-Boats shadowing from this direction.

Just before 2200, "Highlander" heard the shadower astern making her first report and then, almost simultaneously, received "Londonderry's" report that she was investigating an R.D.F. contact four miles astern in the anticipated position. Asdic contact was obtained and the two ships carried out five depth-charge attacks, the results of which are regarded as promising. During the action "Londonderry" was damaged by a torpedo explosion from a non-contact torpedo, but she was able to reach harbour in tow on the 6th. The convoy arrived off Barra Head (*Outer Hebrides.*) without further incident at 1000 on 5th February.

The H/F D/F plot was the hinge of the whole operation and it was gratifying that "Highlander" was able to test her deduction of the shadowing U-Boat's procedure in such a satisfactory manner.

The outward bound convoys suffered more severely than the homeward bound. Convoy O.N.166 was first attacked at 1600 on 21st February, when about 750 miles west-south-west of Cape Clear, and the fight went on until 0725 on the 25th, by which time 12 ships had been sunk, one other being torpedoed but getting in, thanks to the devotion of her master and 15 of her crew. Of these 13 ships, a total of six were torpedoed during attacks made between 0630 and 0730 on three consecutive mornings; on the nights of both the 21st and 22nd attacks were made at about 2130, causing the loss of four ships. The Senior Officer of the escort was U.S.S. "Campbell," but early on the second night of the battle she was "in collision with a U-Boat" from which she obtained 13 prisoners. Her engine room was flooded, but she was able to make St. John's in tow. H.M.S. "Dianthus" also attacked a U-Boat and claims to have sunk it. (*U606 : Oblt.z.S. Hans Dohler*)

Convoy O.N. 167, which like O.N.166 was given a southerly route and had air cover until it was a thousand miles from the United Kingdom, was attacked on the night of the 21st/22nd and lost Nos. 11 and 13. No H/F D/F bearings were obtained before the torpedoings but a U-Boat was detected by R.D.F. as it was attempting to escape on the surface after the attack and depth-charged by F.F.S. "Aconit." Four hours later H/F D/F bearings were obtained and at 0410/22 H.M.S. "Harvester" (S.O.) established R.D.F. contact with a U-Boat after running down a ground wave bearing given by her F.H.4 attachment; the U-Boat was then sighted and attacked with three patterns of depth-charges. It is perhaps significant that the convoy was not reported again. (*There is no record of a loss.*)

A third outward-bound convoy to suffer loss was U.C.1 which consisted of 32 tankers, bound from the United Kingdom to the Dutch West Indies. The convoy was apparently first reported by a U-Boat during the afternoon of the 22nd, when it was about 450 miles west of Lisbon. The U-Boats attacked next day, first sinking a straggler and then torpedoing four in the convoy, two being sunk. The following day the escort, which consisted of four sloops, four U.S.N. destroyers and two frigates, attacked six U-Boats so successfully that, although one U-Boat seems to have shadowed the convoy for another three days, no more attacks developed.

The V.L.R. aircraft mentioned in last month's Report are now operational. Twenty in number, they are stationed in Iceland and at Ballykelly (*Northern Ireland*), with Aldergrove (*Northern Ireland*) and St. Eval (*Cornwall*) as alternative bases.

U-Boat activity has broken out again in the Cape area and a system of convoys, running on a weekly cycle and escorted by corvettes, trawlers and aircraft, has been instituted.

The Prime Minister in his recent speech in the House of Commons spoke at length on the problems of the anti-U-Boat campaign. "The defeat of the U-Boat," he stated, "is the prelude to all effective aggressive operations."

March 1943

More than three quarters of the tonnage sunk during March consisted of ships sailed in convoy, the total of such losses being, by over 100,000 tons, the highest ever recorded. The enemy's main effort continued to be in the North Atlantic but his resources were such that he was able during the month to attack convoys-in the Greenland Sea, in the Indian Ocean and off the coasts of Portugal and Guiana. On 9th March five convoys were engaged, an eastbound and a westbound Transatlantic convoy, a North Russian convoy, a convoy bound from Baia to Trinidad and a convoy on passage from the United Kingdom to Gibraltar.

The convoys most closely beset were S.C.121, H.X.228, S.C.122 and H.X.229, which lost between them 30 ships, excluding stragglers. It was during, the passage of Convoy H.X.228 that H.M.S. "Harvester" destroyed "U444" (*Oblt.z.S. Albert Langfeld*) and was herself sunk by "U432" (*Hermann Eckhard*) which F.F.S. "Aconit" disposed of in her turn. The Commanding Officer of "Harvester," (*Commander A.A. Tait*) an outstanding leader of a group of British, Polish and Free French escort vessels, was unfortunately lost with his ship.

Convoys H.X.230 and S.C.123 were also sighted soon after leaving Newfoundland and attracted packs of U-Boats but nevertheless got through without losing any ships in convoy. S.C.123 was escorted by H.M.S. "Whimbrel" (Senior Officer of Group B2) and H.M. Ships "Whitehall," "Vanessa," "Gentian," "Sweetbriar," "Clematis" and "Heather." A Support Group, consisting of H.M. Ships "Salisbury" and "Chelsea" was in company from 0800 on the 21st March until 1400 on the 24th, and the United States Auxiliary Aircraft Carrier "Bogue," escorted by two United States destroyers, proceeded with the convoy until it was about 175 miles south-east of Cape Farewell.

The weather on the northerly route which the convoy followed made operations very difficult but on four out of six days aircraft were flown off from and successfully recovered by this small carrier.

She and her escorting destroyers parted company at 1900 on 26th March and at 1928 the H/F D/F operator in "Whimbrel" reported a transmission from a U-Boat about twenty miles away and bearing 315° — the convoy's course was then 074°. Within ten minutes another U-Boat was D/F'd bearing 185°, 25 — 30 miles. "Vanessa" was ordered to investigate the first and "Whitehall" the second, both ships being ordered to remain in the suspected area until dark and then to return, if not in contact.

"Whitehall" found nothing and was back in position at midnight, but "Vanessa" was luckier. Her first contact was obtained by asdic at 2000 and, after an hour, was classified as "non-sub." "Vanessa" had just completed her investigations when, at 2056, she sighted a U-Boat bearing 240°, six miles. The U-Boat dived when the range was three miles and was attacked four times by "Vanessa," she failed to regain contact and proceeded to rejoin; steering an evasive course. She was in station at 0300 on the 27th.

During the night of the 27th/28th a few more transmissions from U-Boats between 25 and 30 miles from the convoy were intercepted but all appeared to come from boats astern or on the quarters; from the plot it did not seem that any were overtaking the convoy and after 0438/27th, nothing more was heard. By daylight it was fairly evident that no U-Boats were in touch.

The convoy had air cover for 4 hours during the afternoon of the 27th, and at 1630 a Support Group, of which H.M.S. "Offa" was Senior Officer, joined in a position about 250 miles east of Cape Farewell. The convoy being unmolested, the Support Group was switched to Convoy H.X.230, which was being threatened, and left at 1030 on the 28th.

The safe and timely arrival of the convoy was the result of the action taken during a few critical hours. In the course of the 26th/27th it probably passed through a patrol line of U-Boats and was duly sighted and reported. By expert use of H/F D/F "Vanessa" was guided to the right position and dealt with the reporting U-Boat so faithfully that it was forced under for a considerable time and could neither shadow the convoy nor call up other U-Boats to do so. A hole was, in fact, punched in the line and the convoy passed through it.

Convoy D.N.21 was attacked off East London during the night of 3rd/4th March. After the first attack, in which three ships were hit, the convoy made two 45° turns to port by light but not all the ships saw both or either signals. As a result, when another attack was made after midnight, the convoy was somewhat spread out. The escort consisted of four trawlers, none of which obtained contact.

About the same time a convoy at the other end of the world was being shadowed by two or three U-Boats. This was R.A.53, bound from North Russia to Iceland. Three Fleet destroyers in the escort were fitted with H/F D/F and made good use of it, with the result that the position of the U-Boats could be plotted within fairly accurate limits. At 0830 on 5th March two ships were torpedoed possibly by aircraft and two more were lost later on in rough weather. One of these was a straggler and the other had been damaged in the earlier attack; both were sunk by U-Boats.

H.M.S. "Attacker" formed part of the escort of convoy C.U.1, which, arrived in the United Kingdom on 2nd April. No U-Boats were sighted during the voyage. She had nine Swordfish aircraft available. During the passage 74 landings were made and only three aircraft were damaged. By daylight, aircraft were kept on deck in readiness to investigate H/F D/F bearings but night operations were not carried out, owing to the danger of the ship's position being given away by exhaust flames. Normally, anti-submarine searches made at dawn and dusk covered an area 50 miles ahead and 30 miles on each beam and astern but, on days of greater- danger, supplementary searches were carried out in the forenoon and afternoon to 50 miles depth between limiting lines.

All flying operations were carried out inside the screen, the ship stationing herself between the leading ships of the escort or of the convoy, depending on the wind. The Commander-in-Chief, Western Approaches, considers that, to facilitate manoeuvring of the Escort Carrier, it is preferable for, the Commodore's column to contain only his ship and the Escort Oiler, thus leaving space for the Escort Carrier; to have a lane between columns in case the difficulties of station keeping for the merchant vessels.

In addition to "U444" (*Oblt.z.S. Albert Langfeld*) and "U432," (*Kptlt. Hermann Eckhardt*) sunk by "Harvester" and "Aconit" respectively, United States aircraft destroyed two 'U-Boats during the month. *(On 8 March 1943 – U156 : Korvkpt. Werner Hartenstein and on 22 March – U524 : Kptlt. Walter Freiherr von Steinaecker.)* They have adopted the 100-ft. spacing between depth-charges, which is now also in force in Coastal Command. On the 8th March, a U.S.N. aircraft attacked a U-Boat -in a position 270 miles east of Barbadoes with 325-lb. Torpex filled depth-charges, which broke the vessel in two; the water was covered with debris and about a dozen men were seen swimming. Another United States aircraft, this time a Liberator of the Army Air Force, did much the same to a U-Boat found near the Canary Islands, nine survivors being seen on a raft.

U-Boats have tried methods of approaching to attack varying with weather conditions, visibility and the number of escorts. They have a healthy respect for R.D.F. detection and, in a night attack, if they can reach a position ahead which will allow of a submerged approach, they may dive through the area swept by R.D.F. and surface between the escorts of the convoy to attack at close range. The absence of a rescue ship has again resulted in escort vessels dropping back to pick up survivors, leaving the convoy inadequately protected against subsequent attacks.

It has again been borne out that if escorts have been able to take resolute offensive action against the first U-Boats to make contact with a convoy; the U-Boats attacking later have not pressed home their attacks, possibly through knowing that their predecessors have been roughly handled. In other words, the Escort Commander has retained the initiative and so has avoided dispersion of effort in rescue work and protection of ships which have dropped astern.

There is some evidence of long range torpedo-fire by U-Boats with torpedoes which have altered course inside the convoy area. It is not known if these torpedoes alter course on reaching a certain range or if they are acoustically operated. Prisoner of war evidence suggests that the Germans are developing both types of torpedoes. (*This probably refers to the new anti-convoy torpedoes, later called "Curly" by the Royal Navy.*)

The Commander-in-Chief Mediterranean has found it necessary to point out that U-Boat conditions on the north coast of Africa are quite different from those in the North Atlantic. As the U-Boasts operating in the area of his command do not hunt in packs, escorts must be disposed to detect boats which have sighted the convoy on any bearing, particularly those which are well placed to attack ahead or on the bows of the convoy. In the Mediterranean the task of the escort is moreover complicated by the additional risk of aircraft attacks. There are, therefore, no restrictions on the use of all forms of R.D.F. for air warning in areas where air attack is probable; anti-aircraft armament must be kept at a higher degree of vigilance, particularly at dusk and dawn and in moonlight; to counter the threat of torpedo bomber attack, smoke is used.

A number of convoys running between the United Kingdom and Gibraltar have been attacked by U-Boats in about 15° W. after having been located by Focke-Wulf aircraft. Generally the U-Boats, having placed themselves to intercept the convoy, have attacked individually and not in a pack.

Although the shipping losses for the month have been heavy, there are good reasons for hoping that the situation in the North Atlantic is improving. Advances have been made towards the provision of continuous air cover for transatlantic convoys by the use of Escort Carriers and Merchant Aircraft Carriers, either with the convoys themselves or with Support Groups. In spite of their successes, the U-Boats must have received some pretty hard knocks from both aircraft and surface craft and there is every chance that quite extensive destruction and damage have been achieved, though we may have to wait some months for news to confirm our hopes.

Although it is hoped that the new Asdic sets coming into service will effect an increase in the rate of destruction of U-Boats, there is little doubt that much better results are possible with existing weapons, if used by well-trained and enthusiastic teams. With the scarcity of escorts in all theatres of war, training is apt to be squeezed out but, as more escorts become available, the training periods are undoubtedly the most important necessity and give the best potential improvement in the rate of destroying U-Boats.

Volume 1 of The U-boat Archive Series "What Britain knew and wanted to know about U-boats"
contains a complete re-print of the entire for month April 1943.

The enemy has clearly had some difficulty in explaining away the comparative failure of the U-Boat offensive during April and the task of the apologist must have been made the more bitter by the knowledge that losses of U-Boats have been heavy; as many as a dozen may have been destroyed. On the 7th, H.M. Submarine "Tuna," operating to the southward of Jan Mayen Island, torpedoed one out of four U-Boats which were apparently maintaining a patrol line in that area. (*U644 : Oblt.z.S. Kurt Jensen*) Ten days later, U.S.S. "Spencer" sank "U175" while escorting Convoy H.X.233. This convoy, at one time in some peril, came through with the loss of only one ship, thanks to the efforts of its escort and the opportune arrival of the Third Escort Group (H.M. Ships "Offa," "Penn," "Impulsive" and "Panther").

In the last week of the month there was a considerable slaughter of U-Boats. A Liberator aircraft of 120 Squadron sank one (*U635 : Oblt.z.S. Heinz Eckelmann*) while escorting Convoy H.X.234, a Fortress aircraft of 206 Squadron destroyed another (*U710 : Oblt.z.S. Dietrich von Carlowitz*) on the 24th April in a position to the south-eastward of Iceland and a third (*U227 : Kptlt. Jürgen Kuntze*) was disposed of by a Hampden of 455 Squadron which was flying on an anti-submarine patrol to the northward of the Faeroe Islands. On the 25th, a U-Boat was sunk as a result of co-operation between two newcomers among our counter-measures — the Support Group and the Escort Carrier H.M. Ships "Pathfinder," "Opportune" and "Obdurate," together with H.M.S. "Biter," were sent out to reinforce the escort of Convoy O.N.S.4, which was beset when about 300 miles to the south-east of Cape Farewell. Aircraft from "Biter" found and attacked a U-Boat which "Pathfinder" sank. (*U203 : Kptlt. Hermann Kottmann*) A second U-Boat (*U191 : Kptlt. Herbert Fiehn*) was possibly destroyed during the passage of this convoy, for H.M.S. "Hesperus" made a Hedgehog attack and reported satisfactory explosions. This weapon was also used, apparently with success, by H.M.S. "Hastings," who was escorting Convoy O.N.S.3.

Reports have been received of survivors from a German U-Boat landing on one of the Canary Islands, their boat having apparently been badly damaged by an aircraft attack near Gran Canaria and then scuttled. (*U167 : Korvkpt. Kurt Sturm.*)

Against these losses the enemy can claim the sinking, of 300,000 tons of shipping, a reduction of 292,000 tons as compared with last month. The falling off was not in any way due to a reduction in the enemy's effort, for large packs were operating in the North Atlantic, but individual U-Boats seem to have pressed home their attacks far less effectively than in previous months. Possibly this indicates a decline in their fighting spirit, as well as some reduction in efficiency.

It seems that merely to detect the U-Boats coming in to attack is to have the battle half won. All their efforts appear to tend to the avoidance of detection and once it is apparent that they have failed in this endeavour they seldom press home their attack.

Evidence is, however, accumulating, both from aircraft sightings and from the experiences of escorts, that two or more U-Boats may co-operate in close company, one accepting attack while the other penetrates the protective screen. Aircraft have reported attacking one U-Boat and at the same time sighting another within a mile of the first, while surface craft have detected a U-Boat approaching to attack a convoy and have counter-attacked and put it down, only to find another lying a mile or two astern, ready to take advantage of the confusion caused by the counter-attacks.

Fifteen convoys were attacked and twelve lost ships. In the North Atlantic the greatest single number of casualties during the month did not exceed three, but Convoy O.N.S.5, which had one ship sunk on the 29th; was again assailed during the first week of May and, despite the arrival of a Support Group, lost twelve more. The cost of this success to the enemy, measured in U-Boats destroyed, may well have been extraordinarily high.

The passages of Convoys H.X.231 and H.X.232 are typical of the experiences of the North Atlantic convoys attacked. H.X.231, which sailed on the 25th March, consisted of sixty-one ships in thirteen columns and was escorted by Group B.7, H.M.S. "Tay" (Senior Officer) and H.M. Ships "Vidette," "Loosestrife," "Snowflake," "Alisma" and "Pink." First sighted on the 4th April when in 38°W it was attacked the same night. There was a strong wind and heavy swell from the north-north-west and visibility was increased by bright Northern Lights. As might be expected with a convoy eastbound under such conditions, both attacks came from the starboard side, the first U-boat from the bow and the second from the quarter. Half "Raspberry" was carried out in each case but in each case the U-Boats were not detected. The second and last attack, made next day, was a daylight one and took place about noon in excellent visibility. The attacking U-Boat is thought to have come in submerged from ahead and to have fired from inside the convoy. Like its predecessors it was not detected. Air cover was provided in the course of the day but the enemy remained in contact and attacked again during the night, only to be beaten off by the surface escort. On the next day, the 6th, the Fourth Escort Group, composed of H.M. Ships "Inglefield," "Eclipse," "Fury" and "Icarus," joined, but the enemy's main effort had already been defeated; the surface escort and the air escort, working excellently together, had each made about a dozen attacks.

Convoy H.X.232, which was escorted by H.M.S. "Escapade" (Senior Officer of Group B.7), O.R.P. "Garland," H.M. Ships "Narcissus" and "Azalea" and F.F. Ships "Renoncule" and "Roselys," was reported, like its predecessor, in about 38°W., but the attack took longer to develop, the night after the sighting passing without incident. When the assault was made on the night of the 11th/12th April, there was a wind of Force 4 from the west and visibility was extreme, the moon being up. A number of attacks were delivered, all from the van and up moon, but all except two were frustrated and only three ships were lost. A strong pack of U-Boats was still in contact on the following morning but they seemed to lose touch later in the day, by which time the weather had deteriorated. This may have been due to the arrival of air cover and of the Fourth Escort Group, but it is also possible that the convoy drew away from the U-Boats after the shadower astern had been put down and an evasive turn made. In any case, the U-Boats had probably acquired a respect for the efficiency of the escort.

The month showed what our counter-measures can achieve against the enemy's most strenuous efforts. Promised developments are coming to fruition. There were five Support Groups operating in the North Atlantic during the month, two of them having their own auxiliary carrier, and the number of V.L.R. aircraft available has risen to over thirty. More important, there was a noticeably enhanced standard of group training, better use of H/F D/F was made and co-operation between the surface and air components of the escort was greatly improved. In none of the attacks on transatlantic convoys did the enemy succeed in obtaining anything like the upper hand.

May has been a record month for U-Boat sinkings. Those known to have been sunk numbered at least twenty-four, and the probable rate of destruction was at least one a day. Our merchant shipping losses were, moreover, down to under 250,000 tons. This success is attributed to the stronger protection given to North Atlantic convoys by both shore-based and carrier-borne aircraft and to the use of escort groups as support forces in dangerous areas but these would have been of little avail without the efficiency and team-work achieved by the escorts as a result of training and experience.

At the beginning of May the enemy's U-Boat fleet operating in the North Atlantic was as large as ever and in the first week of the month he concentrated against Convoy O.N.S.5 one of the largest packs ever assembled. The resulting battle cost us eleven merchantmen out of the forty-two which sailed but the enemy paid a very high price.

Convoy S.C.129 was subjected to attacks which may have been proportionately even more expensive to the enemy, though the battle was not on the same scale. Only two merchantmen (*The British "Antigone," 4545 GRT, and the Norwegian "Grado," 3082GRT were sunk by U402 : Siegfried Freiher von Forstner on 11 May.*) out of a convoy of twenty-six were sunk but the enemy may have lost three U-Boats. The Ocean Escort was H.M.S. "Hesperus" (Senior Officer of Group B.2) and H.M. Ships "Whitehall," "Clematis," "Gentian," "Heather," "Campanula" and "Sweetbriar." The convoy, which sailed from Halifax on the 3rd May and was given a southerly route, was probably first sighted about 1400 on the 11th when about 250 miles to the north-westward of the Azores. The U-Boat making the report was D/F'd by "Hesperus" but a sweep failed to find her and at 1800 two ships were sunk in what may well have been a browning attack. (*A shot fired into the middle of a group with the hope of hitting a target.*)

Several R.D.F. contacts were reported during the night but only two of them were afterwards considered to have been with U-Boats. "Whitehall" found and attacked one and "Hesperus" the other. In the latter hunt the U-Boat was brought to the surface after six attacks and, after being a target for depth-charges set to 50 feet, was seen to dive or sink. In the meantime an R.D.F. contact had been obtained with a second U-Boat which was attacked by gunfire; hits with 4•7-in. were made, two of them being at the base of the conning-tower, after which a number of men were seen to be jumping overboard. "Hesperus" subsequently dealt this U-Boat what was described as a "rather half-hearted ram." (*U186 : Kptlt. Siegfried Hessemann on 12 May.*)

Both these U-Boats were considered by "Hesperus" to have been probably destroyed and thereafter the night passed quietly. About noon next day, the 12th, "Hesperus" sweeping along an H/F D/F bearing, hunted and probably sank a third U-Boat, oil and floating wreckage being seen. By this time there may have been about ten U-Boats in contact but it seems that they were so discouraged by this vigorous defence of the convoy that they made only one more attack — at about 2200 — which was frustrated.

The convoy, which had been routed nearly as far south as the Azores, was at this time still out of range of air cover. A Liberator of 86 Squadron was sent out on the 13th from Aldergrove but did not meet it. The aircraft did, however, carry out two attacks on U-Boats when about 1,200 miles from her base. The next day the Fifth Escort Group (H.M.S. "Biter," Senior Officer, and H.M. Ships "Opportune," "Pathfinder" and "Obdurate") joined. On the 16th "Biter's" aircraft and shore-based aircraft hunted repeatedly for a U-Boat which appeared to be shadowing the convoy, but without success. No attack, however, developed. The rest of the passage was "without incident."

Convoy O.N.S.7 was attacked on the 17th and the one ship which she lost was the last to be sunk in a transatlantic convoy during the month. (*The 5196GRT Aymeric was sunk by U657 : Heinrich Göllnitz*) A powerful air offensive was put on almost continuously from end to end of its passage and the U-Boats were so thoroughly put down that only one opportunity for attack was given to a surface escort. In this attack, which followed the torpedoing of S.S. "Aymeric" at 0037 on the 17th, H.M.S. "Swale" used both hedgehog and depth-charges with promising results. (*The U-boat was then sunk by "Swale."*)

The passages of the other transatlantic convoys menaced by U-Boats was an unusually pleasant tale of U-Boats and not merchantmen being sunk. Between them the escorts of Convoys H.X.237 (which lost three stragglers), H.X.239, S.C.130 and O.N.184 are known to have sunk three U-Boats and another three were probably destroyed. Aircraft from U.S.S. "Bogue" and from H.M.S. "Archer" each sank one, and H.M.S. "Broadway" carried out a successful hedgehog attack on the third. This weapon was also responsible for two "probably sunks," the other being by depth-charges. (*U569 : Oblt.z.S. Hans Johannsen was the first U-boat to be sunk by a US Hunter Killer Group and "Archer" sank U752 : Kptlt. Karl-Ernst Schroeter. "Broadway" hit and sank U89 : Kptlt. Dietrich Lohmann, which had attacked Convoy HX237.*)

The enemy made his greatest effort in the North Atlantic against the transatlantic convoys and there suffered his heaviest losses, but he was also active in other parts of the ocean. By way of contrast with the successes just recounted was the attack on Convoy T.S.37, which consisted of nineteen ships.

It was beset when within seventy miles of Freetown on two consecutive nights at the beginning of the month and lost seven ships. With the forces in this area working "all out and then a bit more" under trying climatic conditions, it is still only possible to provide rather weak escorts and the losses in this area must be charged against the comparatively safe passages of the vital transatlantic convoys.

A feature of the past two or three months has been the use of anti-submarine support groups, either with or without escort carriers. They have shown that they are capable of gaining the initiative over concentrated U-Boat packs and have definitely taken their place in the tactics of convoy defence. Experience is showing that a support group attached to a convoy should retain its separate entity and, to defeat a pack attack, should not normally be stationed as a reinforcement of the close escort. It appears probable that ships of a support group are best employed in putting down shadowers, following up aircraft attacks and carrying out searches on H/F D/F information; by night they should be stationed at such a distance outside the close escort that they can deter U-Boats which are gaining bearing on the bows and intercept those which are closing in to attack.

Support Groups formed of Home Fleet destroyers gave invaluable service when this organisation was first instituted this year. These ships have now had to return to fleet duties and Support Groups are formed of sloops, frigates and destroyers as they come forward to join the Western Approaches Command. The Royal Canadian Navy is providing support groups to operate from the western side of the Atlantic.

To sum up, it is probable that historians will note that May, 1943, was remarkable in the Battle of the Atlantic in that escorts and aircraft defeated, at least temporarily, the pack attacks of U-Boats. This was achieved as much by superior leadership and tactics, quick initial action and well-co-ordinated attack and defence as by concentration of forces at the decisive points and by weapon superiority.

FIRST EXPERIENCES WITH ESCORT CARRIERS

It is now possible to give some account of the experiences of the escort carriers. Very good R/T communication on H/F with Swordfish aircraft up to eighty miles allows complete control by the carrier, using fighter direction organisation, and enables her, acting on the information provided by the running commentary, to reinforce the aircraft and guide the surface escorts. The closer the control of the aircraft the greater the traffic on H/F, R/T and a T.B.R. R/T, additional to the convoy wave is required. Escorts detached to hunt can either shift to this wave or have information relayed to them on the convoy R/T wave by the carrier.

It has been found that very close co-operation can be maintained between hunting Swordfish and hunting surface craft and that the carrier captain and the escort group commander, using R/T when out of sight, can also work closely together.

Reports from "Biter" show that the mean speed of Swordfish aircraft in depth-charge attacks was 130 knots — a higher speed than has been recommended. This was due to the aircraft either having to attack at once, if the U-Boat dived, or having to close in quickly if the U-Boat decided to fight it out on the surface.

MERCHANT AIRCRAFT CARRIERS

The first merchant aircraft carrier sailed with Convoy O.N.S. 9. She is the "Empire Macalpine," a grain ship of 8,210 tons, and has a flight deck over her holds. Four Swordfish are carried.

June 1943

The heavy toll taken of the U-Boats in May showed its effects in June. The enemy refrained from attacking the vital North Atlantic Trade Routes and, in fact, continued to demonstrate his inability to exploit the "Wolf Pack" attack against convoys. It is unnecessary to enlarge upon this state of affairs which has been acknowledged in German broadcasts.

It was not unnatural that the lessened activity resulted in a corresponding reduction in U-Boat sinkings, but it is, nevertheless, considered that at least twelve German and three Japanese U-Boats were sunk, eight by surface craft, one by a submarine and six by aircraft.

One of the "known sunks" (*U217 : Kptlt. Kurt Reichenbach-Klinke on 3 June*) was achieved by aircraft from U.S.S. "Bogue" in a position about 550 miles south-westward of the Azores. This and other attacks, taken in conjunction with the general south-westerly trend of outward-bound U-Boats sighted in the Bay of Biscay, suggested that the majority of U-Boats have been moved to this area to get outside the range of V.L.R. aircraft. Though driven from their previous hunting grounds by the operations of these aircraft, U-Boats operating here still have considerable chances of encountering convoys running between North America and North Africa. Convoy U.G.S.10 did, in fact, lose a tanker, this ship with one other sunk off the United States eastern coast making up the sum total of the casualties in the whole of the North Atlantic during the month. In all, three trans-Atlantic convoys and one S.L. convoy were shadowed by U-Boats and one O.S. and one S.L. convoy by aircraft. There was apparently no follow-up by

U-Boats on the aircraft sightings, and only one aircraft attack on a convoy by nine Focke-Wulfs. Two ships were sunk by U-Boats in Mediterranean convoys, and one in a Cape — Durban convoy. Another was lost out of a Sydney — Brisbane convoy.

On the 12th June it was noticed that U-Boats had started to make the passage to and from their bases in the Bay of Biscay in groups of three to five U-Boats. Coastal Command laid on special patrols with all the aircraft available from 18 and 19 Groups which were not required for convoy escort. On the 21st June the Second Escort Group (H.M.S. "Starling," Senior Officer and H.M. Ships "Woodpecker," "Wild Goose," "Wren" and "Kite") began operations in the Bay area in co-operation with Coastal Command aircraft. Their success three days later is related below.

The first conclusion as regards the effects of group sailings by U-Boats is that the total number of U-Boats sighted is approximately the same as if they were proceeding independently but that the conversion of sightings into attacks is low. This is to be expected, as each aircraft can normally only attack one U-Boat. Should the U-Boats choose to fight, the group is a formidable adversary to a single aircraft. Should they choose to dive, the group should be able to provide better mutual warning, but should a few ships or reinforcing aircraft arrive on the scene the advantage is with the hunters in having several U-Boats "pinned down." The hunting group or surface escort is largely dependent for its success on the time which it takes to reach the locality of the U-Boat and the accuracy of the position from which it starts its hunt. Good communication and co-operation between ships and aircraft is of the greatest importance, as the chances of success increase enormously if the aircraft can home the ships on to the right position and/or mark the position with an efficient marker buoy. The other necessity is that the U-Boat shall be kept submerged by the aircraft until the ships arrive on the scene, for then the submerged U-Boat will only be a few miles from her point of submergence. The good co-operation of A.S.V.-fitted aircraft with the hunting group by night achieved a considerable measure of success in the Mediterranean.

On the 24th June the Second Escort. Group, acting as a striking force in co-operation with aircraft engaged in the Bay offensive, destroyed two U-boats in the space of nine hours. (*U119 : Kptlt. Horst von Kamecke and U449 : Oblt.z.S. Hermann Otto.*)

At 0800 "Starling" obtained an echo which was classified as "submarine." Ordering the other ships to patrol round her as protection from attack from other U-Boats and to ensure that the one "in the net" did not escape, "Starling" carried out a deliberate attack with a ten-charge pattern set to 150 and 300 ft. The U-Boat, apparently blown to the surface, appeared a thousand yards astern as the noise of the last detonation died away. The whole group opened fire on her. It was observed that she was going slow ahead apparently under full control and that no attempt was being made to abandon ship. "Starling" therefore rammed her, striking her abreast the conning-tower at an inclination of 90° when travelling at about 10 knots. Ten minol-filled depth-charges, set to 50 and 140 ft., were dropped when the U-Boat, clearly visible, had reached the level of the quarter deck after passing under the ship. "Woodpecker" then fired two deep patterns in the position in which the U-Boat had been last seen. Locker doors and other floating wreckage (*from U119*) marked in German were afterwards picked up by "Starling."

About two hours later, while "Starling" was still dealing with the necessary damage control operations, "Wren" obtained another contact. Ten attacks were made by the ships of the Group other than "Starling," who, with her Asdics out of order, stood by waiting for another chance to ram. It was not given and after about an hour the Senior Officer, suspecting that depth-charges were being wasted on S.B.T.s, transferred to "Wild Goose."

He was soon rewarded by a "perfect submarine echo" which "Wren" obtained about 1300. A series of attacks was carried out between 1311 and 1501, the first being a barrage attack by "Wild Goose," "Wren" and "Kite". The attack at 1501 apparently caused the U-boat to disintegrate; the firm echo, which had been held "with the utmost confidence" suddenly became woolly and "non-sub," disappearing at 1505. An hour later oil and wreckage in large quantities came to the surface. (*This was U449 : Oblt.z.S. Hermann Otto*)

On the return of the Second Escort Group to Plymouth a conference was held to discuss the best method of co-operation between aircraft and a Support Group acting as a Hunting Group. The views of this conference confirmed experience in the Mediterranean where it had been found that there must be aircraft to "connect" the surface force with the position of an aircraft making the sighting. To give the geographical position is of little use and the sighting aircraft is only occasionally able to remain in the area long enough to home the surface craft. To ensure that the group gets in touch with the U-Boat, as soon as 'the "follow-up" is begun an aircraft should work under the orders of the Senior Officer and, if possible, be flown by a pilot known to him.

Of the other U-Boats sunk during the month — on the 2nd June, "U 521" (*Kptlt. Klaus Bargsten*) was sunk by U.S.S. PC-565 in a position 140 miles east of Hampton Roads. Two more were sunk in the Faeroe Islands area, one (*U308 : Oblt.z.S. Karl Mühlenpfordt*) by H.M. Submarine "Truculent" and the other (*U417 : Oblt.z.S. Wolfgang Schreiner*) by an aircraft of 206 Squadron which was herself destroyed. Aircraft of 120 Squadron sank another on the 24th June, in a position 350 miles south by west of Reykjanes.

Another sinking had been achieved ten days earlier by H.M. Ships "Jed" and "Pelican" who, while escorting Convoy O.N.S.10, sank a U-Boat 750 miles west of the Butt of Lewis. A report of the action has not yet been received. (*U334 : Oblt.z.S. Heinz Erich was sunk.*)

On the 16th June, "U 97" (*Kptlt. Hans-Georg Trox*) was sunk by aircraft in the area off Haifa where the U-Boats achieved some slight success against shipping during the month.

The defeat of the U-Boat is still a first charge on the resources of the United Nations. June was a good month in Anti-U-Boat Warfare, largely because the enemy had retired to lick his wounds and think about the next move. His intermediate move is evidently to attack in many areas and try to cause us to disperse our forces both surface and aircraft. His only hope of ultimate success, however, is effective attack on the North Atlantic life line and we may be sure he will return to this with both new equipment and modified tactics.

July 1943

There is every reason to be highly satisfied with the results for July. In May U-Boat, pack tactics were defeated as the rate of loss was unacceptable for the dividend paid in June the U-Boats were either withdrawn to their bases or were dispersed to widely-spread areas and attacks on shipping were few, except for an abortive effort against United States convoys to North Africa; in July, however, in spite of the dissipation of the enemy's effort over a great area and the infliction on us of shipping losses approximately equal to the average for the first half of the year, the killings of U-Boats if the Italian losses are included — exceeded the record total of May. The chief credit for this achievement must be given to the aircraft of Coastal Command based in the United Kingdom and to the British and United States aircraft operating from Gibraltar and Morocco. Their crews have not only faced the increased anti-aircraft fire of U-Boats proceeding in formation on the surface but they have also achieved a percentage of kills to attacks of over 25 per cent.

During the month 18 U-Boats were destroyed in the approaches to the Bay of Biscay, all but two of them by aircraft unassisted by a surface force. The crowning success was achieved on the 30th when a whole group of three outward-bound U-Boats was sunk, two of these being supply U-Boats, of which the enemy is very short. (*U461 : Kptlt. Wolf-Harro Stiebler, U462 : Oblt.z.S. Bruno Vowe and U504 Kptlt. Wilhelm Luis*)

At 0714 on the 30th July, when the Second Escort Group was proceeding at 15 knots on a course of 149°, H.M.S. "Wild Goose" obtained an H/F D/F bearing of 216° and the group thereupon altered to this bearing. At 0757 a signal was intercepted from an aircraft reporting herself over three U-Boats in position 44°00'N., 10°35'W., this being followed at 0804 by a second H/F D/F bearing of 225°, and at 0817 by a third of 244°, this being described as "first-class." The group maintained its course of 240° until 0927 when more H/F D/F bearings caused an alteration of 3° to starboard. After 0817 aircraft reports were constantly being received.

At 0947 what appeared to be a depth-charge explosion over the horizon was sighted fine on the port bow and the ships went to action stations, speed being increased to 18 knots. Within the next quarter of an hour definite depth-charge explosions were seen ahead and the Senior Officer in H.M.S. "Kite" hoisted the General Chase. (It is believed that this is one of the rare occasions since the days of Nelson on which this signal has been used.) At 1005 the enemy were sighted, his force consisting of two 1,600-ton U-Boats and one of smaller size. "Kite" opened fire at a range of over 13,000 yards, and was quickly followed by the other ships, the group firing 121 rounds of 4-in. A hit was observed in "Kite" at 1015 and almost simultaneously the aircraft circling the position reported "U-Boat no more." This U-Boat was "U462," (*Kptlt. Bruno Vowe*) the chief credit for her sinking going to a Halifax aircraft of 502 Squadron; her end was hastened by scuttling. "U461" (*Kptlt. Hinrich Oskar Bernbeck*) had already been destroyed by Sunderland aircraft "U" of 461 Squadron. At 1030, when the group closed the position, it passed close to the dinghies into which the survivors were packed. The Senior Officer ordered H.M. Ships "Woodpecker," "Wild Goose" and "Woodcock" to form a square patrol, H.M.S. "Wren" being at the same time ordered to join him. By 1034 contact had been obtained and "Kite" carried out the first attack, "Wren" following with an attack at 1040. The survivors from "U461" and "U462" were not far off from these patterns but after the water had subsided their dinghies were still to be seen rocking gently in the swell.

Contact was then lost and regained intermittently until 1132 — asdic conditions were described as very poor — but at 1149 "Kite," in firm contact, dropped a pattern set to 350 and 550 ft. Contact was lost at 600 yards and the Senior Officer, being of the opinion that the U-Boat had gone deep and had taken swift avoiding action from the three normal attacks — and could not therefore be a large supply U-Boat — decided to apply the creeping attack which had been successfully used on the 24th June. At 1258, therefore, "Woodpecker" fired a 22-charge pattern set to 500 and 750 ft. under "Kite's" direction; a quantity of oil was seen to come to the surface after the attack. "Wild Goose" made a similar attack at 1342 and contact then faded. A search made in the area revealed much oil and wreckage which included a uniform jacket, a human lung and some well-cured bacon. The survivors from the other U-Boats, who by this time had been in their dinghies for over four hours, were then collected.

To continue the story of this patrol, the next day passed quietly but at 0900 on the 1st August a signal was intercepted from an aircraft reporting herself over a U-Boat in position 45°50'N., 09°40'W. The group was close to this position but, before it could close, the aircraft reported that she had to return to base owing to shortage of fuel and nothing came of the sighting. The group continued on the course of 350° to which it had altered until 1246, when a Catalina aircraft reported a U-Boat bearing 132° 34 miles. Course was then altered to 180°.

This aircraft skilfully homed the group on and at 1430 two smoke floats were sighted, the guiding Catalina having dropped a fresh float close to one which, was dying down. The group passed both floats on a course of 270° at asdic sweeping speed and ten minutes later sighted a

Sunderland aircraft attacking a U-Boat. Very soon after the depth-charges had been dropped, the Sunderland crashed into the sea and it was afterwards learnt that both pilots had been killed by the U-Boat's gunfire. It seems likely that aircraft-captain died at the moment at which the depth-charges were released. The group closed the position and in a few minutes was picking up survivors from "U 454." (*Kptlt. Burkhard Hackländer*)

Reference was made in the last Report to the withdrawal of U-Boats to the southward and to their operations in the Azores area. Conditions in this part of the Atlantic were good during July, but if any U-Boat crews were looking forward to pleasant work in good weather, they must have had some disappointments. Convoys bound to and from the United States passed unscathed through the area, leaving behind them five U-Boats sunk by aircraft from the U.S. escort carriers, "Bogue," (*U527 : Kptlt. Herbert Uhlig*) "Santee" (*U43 : Kptlt. Hans-Joachim Schwantke*) and "Core." (*U67 : Kptlt. Günther Müller-Stockheim*)

Further still to the southward, H.M. Ships "Rochester," "Balsam" and "Mignonette," who were escorting Convoy O.S.51, sank "U135" (*Friedrich Hermann Praetorius*) in a position between the Canary Islands and the West Coast of Africa.

In the Mediterranean, H.M.S. "Inconstant" sank "U409" (*Kptl. Hanns-Ferdinand Massmann*) on the 12th July in the Algiers area and on the 6th July the escorts of Convoy K.M.S.18 probably disposed of another. The sinkings achieved in the course of the Sicilian operations are not yet known for certain but two German may have been sunk. Five Italian U-Boats are known to have been accounted for, one of them having been towed into Malta.

In the successful daylight raid on Trondheim by United States Fortress aircraft on the 24th July, one large U-Boat is known to have been sunk. (*U622 : Kptlt. Horst-Thilo Queck*)

The result of operations still further afield must have been equally unsatisfactory to the U-Boat command. Recently one of the most profitable areas for U-Boats has been the coast of Brazil. During July a vigorous air offensive deprived the enemy of this "soft spot" which he had been exploiting for some time; so powerful was the effort made by United States and Brazilian aircraft that no fewer than six U-Boats were sunk in this area during the month.

There has apparently been a great reduction in the number of U-Boats making the passage north on their first operational patrol. It is thought that instead of the usual monthly number of about 20, not more than five entered the Atlantic outward bound from Kiel. It will, therefore, take the enemy all the longer to recover from the blows of the past three months which have cost the Germans over 80 U-Boats. The boats of the Biscay flotillas, thinned by this slaughter, are apparently delayed in harbour while equipment and armament are being improved and increased; the U-Boats, which should have started operations this month, joining the Biscay flotillas at the end of their first patrol, remain in the Baltic, perhaps for the same purpose.

Despite their losses, outward-bound U-Boats are still crossing the Bay area in company and on the surface — long may they continue to do so. Proceeding in groups of three to five, often in vic-formation, they rely on tight turns at high speed and concentrated "flak" to keep attacking aircraft at bay. The U-Boat singled out for attack always endeavours, by a last-moment turn, to present a beam-on target to the aircraft when the latter is committed to her line of attack; by this manoeuvre, while still supported by the fire of her consorts, she gives full play to her own anti-aircraft armament.

This policy of fighting it out on the surface has greatly increased the hazards to be faced by our aircraft; it has also presented them with an increased number of "Class A" targets, of which they have taken full advantage, pressing home their attacks with the greatest determination in the face of accurate fire. Many aircraft have suffered casualties and several have been shot down but the survivors of at least three of these have had the satisfaction of knowing that their gallantry has been rewarded by a kill. It is interesting that the A.A. fire has been more effective from single U-Boats than from groups.

Reports from the United States Air Command in Moroccan Sea Frontier show that the policy of instituting searches in an area of radius 80 miles from the plotted position of a D/F fix has proved much more fruitful than air patrols or sweeps of possible U-Boat areas.

The U-Boat is being hit and hit hard whenever an aircraft attacks her on the surface in the Atlantic; whenever a group of three or more ships can obtain contact with a submerged U-Boat and have time to hunt her, her destruction is pretty well assured. The U-Boat's life has indeed become precarious. There are still a few "soft spots" where the enemy can sink a small proportion of the shipping passing through an area without being unduly worried by the accuracy of attacks by aircraft or surface forces, but in Western Approaches Command, in the Fleet and in Coastal Command in particular the emphasis on anti-submarine training has clearly borne much good fruit. Elsewhere there are difficulties in fitting in training owing to shortages and the lack of training submarines but the need is great and opportunities must be made, even if some operational commitments are not fully satisfied. A few fully efficient anti-submarine craft are worth a large number of "fifty-percenters."

August 1943

In the last month of the fourth year of the war, for the first time, more U-Boats than merchantmen were sunk. Twenty German and Italian and two Japanese U-Boats were destroyed, as against 13 merchant ships sunk by U-Boat attack. The month opened with the sinking in the Bay area of four U-Boats in two days by aircraft of Coastal Command, but these successes (culminating in nine sunk in one week) marked the end of the six weeks' slaughter which began in the last week of June. Fewer U-Boats were subsequently crossing the Bay and those that made the passage apparently hugged the coast of Spain and surfaced only at night. Two and possibly three more U-Boats are, however, likely to have been destroyed in this area of the North Atlantic. On the 25th August, H.M.S. "Wanderer," who was escorting Convoy O.G.92, sank "U523" (*Kptlt. Werner Pietzsch*); this U-Boat, under orders for the Far East, had had to put back for repairs and was caught as she made the passage for the second time. Three days later H.M.S. "Grenville," on offensive patrol to the westward of Vigo, made a promising attack on what may have been a Japanese U-Boat inward-bound to the Biscay ports and, on the 30th, H.M. Ships "Stork" and "Stonecrop," part of the escort of Convoy S.L.135, probably destroyed a German U-Boat. (*U634 : Oblt.z.S. Eberhard Dahlhaus*)

In northern waters a Sunderland aircraft of 423 Squadron sank "U489," (*Obltl.z.S. Adalbert Schmandt*) being herself shot down. Happily, destroyers were at hand to rescue six of the aircraft's crew and to take prisoner 23 survivors from the U-Boat.

United States carrier-borne aircraft continued to operate with success in the Azores area against the U-Boats moved, after the disasters of the spring, from more northerly waters and destroyed five. Further south, aircraft operating from West African bases had a most satisfactory month. One and perhaps two fully successful attacks were made, though the certain kill was only achieved at the cost of the destruction of the attacking Liberator and its entire crew. (*U468 Oblt.z.S. Klemens Schamong. The pilot was awarded the Victoria Cross on account of reports given by men of U468.*)

On the other side of the Atlantic, United States aircraft and ships operating in South American waters also had a successful month in what was not long ago a "soft spot," destroying three U-Boats between the Caribbean and Rio de Janeiro.

From one of the few remaining "soft spots" — the area south of Madagascar — came refreshing news of the destruction of a U-Boat by Catalina aircraft. This is the first "kill" reported this year from an area where losses have occurred persistently, though they have been small compared with the amount of shipping. (*U197 : Kptlt. Robert Bartels*)

In the Mediterranean two U-Boats, one German and one Italian, were destroyed in the neighbourhood of Pantellaria. H.M.S. "Easton" and H.H.M.S. "Pindos" accounted for "U458," (*Kptlt. Kurt Diggins*) while to U.S.S. "Buck" fell what is likely to be the last sinking of an Italian U-Boat.

Two Japanese U-Boats were claimed as sunk in the South-West Pacific, one by a United States destroyer and another by a corvette of the Royal New Zealand Navy assisted by aircraft. Six prisoners are reported to have been taken from the latter boat.

In August, the enemy's U-Boats sank but 13 ships — only five in convoy and only one in the Atlantic north of the Equator. The sinking of so many supply U-Boats has forced him to recall operational U-Boats before the normal time: the weight of the offensive in transit areas has compelled him to try antidotes such as the improvement of the anti-aircraft defence and technical equipment.

Last month aircraft losses rose considerably in the Bay area, most of them probably being due to enemy aircraft and not to U-Boats; and one of Germany's new "secret weapons" — a rocket-projected glider — sank one of the ships co-operating with the aircraft. If U-Boats are going to affect materially the outcome of the war, the Germans must sooner or later resume attacks on transatlantic shipping. The real battle will then be joined again. Meanwhile, the enemy is accumulating a formidable number of U-Boats in their home bases, but their crews' morale must be severely strained; our power to defeat him is rising and we may now look with considerable confidence on the eventual outcome. The importance of sinking U-Boats, even at the cost of a reduced scale of protection to shipping, is more than ever apparent.

September 1943

The lull in the German U-Boat campaign lasted until 19th September, although H.M.S. "Puckeridge" had been sunk (*by U617 : Kptlt. Albrecht Brandi*) close eastward of Gibraltar and some 35 — 40 attacks had been carried out by aircraft and surface forces in various areas, with very little evidence on which to give provisional assessments higher than two sunk and four damaged.

On the 19th September, O.N.S.18 (27 ships) and O.N.202 (38 ships) were 5.5 and 3.5 days out from the United Kingdom respectively. That evening there were indications that one or both convoys had been sighted by U-Boats. Fortunately it was possible to join these two convoys on the 20th September and reinforce their combined escort with a support group. Thus was the stage set for the renewal of North Atlantic convoy battles after a four months' lull. Except for the use by the enemy of an acoustic homing torpedo fired at chasing anti-submarine vessels there was no evidence of new tactics or technical developments.

Escort groups working with Coastal Command aircraft in the Bay offensive were withdrawn to support North Atlantic convoys, but the aircraft operations continued. The German counter-measures of maximum submerging tactics, accepting a long delay in making the passage of the Bay, and the routeing of a proportion of the U-Boats close to the coast of Spain, achieved a measure of immunity which was increased by a spell of bad weather at bases, causing night flying to be cancelled, and by our inability to provide a sufficiently strong effort with available Wellington aircraft, the only ones fitted with Leigh lights. This had been foreseen many months ago but there have been technical and production hitches delaying the fitting of Long Range aircraft with searchlights. There were, however, 24 U-Boat sightings in the Bay and 12 attacks, of which 9 were by the L.L. Wellingtons. One U-Boat was sunk by day and one damaged U-Boat entered Vigo (*Spain*) and has since been interned; this damage is attributed to an attack by a L.L. Wellington from Gibraltar. (*U760 : Kptlt. Otto-Ulrich Blum*)

The most profitable areas for killing U-Boats are (a) the vicinity of convoys on which packs are massing, (b) the refuelling areas if they can be found and the U-Boats surprised, (c) the transit areas. The first two exist only intermittently whilst the transit areas are constant probability areas.

In areas where U-Boats are operating singly in patrol areas to intercept shipping, they must approach the escorts when approaching the convoys. When the U-Boat has been located it is well worth while detaching most of the escorts and laying on as many aircraft as possible to destroy it, since the convoy is safe until it enters the next U-Boat's patrol area. It is most important to destroy U-Boats operating far from their bases, even at the expense of some shipping losses.

In September, although shipping losses were small, there is no certainty that we sank more than four German U-Boats and caused the internment of another. In the previous four months the total score was over 100 and the enemy must be seriously alarmed. A vigorous offensive must be maintained to break his morale.

U-Boats achieved a measure of surprise with their acoustic torpedo, but the weapon has many limitations such as speed, homing radius and inability to distinguish between propellor and other noises.

The outstanding event of the month was the surrender of the Italian Fleet. By the end of the month 29 Italian U-Boats were under British control.

THE ATTACKS ON CONVOYS O.N.202 AND O.N.S.18

On 19th September Convoy O.N.S.18, consisting, of 27 ships, escorted by H.M.S. "Keppel" (Senior' Officer, Group B.3), H.M. Ships "Escapade," "Narcissus," "Orchis" and "Northern Foam" and French ships "Lobelia," "Roselys" and "Renoncule," with "Empire MacAlpine" in company, was about 475 miles west by south of Rockall, Convoy O.N.202 being about 60 miles to the east-north-east. This convoy of 38 ships was escorted by Group C.2 (H.M.C.S. "Gatineau" (Senior Officer), H.M. Ships "Icarus," "Lagan," "Polyanthus" and "Lancer," and H.M.C. Ships "Drumheller" and "Kamloops") During the day it became evident that the convoys were being shadowed and that night attacks developed against both of them. Group B 3 drove off the U-Boats which attacked O.N.S.18 persistently from about 2230 onwards and possibly damaged one of them. O.N.202 was attacked later that night and at about 0400/20 "Lagan" was torpedoed (*by U270 : Paul-Friedrich Otto*). She had been detached to follow up an H/F D/F bearing and had obtained a Radar contact which had faded when the range was about 3,000 yards. She was within about 1,200 yards of the assumed diving position when she was hit by a torpedo which blew off her stern — the first indication that the enemy was using a new weapon in the acoustic homing torpedo. She was taken in tow and reached harbour on the 24th.

At about 0800 two merchant ships were torpedoed one sinking almost immediately while the other was abandoned in a sinking condition. (*Theodore Dweight Weld and Frederick Douglass sunk by U238 : Horst Hepp*)

During the forenoon the two convoys were ordered to join, forming one convoy of 63 ships, this being done during the late afternoon in poor visibility. "Escapade," damaged by a premature explosion of her hedgehog, had had to return to harbour, but the combined escorts were now supported by the 9th Escort Group (H.M.S. "Itchen" (Senior Officer), and H.M.C. Ships "St. Croix," "Sackville," "Chambly" and "Morden") and throughout the day were covered by aircraft of 120 Squadron, which made eight sightings and attacked four times. That evening two of the escort were sunk with heavy loss of life. "St. Croix" was torpedoed (*by U305 : Rudolf Bahr*) at about 2100 while hunting a U-Boat; she was hit again an hour later and sank.

Within two hours "Polyanthus," who was screening the rescue ship astern of the convoy, was torpedoed (*by U952 : Oskar Curio*) while following up a Radar contact. "Itchen" was narrowly missed by a torpedo (*from U305: Rudolf Bahr*) when circling the wreck of "St. Croix."

Despite these losses, the attempts which the U-Boats made on the convoy during the night all failed, and it is thought that one counter-attack by "Keppel," "Itchen" and "Narcissus" resulted in one U-Boat being seriously damaged. Early on the 21st the convoy was re-routed to the southward in order to get within range of Newfoundland-based aircraft. Owing to the previous routeing signal being received corrupt, the convoy was some 100 miles to the southward of the intended route and in the thick fog prevailing was unable to regain the route ordered. Liberators from Iceland continued to give the convoy what protection they could until prevented by the fog. This weather did not prevent another fierce night battle. The U-Boats, estimated to be 15 or 20 in number, had the worst of it, for they sank nothing and in the early hours of the 22nd one of the pack was rammed and sent to the bottom by "Keppel." "Chambly" obtained hits with her 4-in, gun on another.

With first light on the 22nd, Liberators arrived from Newfoundland, giving cover throughout the day and making four sightings and two attacks. At about 1820/22 the Senior Officer reported that there were still a few U-Boats in contact and that they were being chased. They nevertheless attacked again that night in strength and, though many of them were driven off, the defence was twice penetrated. Just after midnight, "Itchen" was sunk, two merchantmen being torpedoed about the same time, and two more merchant ships were lost at about 0730/23.

The enemy did not, however, escape unscathed, as one of the 12 U-boats then in contact with the convoy was probably sunk by "Northern Foam," one possibly sunk by "Lobelia" and three probably damaged by "Chambly," "Renoncule" and "Northern Foam" respectively. The U-boats kept in contact during the 23rd but the attacks made by the escorting Liberators from Newfoundland, which again gave cover throughout the day, so deterred them that their attacks on the night of 23rd/24th were half-hearted and they probably lost another of their number, as a result of attacks by "Sackville," without causing any loss to the convoy. After this they lost touch with the convoy and the number of attacks on Atlantic convoys was small and the losses inflicted negligible.

The enemy's propaganda has continually stressed the point that his attacks on our shipping have resulted in such heavy tonnage losses that they are beyond our shipbuilding capacity to replace. It may, therefore, be of interest that at the beginning of October, United Nations merchant Ship construction had wiped out, not only the accumulated tonnage losses caused by enemy action since 3rd September, 1939, but the marine losses as well. United States shipyards have played, and are playing, the major part in this highly satisfactory performance. Their share of the total new construction at the end of September, 1943, was about 74 per cent.; that of the United Kingdom about 20 per cent.; and Canada about 6 per cent.

Enemy propaganda claims of Allied shipping losses continue to be of a grossly exaggerated character, for example, on 13th October, 1943, the German Telegraph Service (D.N.B.) put out the following: — "During the past few weeks the naval war situation has developed considerably. Since 1st August, German naval and air forces have sunk no fewer than 140 vessels of 785,000 G.R.T and damaged 284 vessels of 1,370,000 G.R.T.; some of these were damaged so heavily that their total loss may be assumed, and the others will be out of commission for some time, so that Anglo-U.S. available shipping has been decreased by 424 vessels of 2,155,000 G.R.T."

So long as the net increase of United Nations merchant shipbuilding continues to be over 1,000,000 gross tons per month, as at present, they can face even such claims with equanimity.

October 1943

Events in October made it clear that in the North Atlantic the enemy was maintaining his old pack tactics but not the determination that formerly went with them. He must have counted highly on the acoustic homing torpedo; its success might have sent our merchant shipping losses up towards last winter's totals — and almost equally important — might have refreshed the morale of U-Boat crews drooping under nearly six months' continuous adversity. The idea of drawing off and disabling the escorts and then sinking the convoy at leisure was a good one but, thanks to the determination and skill of our escort vessels and their group leaders, the first promising results were not maintained and during October the new weapon had singularly little success.

By way of counter-measure we have developed a towed noise-making device, christened "Foxer," but experience has so far been lacking as to its efficacy. It has to be accepted that foxers interfere with asdic results and, as an alternative, ships have been instructed to use the "indirect" or "step-aside" approach to a contact when the range is between 4,000 and 5,000 yards. It is known that the noise from the foxer can be clearly heard throughout a submarine and it is important that the device should be used at the present time, if only to undermine the U-Boat crew's faith in the efficacy of their new weapon.

Recent events have shown the importance of early information being received from sea which may assist in determining the value of any new tactics adopted by escorts or by the enemy. The Commander-in-Chief, Western Approaches, has issued instructions that, when anti-submarine vessels report successful attacks on U-Boats, they should include brief details of the methods of destruction and any notable points regarding tactics. It is also of importance that confirmation of the use of acoustic torpedoes should be signalled, with any information as to their characteristics and also as to the results obtained by using foxers.

The convoys with which the enemy was in contact in the North Atlantic were SC.143, O.N.206 and O.N.S.20. The east-bound convoy of 39 ships sailed from Halifax on 28th September, under the escort of C.2 Group (H.M.C.S. "Kamloops," Senior Officer) and proceeded without incident until the afternoon of 7th October, when O.R.P. "Orkan," who, with H.M.S. "Musketeer" (Senior Officer) and H.M. Ships "Oribi" and "Orwell" formed the 10th Support Group, obtained a D/F bearing about 30 miles ahead of the convoy. A sweep by

"Musketeer" and "Orkan" was, however, without result. Another close H/F D/F bearing to the northward was also investigated by them but no contact was made, though what was probably a torpedo explosion occurred in the Polish destroyer's wake.

It was evident that night that the convoy was being shadowed from astern but the sweeps which the ships of the Support Group made still failed to bring them into touch with the enemy. In the early morning of the 8th "Orkan" was torpedoed (*by U758 : Helmut Manseck*) — probably not by an acoustic homing torpedo — and sank with heavy loss of life, only one officer and 43 ratings being saved. (Unhappily the commanding officer of O.R.P. "Orkan," Commander Stanislaw Hryniewiecki, was lost with his ship. This officer greatly distinguished himself in the 1919-20, being awarded the "Order of Virtui Militari" and, on two occasions, the "Krzyz Walecznych." In 1939 he was in command of O.R.P. "Gryf," which was sunk by aircraft attack. Escaping in a fishing boat to Estonia, he was interned but later managed to escape.)

By that time it was estimated that 15 U-Boats were in the vicinity of the convoy but, thanks to the efforts of the Support Group and the air escort, they were never allowed to get into attacking positions. This pack of U-Boats had already lost three of its number to the aircraft which had patrolled the areas, to the westward of the convoy, in which it was suspected that the enemy was concentrating his forces. In the course of operations on 8th"October, three more U-Boats were destroyed, one by Liberator aircraft R/86, one by Liberator aircraft Z/86 and T/120 and a third by a Sunderland "J" of 423 Squadron, R.C.A.F.

Under this pressure the pack dropped astern during the night of the 8th/9th, except for one U-Boat which made a long-range attack from the starboard bow at 0630/9, s.s. "Yorkmar," No. 111, being sunk (*by U645 : Otto Ferro*). The U-Boat, though not attacked, did not tempt fortune again and the convoy arrived off Oversay on 11th October, without further incident.

On the next day Convoy O.N.206, consisting of 56 ships sailed under the escort Of Group B.6 (H.M.S. "Fame," Senior Officer, and H.M. Ships "Vanquisher," "Deveron," "Grenadier" and "Engadine," and H.Nor.M. Ships "Rose" and "Potentilla." By the time it had reached the danger area the enemy had made up his losses and increased his pack to nearly 20. The first sign that contact had been made with the convoy was an H/F D/F bearing obtained during the evening of 15th October; this resulted in a hunt and attacks by "Vanquisher" and H.M.S. "Duncan," Senior Officer of Group B.7, which had joined as a Support Group during the previous day. On the 16th, aircraft of 59 and 120 Squadrons gave cover and sank one U-Boat, (*U844 : Oblt.z.S. Günther Möller*) from which "Duncan" rescued 15 survivors, and probably sank another. This latter attack was made by Liberator aircraft, S/59, which afterwards had to come down in the sea, the crew being rescued by "Pink." Very strong forces gave air cover on the 17th. Two Liberators from Iceland acted as a close escort to the convoy, two sweeps, each by five aircraft, were made to the north-eastward of the convoy and, five more aircraft swept the convoy's track; one U-Boat was destroyed by the joint action of Liberator aircraft D/59, which formed part of the close escort, and Liberator aircraft H/120, which was engaged on a sweep. By the evening the U-Boats were no longer in contact. (*Probably U964 : Oblt.z.S. Emmo Hummerjohann*)

Group B.7 was therefore ordered to go to the support of Convoy O.N.S.20, which, after being sighted by the enemy on the 16th, had been diverted to the northward to clear, the route of O.N.206. One of the covering aircraft, Y/86, attacked and sank a U-Boat during the afternoon, but at about 2141/16, a merchantman (*Essex Lance*) was torpedoed and sunk (*by U426 Christian Reich*). This was the enemy's only achievement and was more than offset by the destruction next day of two U-Boats, one by H.M.S. "Byard," who thereby earned the distinction of being the first B.D.E. to sink a U-Boat, and the other by H.M.S. "Sunflower." From a preliminary report it appears that "Byard's" U-Boat ("U841") (*Kptlt. Werner Bender*) had been surprised by an aircraft as she was closing the convoy. The aircraft attacked and, though the U-Boat took avoiding action and dived, her batteries were damaged and water began to leak in through a torpedo tube and one of the oil supply hose connections. About half an hour later "Byard" made contact and attacked with depth-charges, which, enlarging the leaks, caused more water to come in and upset the trim. The connection for blowing the tanks by means of the Diesels, which had already given trouble, then failed, and the Captain gave the order to surface. The crew abandoned ship under fire from the frigate and the U-Boat was scuttled. Twenty-seven survivors were picked up. For two more days the U-Boats kept in contact with this convoy of 58 ships, but the escort (Fourth Escort Group, H.M.S. "Bentinck," Senior Officer), with Group B.7 in company, were too strong for the pack and the Convoy reached harbour without further molestation. (*The other boat was U 631 : Oblt.z.S. Jürgen Krüger sunk by H.M.S. "Sunflower"*)

In his operations against our North Atlantic convoys the enemy lost about twenty U-Boats and the total sinkings for the month were probably twenty-seven. There was a lack of kills in the Bay of Biscay owing to the extreme caution displayed by the U-Boats, which were still following "maximum submergence" tactics and surfacing by night for the shortest possible time for battery charging. This greatly increases the time which they take to pass through the danger area, but it naturally reduces their chances of being sighted and attacked by aircraft, since searchlight-fitted Wellingtons are at present the only type capable of efficient night patrol and their range is, of course, limited. As it was, there were five sightings by day and 14 by night, 13 of the sightings being followed by attacks. There were no sinkings by aircraft in the Bay area, but a searchlight-fitted Wellington, based at Gibraltar and assigned to "Percussion," sank a south-bound U-Boat off Oporto on the 24th October.

The total figures for Coastal Command, Gibraltar and Moroccan Sea Frontier air operations were 57 sightings leading to 43 attacks. Seven aircraft were lost, three being known to have been shot down by U-Boats and one by enemy aircraft. Aircraft from United States Ships "Card," "Core" and "Block Island," who were operating offensively to the northward of the Azores carried out attacks which are claimed to have resulted in eight "kills" and four "probables." H.M. Ships "Fencer," "Tracker" and "Biter" also operated in the North Atlantic.

Convoy H.X.262 was the first to be escorted by aircraft based on the Azores.

"U 533," (*Kptlt. Helmut Hennig*) one of the half-dozen German U-Boats operating against shipping proceeding through the Persian Gulf, was sunk in the Gulf of Oman by a Bisley aircraft of 500 Squadron on 16th October one survivor being picked up. This is encouraging evidence that our killing power in potential "soft spots" is improving.

November 1943

The renewal of the U-Boat offensive in the North Atlantic, which started in September, has proved a costly failure to the enemy, who appears to have adopted new tactics which have greatly reduced his attacking power. It is now so rare an occurrence for a U-Boat to be sighted on the surface in daylight that it may safely be assumed that U-Boats now spend the hours of daylight in avoiding our air patrols by remaining submerged, surfacing only at night to charge batteries and to follow up and attack any convoy within reach. To compensate for this loss of mobility, enemy long-range aircraft are, it seems, being used to locate our convoys and it is likely that small groups of U-Boats will be disposed along their probable course.

As most of the enemy's long-range aircraft are based in France, the routes between the United Kingdom and Gibraltar saw the greatest activity. Four north-bound convoys — S.L.138 / M.K.S.28, M.K.S.29A, S.L.139 / M.K.S.30 and S.L.140 / M.K.S.31 — at sea during the month were attacked. The enemy gained little from these operations. One merchantman (*Norwegian "Hallfried" sunk by U262 : Heinz Franke*) in S.L.138 / M.K.S.28 was sunk on the 31st October, when the convoy was about 500 miles west of Cape Finisterre, but two of the small group of U-Boats were detected and hunted, one by H.M. Ships "Rochester" and "Azalea," and the other by H.M. Ships "Whitehall" and "Geranium"; "Whitehall" obtained one hedgehog hit and the usual evidence of a kill. (*U306 : Kptlt. Klaus von Trotha*)

The attack on Convoy M.K.S.29A provided Azores-based aircraft with their first kill, a Fortress of 220 Squadron destroying a U-Boat at daybreak on the 9th November. H.M.S. "Havelock" hunted and probably damaged a U-Boat, (*U707 : Oblt. z.S. Günter Gretschel*) which was found on the surface about the same time. The convoy suffered no loss.

The enemy made a much greater effort against the next north-bound convoy, S.L.139/ M.K.S.30, escorted by the 40th Escort Group, but it passed through the danger area without losing a single merchant ship by U-Boat action, though H.M.S. "Chanticleer," one of the escort, had her stern blown off by an exceptionally violent explosion. (*U515 : Werner Henke*) An acoustic torpedo may have hit, but something more than this appears to have "gone up" under the ship.

The convoy was reported as being shadowed by aircraft two days after the two parts had joined and, as it was suspected that a considerable force of U-Boats might be laid across its route about 500 miles westward of Oporto, the escort was strongly reinforced. A total of no less than 26 ships were ultimately involved in this operation. The convoy was in the danger area from about the 18th to the 20th November, but the strength of the surface escort and the provision of continuous air cover, by day and night, were too much for the U-Boats. Between 20 and 30 were probably concentrated for the attack. At least two of them were sunk or probably sunk and one other attack, about which information is still awaited, is regarded as promising. On the 21st, when the convoy was about 400 miles west-north-west of Cape Finisterre, an attack with glider bombs was made and two merchant ships were hit, one being abandoned and the other getting in.

The danger area for S.L.140 / M.K.S.31 appeared to lie slightly further south, at a point about midway between the Azores and Lisbon. The convoy, which left the rendezvous to the westward of Gibraltar on the 24th, was shadowed by enemy aircraft on the 26th and 27th November. It was escorted by B.1 Group, supported by the Second and Fourth Escort Groups. The Second Escort Group was brought over from Argentina, arriving just in time. The Fourth Escort Group first refuelled at the Azores and then operated in the area ahead of the convoy before joining. On the night of the 27th/28th November the convoy passed through the danger area. At least nine attacks were beaten off without loss and H.M.S. "Dahlia" reported one most promising attack.

These were not the only convoys which proceeded without loss through concentrations of U-Boats. At the end of October the main U-Boat concentration was about 600 miles east of Newfoundland. Early in November it became evident that the Newfoundland concentration had scattered and then re-disposed itself further east. Convoy S.C.146 was diverted slightly to the southward, but Convoy H.X.265, which was not far ahead of the slow convoy, was to fight its way through, its escort having the support of the Fifth and Seventh Groups. The dispositions used were to throw the support groups out on the threatened bow and spread them at a distance of 60 miles and 120 miles respectively from the convoy; the Escort Carrier with the Fifth Escort Group remained with the convoy. The S.C. convoy maintained strict R/T silence while the H.X.

convoy and the Support Groups were told to use R/T freely. It is suspected that the enemy is taking bearings on our R/T wave in order to locate convoys and it was hoped to draw the U-Boats from the slow convoy and hit them hard with the Support Groups, but unfortunately nothing came of it and both convoys passed the U-Boats without incident.

About the beginning of the month an attempt to pass a small force of U-Boats into the Mediterranean was largely frustrated. One U-Boat was sunk by a Gibraltar-based aircraft, another was attacked from the air in the Western Approaches to the Straits, a third was sunk just westward of the Straits as a result of attacks separately carried out by H.M. Ships "Imperialist" and "Douglas." H.M.S. "Fleetwood" and aircraft were responsible for the sinking of a fourth, which had just made the passage. The Captain of this U-Boat gave up the struggle after three days of continuous harassing and scuttled his boat, the crew swimming to some Spanish fishing craft. *(U340 : Oblt.z.S. Hans-Joachim Klaus and U732 Onlt.z.S. Claus-Peter Carlsen. Paul Kemp in "U-boats Destroyed" Arms and Armour Press, 1997 mentions an interesting twist in this account.)*

The high degree of caution displayed by the U-Boats when making the Bay passage has resulted in comparatively few sightings by the patrols which we have maintained by night and day. It is estimated that during the Bay passage from the coast of France to about 15° West, the U-Boats make about 80 miles a day, surfacing for about three hours by night to get a charge into the batteries.

The Caribbean, South Atlantic and Indian Ocean areas have been comparatively quiet. United States aircraft have made two kills in the Ascension Island area. A Catalina made a promising attack off Cochin at the beginning of the month. There have been signs of U-Boat activity in the Gulf of Aden and the Caribbean, where three attacks were made on shipping north of Colon on the 23rd/24th November. There was also evidence that the coasts of Brazil and West Africa were not entirely free from U-Boats; their numbers were small and their successes meagre.

The extremely cautious tactics now adopted by the U-Boats have naturally restricted our opportunities for attack. It is estimated that 10 U-Boats, in addition to those sunk in the Ascension Island area, have been destroyed and there have also been five or six promising attacks, on which further information is awaited. Two were sunk on the 6th November by the Second Escort Group, which had H.M.S. "Tracker" in company. Both kills were made by "creeping attack," a skilful means of hitting at the deep diving U-Boat introduced and perfected by the Senior Officer of the Group.

The U-Boat kills for November at present stand at 12, eight being sunk by ship and four by aircraft. The corrected figures for October are 27 German U-Boats sunk or probably sunk, eight having been destroyed by ship and 19 by aircraft.

The lack of day sightings and D/F's experienced during these operations confirmed that the enemy had adopted tactics of maximum submergence by day. It seems probable that pack attacks will continue, but possibly any one pack may attack for one night only, since the U-Boats appear to be so reluctant to surface in daylight in order to regain touch with the convoy. It is, however, possible, as already mentioned, that the enemy will endeavour to station small groups along the probable line of advance of a convoy and, in case of any such disposition, each group would be directed to a night attack by V.L.R. shadowing aircraft. It is clear that the enemy intends to reduce the effectiveness of surface escorts by attacking them as often as possible with U-Boats and aircraft. Our measures against the acoustic homing torpedo are proving effective, at any rate for the time being; it remains to be seen to what extent we are able to counter the glider bomb.

The change in tactics which became apparent in November was forced upon the enemy by his predominant and urgent need to avoid or repel attack by aircraft. To complete his discomfort it is necessary to concert measures which will deprive the U-Boat of its time on the surface under cover darkness and also of the assistance of long-range aircraft. The latter problem may be solved by C.V.E.s carrying more fighter aircraft.

The extension of our successful daylight measures to the hours of darkness is more difficult to achieve. A Liberator squadron has now been equipped with Leigh Lights and we now have five squadrons of Leigh-Light Wellingtons. The possession of bases in the Azores means that Gibraltar convoys will remain within range of the latter type of aircraft throughout most of their voyage. The problem of correctly identifying A.S.V. and Radar contacts makes co-operation between ships and aircraft by night extremely difficult and the ship "follow-up" in the dark will need a great deal of training and skill. Western Approaches are trying out schemes of identification and certain tactical dispositions to help to increase the effectiveness of our night effort and thus obtain more kills.

RESCUE OF SURVIVORS FROM U-BOATS

After destroying a U-Boat, a Commanding Officer may be in doubt as to whether to let the survivors "swim for it" or not. The risk of attack by another U-Boat or by aircraft, the need to rejoin a convoy passing through a danger area, the condition of his ship and the state of the weather must be set against the value of the prisoners taken.

The Intelligence Division of the Naval Staff has built up an extremely efficient system of interrogation of prisoners of war and the interrogating officers have, by their skill and patience, obtained information of the greatest value. Some prisoners have an invincible security-consciousness, others are merely bad-mannered or stupid, but the majority make a useful contribution to our intelligence.

In the past year, prisoners taken from U-Boats have provided information on the following subjects, among others; patrol lines and pack tactics, "Gnat" and "Curly" torpedoes, submarine bubble target, Radar decoy balloons, search-receiver listening gear, W/T organization, diving depths, speeds and angles, and anti-aircraft armament and tactics.

It is, of course, not only the information itself which is of such value; it is the obtaining of it early, in time to plan well ahead and to prepare counter-measures which will quickly defeat the enemy's devices and so reduce our losses.

December 1943

Only six U-Boats were sunk or probably sunk in December. The events of the month made it clear that the era of good hunting by day has passed, for the enemy now moves stealthily by night and rarely dares to show himself in the daytime for fear of attack from the air. It is only when weather conditions are patently unsuitable for flying that the U-Boat may be so bold as to proceed on the surface by day. Even so, the enemy took little advantage of the generally foul weather, which caused many convoys to become disorganised and several to be badly scattered.

North Atlantic

The activity on the Gibraltar — United Kingdom convoy route died away at the beginning of the month and the U-Boats moved to the north-westward. If they hoped to intercept our transatlantic convoys they had little success. During the month there were only three incidents in this area. On the 7th, Convoy O.N.214 was probably reported by a U-Boat when about 600 miles south-west of Ireland but, as nothing more happened, it seems likely that the enemy was driven off by the escort, of which H.M.S. "Havelock" was Senior Officer. The main force of U-Boats was thought to have been to the northward of the position of the convoy at the time. Sixteen days elapsed and then, on the 23rd, Liberator "O" of 120 Squadron attacked a U-Boat proceeding on the surface not far from Convoy T.U.5. (*But it survived to celebrate Christmas*) Finally, on the last day of the year, a straggler from Convoy O.N.217 was torpedoed about 200 miles south of Iceland. (*Empire Housman by U744 : Heinz Blischke*)

Towards the end of the month the centre of activity had moved southward again. On the 24th, U.S.S. "Leary" was torpedoed and sunk, (*by an acoustic torpedo fired from U275 : Helmut Bork*) unfortunately with heavy loss of life, when operating with the escort carrier U.S.S. "Card" in a position about 600 miles west of Cape Finisterre. U.S.S. "Schenk," another of "Card's" escort, attacked no less than five U-Boats in the vicinity and possibly sank two of them. H.M. Ships "Hurricane" and "Glenarm,", who were acting as a Support Group, were sent into the area; on the 24th "Hurricane" was hit aft, . (*by U415 : Kurt Neide*) probably by a "Gnat," and was eventually ordered to be abandoned and sunk. Convoy O.S. 62/K.M.S.26, which was approaching the area, was diverted to the westward. Early on the 26th an aircraft from H.M.S. "Striker," who formed part of the escort, detected a U-Boat by A.S.V., but the convoy was not apparently reported. U.S. Ships "Block Island" and "Core" operated in the area in which it was suspected that the U-Boats were concentrated and U.S. Ships "Parrot" and "Bulmer," two of the escorting destroyers, claimed the sinking of a U-Boat on the 30th. (*Which escaped*) In anticipation of trouble, the escort of Convoy S.L.143/M.K.S. 36 was reinforced, but the U-Boats apparently failed to make contact when it passed through the area on the night of 30th/31st.

South Atlantic and West Coast of Africa

On the 13th a U-Boat was sunk by U.S.S. "Clemson" about 600 miles north-west of the Cape Verde Islands. From its course it is possible that it was making for the South Atlantic. Another U-Boat which was sighted was possibly bound for the same area. A third southbound U-Boat was found by aircraft from U.S.S. "Bogue" in a position about 500 miles south-west of the Azores and destroyed. (*Only one boat seems to have been sunk, U172 : OL Hermann Hoffmann*)

The West Coast of Africa was quiet until the 17th December, when a series of attacks were made by F.F.S. "Commandant Drogu," after two ships had been torpedoed. (*"Kingswood" and "Phemius", both torpedoed by U515 : Werner Henke*) Other vessels joined in the hunt and it was reported that the U-Boat had been damaged to the extent of leaving an oil streak. On the 24th December, however, another ship (*Dumana, also U515*) was torpedoed off Liberia, almost certainly by this same U-Boat.

Mediterranean

On the 11th December, while Convoy K.M.S.34 was proceeding along the Algerian coast, H.M.S. "Cuckmere" was torpedoed, (*by U223 : Karl-Jürg Wächter*) but was able to reach Algiers. At 0710 on the 12th, H.M.S. "Tynedale" was torpedoed and sunk, (*by U593 : Gerd Kelbling*) and later in the day H.M.S. "Holcombe" was also lost. The U-Boat "U593" was hunted to exhaustion and destroyed the next day by H.M.S. "Calpe" and U.S.S. "Wainwright." On the 16th, Convoy G.U.S.24 was attacked when about 40 miles north of Oran; one merchantman was torpedoed hut reached harbour. Another hunt to exhaustion, but less prolonged, ensued, ending in the destruction of "U73" (*Oblt.z.S. Horst Deckert*) by U.S. Ships "Wolsey," "Trippe" and "Edison." In both cases the U-Boat attack was immediately followed by an intensive and skilfully controlled anti-submarine operation, in which air and surface forces were well co-ordinated.

General Remarks

The destruction of these two U-Boats shows what can be done if escorts "supporting" a convoy cling to their contact and hunt it to exhaustion. With the enemy's lack of mobility, resulting from the tactics of maximum submergence by day, it is essential that this should be done even though it takes more than twenty-four hours. Only when the dual role of A.A. and A/S escort is imposed upon a ship and air attack threatens must this policy be disregarded. Thanks to our offensive efforts, particularly those of our aircraft, we have for the time being, at least, been able to frustrate the power of the U-Boat arm.

Opportunities for achieving a kill, being rare, must not be thrown away. Unfortunately it is apparently still possible in some parts of the world for a U-Boat to torpedo ships not far off-shore and survive. The power to destroy a U-Boat is now largely a matter of efficiency, attention to detail and training. On the whole all ships are equally well armed and equipped for anti-submarine operations, but the results obtained by them still vary enormously. Much of this difference may be attributed to unfamiliarity with new types of ships or equipment and only hard and constant training will overcome this.

Opportunities for kills are unlikely to increase since the skill of the U-Boats in avoiding action is unlikely to grow less, and every effort must be made to ensure that a U-Boat detected is a U-Boat sunk.

January 1944

The Azores Area

The number of U-Boat sinkings known or claimed during January showed a welcome increase over the low December figures. The larger proportion occurred in the area to the north-eastward of the Azores, where, at the beginning of the month, the enemy had stationed about a dozen U-Boats. Toll was duly taken by the United States Task Groups operating in this area and by convoy escorts and the enemy obtained no recompense in merchant shipping sunk. The month opened with an effective attack by U.S. Ships "Goldsborough" and "Kearney" and aircraft from U.S.S. "Core." On 'the 8th the escort of Convoy O.S.64 / K.M.S.38 (Group B.4,

H.M.S. "Helmsdale," Senior Officer, and the Sixth Escort Group, H.M.S. "Nene," Senior Officer) detected a U-Boat close to the outer screen. A prolonged hunt followed. After eight attacks had been made by H.M.S. "Bayntun" and H.M.C. Ships "Camrose," "Snowberry" and "Edmundston," the U-Boat was heard apparently trying to blow its tanks and contact then faded, some wreckage being afterwards found. (*U757 : Kptlt. Friedrich Deetz was sunk.*)

Next day the escort scored another probable success, again after a lengthy hunt. The attacks began at 0435 on the 9th, but it was not until noon that H.M.S. "Winchelsea," who had H.M. Ships "Abelia" and "Burdock" in company, could report that the U-Boat had been severely damaged and possibly sunk. The enemy continued to keep in touch and on the nights of the 11th / 12th and 12th / 13th January contacts were made and hunts, in which H.M.C. Ships "Lunenburg" and "Edmundston" took part, ensued. (*The U-boat escaped*)

The United States Task Groups were meanwhile operating profitably in the area about 400 miles east-north-east of the Azores. On the 11th aircraft from U.S.S. "Block Island" claimed the sinking of a large U-Boat (*which escaped*) and three days later the same escort carrier reported encountering three U-Boats. U.S. Ships "Parrott" and "Bulmer" carried out attacks and the sinking of another U-Boat was claimed. Later in the same day, the 14th, "Block Island" picked up 43 survivors from a U-Boat which had been destroyed by an aircraft. (*U231 : Kptlt. Wolfgang Wenzel*) This was the achievement of a Leigh Light Wellington of 172 Squadron, which, during a patrol from the Azores, had attacked the U-Boat shortly after midnight in a position about 465 miles north-north-east of San Miguel.

Despite these losses the enemy maintained his force in the area and the escorts of the next southbound convoy, O.S.65/K.M.S.39, made contact in much the same position as had "Bayntun," "Camrose," "Snowberry" and "Edmundston." On the 19th January H.M.S. "Violet" and F.F.S. "Roselys" carried out attacks ahead of the convoy and two Hedgehog attacks were made, the second being followed by an explosion. (*U641 : Kptlt. Horst Rendtel*)

On the 16th an aircraft from U.S.S. "Guadalcanal" — a newcomer to the area — had reported a sinking in a position about 300 miles west-by-north of Flores. (*U544 : Kptlt. Willy Mattke*)

The North – Western Approaches

After the middle of the month it was appreciated that the 20 or so U-Boats which had been strung out between 50° N. and 61° W., about 700 miles west of Ireland, would probably move slowly in towards the North-Western Approaches in an endeavour to locate our convoys. This return to the scene of the convoy battles of 1940/41 did not have any success. Additional anti-submarine precautions were taken in the entrance to the North Channel and a U-Boat — probably the only one in this particular area — was attacked by H.M.S. "Portchester Castle" in a position only 30 miles north-west of Malin Head. The escorts of Convoy H.X.275 sighted and attacked one of this group on the evening of the 25th in a position about 400 miles west of Cape Clear.

The extremely foul weather which prevailed during the last week of the month impeded operations against these U-Boats, but some successes were obtained. On the 28th Sunderland aircraft D/461, R.A.A.F., reported sighting 30 men in the water after an attack with six depth-charges, and about 180 miles west-south-west of Blacksod Bay on the 31st Captain (D), Second Support Group, successfully carried out one of his "creeping" attacks about 320 miles west-south-west of Cape Clear; there were some extra explosions and much oil, wreckage and the usual human remains were seen. (*U571 : Oblt.z.S. Gustav Lüssow*)

The North – Russian Convoys

In the last week of the month two convoys, J.W.56A and 56B, were on their way to North Russia J.W.56A had actually left Loch Ewe on the 12th but it was badly scattered by storm when east of Iceland and the ships were ordered to put back to Akureyri. On the 21st the convoy set out again. It now numbered 15, three ships of the original convoy having proceeded to Loch Ewe. The escort consisted of Captain (D) 26 in H.M.S. "Hardy," H.M. Ships "Venus," "Virago," "Savage," "Offa," "Obdurate," "Vigilant," " Inconstant," " Dianefla," "Poppy," "Ready" and " Orestes" and H.Nor.M.S. "Stord." On the 25th, when the convoy was about 200 miles north-north-east of North Cape, Captain (D) 26 reported that it was being shadowed by three or possibly four U-boats. At 1330/25th about half a dozen U-boats began a pack attack which lasted until 0730 next morning. It was thought that some U-boats attacked submerged from the bow or ahead as, though both Radar and asdic conditions were good, comparatively few Radar contacts were reported. As a result of these attacks three merchantmen were sunk and "Obdurate" was damaged by a near miss from a "Gnat" torpedo (*fired from U360 : Klaus Becker*) while investigating a Radar contact. British and Russian minesweepers were sailed to give additional support and Russian destroyers were also ordered to join at the first light on the 27th. No more attacks were made and the convoys entered Kola Inlet late on the night of the 27th/28th. (*The three sunk merchantmen were: "Penelope Barker," "Fort Bellingham" and "Andrew G. Curtin," which were sunk by U278 : Joachim Franze, U360 : Klaus Becker and U716 : Hans Dunkelberg.*)

At this time J.W.56B was about 150 miles west-south-west of Bear Island. During the 29th, it was reported that aircraft were shadowing the convoy and homing U-Boats to it, two of them being in contact by that evening. The Escort (H.M.S. "Whitehall," Senior Officer, and H.M. Ships "Westcott," "Cygnet," "Oxlip" and "Seagull," together with Captain (D) 3 in H.M.S. "Milne" and H.M. Ships "Mahrattah," "Opportune," "Scourge," "Musketeer" and "Meteor" and H.M.C.S. "Huron") was further strengthened by the arrival of destroyers from the escort of J.W.56A. During the night of the 29th/30th five or six U-Boats and three aircraft operated in the vicinity but found the defences too strong for them. "Hardy" was, however, torpedoed early in the morning of the 30th, (*by U957 : Gerd Schaar and later by U258 : Leopold Koch*) a hit right aft causing an explosion of the after magazine. All except 40 of the ship's company were saved and Captain (D) transferred first to "Venus" and then to "Vigilant." The enemy kept in touch during the 30th and made some attacks during the night, but these were beaten off and the convoy arrived intact at the entrance to Kola Inlet early on 1st February.

Detailed reports of the passages of these convoys have not yet been received in the Admiralty but it appears that, though the enemy succeeded in sinking a destroyer and three merchantmen and damaging another destroyer, the cost was made reasonably high and it seems likely that one U-Boat was sunk and a number of others more or less severely damaged.

Bay of Biscay Area

The first week of the month brought a welcome crop of sightings and attacks in the Bay area. A Sunderland aircraft, U/10, R.A.A.F., sank a U-Boat (*U426 : Kptlt. Christian Reich*) there on the 8th but the weather then enforced a drastic curtailment of flying and it was not until the 29th that another success was reported, a Polish Wellington, G/304, making a night attack on a U-Boat which was reported as being left disabled on the surface.

The Present Position and Future Developments

The month, by itself, can be considered satisfactory, but, as a pointer to the future, it gives no encouragement for undue optimism. Seven convoys were attacked, one suffered loss and the enemy may have lost a dozen U-Boats. The December figure was thus doubled. The improved weather at the beginning and at the end of the month was no doubt a contributing factor. In the review of that month it was stated that the era of good hunting by day seemed to have passed owing to the enemy's tactics of moving stealthily by night, and rarely showing himself in the daytime for fear of attack from the air. The fact that the kills by Sunderland aircraft on 8th (*U426 : Kptlt. Christian Reich*) and 28th January (*U571 : Oblt.z.S. Gustav Lüssow*) were both made in the daytime suggests that this may have been an over-statement based on too low an estimate of the morale of U-Boat captains at the present time. Reports from both aircraft and surface craft suggest that the U-Boat was poking his nose out of the water a little more confidently than in previous months.

It seems, however, that the ascendancy which we have achieved so laboriously still extends to the point of making the U-Boat shy at the sight of an escorting carrier or aircraft. Convoys have been reported and then after a few hours allowed to draw away, but U-Boats have shown more determination against independents.

The present calm may be deceptive and the time more critical than appears at first sight. By a great weight of effort, we are keeping the U-Boat down but the enemy shows some signs of a renewed determination to overthrow our present superiority. It is for every ship to see that the U-Boat arm is not merely kept in subjection but broken in pieces. This can only be achieved by good drill, skilful seamanship — and a spice of luck.

Anti – U-boat Operations in the Mediterranean

Activity was on a much reduced scale. Two U-Boats were operating off the. Algerian coast at the beginning of the month but neither carried out any attacks. Another U-Boat was patrolling off the "Toe of Italy" but, after being sighted by aircraft and hunted by six destroyers — one of them Italian — it apparently withdrew. The Anzio landings do not seem to have been expected by the enemy for there was no evidence of U-Boats being in the area until the 26th, when one was D/F'd. It is thought that there may be three U-Boats in the area now but no attacks had been made up to the end of the month.

Between 7th and 12th January the most prolonged anti-U-Boat operations yet carried out in the Mediterranean took place off the Spanish coast. Starting from a D/F fix west of Oran, they extended to the Almeria — Cartagena area and eventually ended to the north-westward of the Balearic Islands. Many sightings and fixes established the presence of three U-Boats and it was surmised that two of these had recently made the passage of the Strait of Gibraltar. Aircraft made 10 attacks and surface craft one, but it is not thought that any of the U-Boats were more than damaged.

About the middle of the month it appeared that another U-Boat was attempting to enter the Mediterranean and a patrol was again maintained between Oran and the Spanish coast. After several attacks had been reported to the westward of Gibraltar the patrol was moved closer eastward of the Strait.

After the Anzio landings had been made, reinforcements of anti-submarine aircraft were sent to Corsica and Naples and a flight of Leigh-light fitted Wellington aircraft to Sicily; one attack was made by one of the latter aircraft on a U-Boat in the Tyrrhenian Sea.

The great volume of shipping now passing through the. Mediterranean may not be generally realized. In October and November, 1943, there were respectively 203 and 231 ships in. the Mediterranean, compared with 253 and 212 in the Atlantic. This does not seem to be lost upon the enemy.

February 1944

The outstanding event of a highly successful month was the patrol of the Second Support Groups in the course of which six U-Boats were sunk. H.M.S. "Spey" (Senior Officer, Tenth Escort Group), striking quickly, carried the enemy's discomfiture in the North Atlantic a stage further by sinking two U-Boats on consecutive-days.

The Second Support Group's Patrol

The Second Support Group destroyed its first U-Boat (*U592 : Oblt.z.S. Heinz Jaschke*) on the 31st January, when acting as an anti-submarine screen for H.M. Ships "Nairana" and "Activity." The contact was made by H.M.S. "Wild Goose," whose quick appreciation probably saved "Nairana"; H.M. Ships "Magpie" and "Starling" joined and, a little over an hour later, after a 26-charge and a 22-charge pattern had been dropped, all the necessary evidence of death appeared. The second sinking was on the 9th February, when the escort carriers and sloops were with Convoy S.L.147 / M.K.S.38. (*U734 : Oblt.z.S. Hans-Jörg Blauert*) It began with a sighting by "Wild Goose," who at once obtained asdic contact. H.M.S. "Woodpecker" joined and dropped a 22-charge pattern; by the time "Starling" had closed it was all over.

Next day two more U-Boats we're destroyed. (*U545 : Kptlt. Gert Mannesmann and U666: Oblt.z.S. Ernst-August Wilberg*) H.M.S. "Kite," sent to investigate H/F D/F bearings, made simultaneously a radar contact and a sighting and then, having at once adopted the correct procedure, counter-mined a "Gnat." The hunt which ensued lasted eight hours. "Magpie" joined at about 0900, after it had been in progress for three hours, and "Starling" and "Wild Goose" came on from another kill at about noon. The enemy was tough and wily and survived two creeping attacks; by going slow, mainly down wind and sea at considerable depth; it made it difficult, in the weather then prevailing, to hold the directing ship in position for the time required. It was eventually destroyed by a creeping attack by "Magpie" and "Starling," in which both hedgehog and depth-charges were used.

The U-Boat which "Starling" and "Wild Goose" had already sunk when they joined in this hunt had been forced deep and destroyed three hours later by the second of two creeping attacks.

The fifth U-Boat was sunk as the result of attacks by "Woodpecker" and "Wild Goose." The hunt lasted about two hours, two 10-charge patterns and a 22-charge pattern being dropped. (*U424 : Oblt.z.S. Günther Lüdders*)

After supporting Convoy H.X.278 the Group was detached on the 17th February and sent to reinforce the escort of Convoy O.N.224, which was passing through a dangerous area. Two U-Boats endeavoured to attack the convoy during the night of the 18th/19th; their efforts were half-hearted but they were allowed to go more or less unscathed and at first light on the 19th the Second Support Group turned back astern of the convoy to look for them. It had just altered course to rejoin when at 1007 "Woodpecker" obtained an asdic contact. "Starling" confirmed and, in extremely bad asdic conditions, the ships began to hunt a U-Boat which, by continued alterations of course, did its best to prevent the sloops from getting into their favourite astern position. The asdic teams held on to her for six hours, three creeping and two ordinary attacks were made and then, at about 1630, contact was lost and could not be regained. Captain (D), Second Support Group, was preparing for a test of endurance but the U-Boat gave up the struggle after about half an hour and surfaced. By way of contrast the fate of the crews of the five other U-Boats, who had all come to be described briefly as "wreckage and human remains," every single man from this sixth U-Boat — "U 264" (*Kptlt. Hartwig Looks*) — was picked up.

On its return to Liverpool the Group received the honour of being cheered into harbour. Unhappily "Woodpecker" was not with her sister-ships. Torpedoed on the 19th February, (*by U256 : Wilhelm Brauel*) she sank in tow early on the 27th when about ten miles from the Scilly Isles.

Two Quick Kills by the Tenth Escort Group

In his report of proceedings, Captain (D), Second Support Group, recorded that, as he was approaching Convoy O.N.224 on the afternoon of the 18th February, he heard by R/T the Senior Officer, Tenth Escort Group, in "Spey," making "a very swift and pretty kill." Twenty-four hours later "Spey" repeated her success; in both cases a single 10-charge pattern sufficed.

The Tenth Escort Group had been detached to sweep to starboard of Convoy O.N.S.29 and was returning when, at 1523/18, "Spey" obtained contact by asdic at 1,700 yards range and quickly classified it as "submarine." It was held down to "instant echoes" on the main set; echoes on the "Q" attachment were heard from 300 yards, but the first and range operators had the situation well in hand and it was considered that the order "Switch to Q" at such short range would probably have upset the rhythm of their attack at the critical point. Ten charges were dropped. Contact was regained at 300 yards range and at 500 yards a U-Boat broke surface in the middle of the pattern. "Spey" opened fire, to which some return was made, and, not believing that the U-Boat could have been mortally damaged by a single pattern, steered close across her bows to lay another shallow pattern round her. It then appeared that she had no more fight in her and only half a pattern was dropped. A number of survivors were picked up and the U-Boat was found to be "U406." (*Kptlt. Horst Dietrichs*) Twenty-three hours later the Group was on its way to join Convoy O.N.224. At 1426/19 "Spey" obtained a "submarine" contact at a range of 1,800 yards and began an attack at 750 yards. Charges were set at 50ft. and 140ft. At about 700 yards range, firm contact by "Q" was obtained and the operators were at once switched over. The 147B (*Depth Predictor*) was started, its beam being depressed to 15°. At 600 yards the 147B was set to "step-up" and at 500 yards three echoes appeared showing a depth of 350 ft. On this being reported the settings of the depth-charges were ordered to be altered to 250 ft. and 385 ft. The depth-charge party had just time enough to do it.

Contact was lost on the main set at 350 yards but was held by "Q" right down to "instant echoes." Owing to the last minute changes of the depth settings, which had also to be applied to the speed/depth plate of the range recorder, there was not time to apply slant range correction and the ten-charge pattern was therefore fired by recorder, the last inch of the main trace being used. Contact was regained at 300 - 400 yards and at 800 yards the U-Boat broke surface at a very steep angle, bows first. This U-Boat— she was "U386" (*Oblt.z.S. Fritz Albrecht*) — had much more fight in her than the boat of the previous day, and not only replied to "Spey's" fire but made some effort to escape on the surface. "Spey" closed and straddled the boat with a shallow pattern and eventually her bows reared up and she sank stern first. Sixteen of the crew, including the captain, were rescued.

Contrast of Methods

The contrast in the methods employed by these two highly efficient groups is interesting. The Second Support Group took an average of four hours and 106 depth-charges to sink each of its six U-Boats. "Spey," fitted with the latest type of asdic set, including the Type 147B depth-predictor, destroyed both her boats in a matter of minutes, forcing them to the surface with single ten-charge patterns. The common factors in both groups' successes were good seamanship, efficient use of asdics and the highest standards of depth-charge drill — the information given by "Spey's" depth-predictor would have been wasted if the depth-charge party had not been able to change the settings in time. On the other hand the Second Support Group's methods require exceedingly close co-operation between ships and almost unlimited time and depth-charges; to force the U-Boat deep is essential to a creeping attack.

It is obviously tactically advantageous to kill the quarry as quickly as possible and the latest developments in asdic sets and anti-submarine weapons are designed to assist in the accomplishment of this object. The danger of the creeping attack lies in the fact that it tends to develop into a long, drawn-out struggle during which asdic conditions or weather may deteriorate, thereby causing the hunting vessels, to lose contact and giving the U-Boat an opportunity to escape.

The passage of Convoys O.N.224 and O.N.S.29 completed the triumph of the Groups. At the beginning of the month the enemy bad a line of U-Boats disposed roughly between 61°N. and 48°N. and 400 - 500 miles west of Ireland . The losses inflicted by the Second Support Group and the weight of our air offensive caused the enemy to withdraw to the westward. Aircraft shadowing Convoys O.N.224 and O.N.S.29 disclosed his intentions. The fast convoy consisted of 81 ships escorted by Group C.1 (H.M.C.S. "Assiniboine," Senior Officer) and the slow convoy of 46 ships, its escorting Group being B.6 (H.M.S. "Fame," Senior Officer). As they drew near the dangerous area they were reinforced, O.N.224 by sloops of the Seventh Escort Group in addition to those of the Second Support Group and O.N.S.29 by destroyers of the 18th Group, the Tenth Escort Group being sent first to O.N.S.29 and then moved to support O.N.S.24. With their escorts thus strengthened, the convoys passed without loss through the concentration of U-Boats, three of which were destroyed.

Other Successes in the North Atlantic

To complete a highly successful month in the North Atlantic, H.M.C.S. "Waskesiu" sank "U257" (*Kptlt. Heinz Rahe*) when operating with the Sixth Escort Group in support of Convoy S.C.153 and on the 26th H.M. Ships,. "Affleck" and "Gore" destroyed "U91." (*Kptlt. Heinz Hungerhausen*) In the former action the Commanding Officer of the Canadian ship had the courage of his convictions and hung on to his contact when the Senior Officer of the Group was

88

unable to confirm it. Dropping another pattern, he brought the U-Boat to the surface and he and his Senior Officer engaged her with gunfire until she sank.These successes have provided us with a satisfactory number of prisoners of war, which had been in short supply for some months. Their value as sources of intelligence, always great, is particularly high at the present time.

North Russian Convoys

The passage of Convoy J.W.57 was distinguished by the sinking of a U-Boat (*U601 : Oblt.z.S. Otto Hansen*) by Catalina M/210 Operating at extreme range — about 750 miles from its base at Sullom Voe — and in waters, in which the enemy have had comparatively little to fear from the air, M/210 found the U-Boat about 250 miles north-west of the Lofoten Islands. It dropped one of the two charges which it carried 15ft. on the U-Boat's starboard quarter, level with its stern, and the other 5ft. to port of the conning-tower. The U-Boat sank in about 30 seconds. Eight or 10 survivors and wreckage were seen but they were soon lost to sight in a snow storm. Convoy J.W.57 passed through a heavy concentration of U-Boats without losing any merchantmen but H.M.S. "Mahratta" was torpedoed and sunk. (*By U990 : Kptlt. Hubert Nordheimer*)

Other Areas

In the Iceland — Faeroes area, two U-Boats were probably sunk on the night of 10th/11th February, one by Wellington aircraft O/612 and the other by Wellington "D" of 407 Squadron. (*U545 : Kptlt. Gert Mannesmann and U 283 : Oblt.z.S. Günther Ney*)

The Bay of Biscay, the Azores area and the South Atlantic were comparatively quiet. On the 6th, however, U.S. Liberators from Ascension Island sank a German U-Boat, (*U177 : Korvkpt. Heinz Bucholz*) from which U.S.S. "Omaha" picked up survivors. From the other areas only one likely attack was reported — one made by aircraft from U.S.S. "Croaten" on the 15th in 27°40'N., 40°40'W.

The sinking of "U761" (*Oblt.z.S. Horst Geider*) on the 24th February to the westward of Gibraltar, was particularly satisfactory. The U-Boat was detected by two United States Catalinas as she was attempting the passage of the Strait. The aircraft were fitted with the M.A.D. device. They dropped a smoke float which was sighted by H.M. Ships "Anthony" and "Wishart," who were patrolling about a mile away. Asdic contact was gained and lost and, after a hunt lasting about 40 minutes, the U-boat was again detected by aircraft. After they and the destroyers had attacked she came to the surface and eventually blew up.

The Indian Ocean

In the Indian Ocean, in which eight of the 10 ships lost in the month were sunk, our counter-measures had greater success than for some time. H.M.A. Ships "Launceston" and "Ipswich" and H.M.I.S. "Jumna," escorting Convoy J.C.36, attacked and probably sank a Japanese U-Boat off Vizagapatam on 11th February. The next day H.M. Ships "Petard" and "Paladin" destroyed another Japanese U-Boat north of Addu Atoll, though not before it had torpedoed a ship in convoy which sank with very heavy loss of life.

H.M. Submarine "Tally-Ho," operating in the Strait of Malacca, claimed the sinking of a third off Penang, although she was not able to establish its nationality. The activities of German U-Boats in this area are likely to be considerably hampered by the sinking of a supply ship — the tanker "Charlotte Schliemann" — by H.M.S. "Relentless," who was following up a sighting report by a Catalina from Mauritius.

Inshore Operations

There has again been some indication that the enemy is probing our anti-submarine defences inshore. In January he sent a U-Boat within 30 miles of Malin Head and this month H.M.S. "Warwick" was sunk (*by U413 : Gustav Poel*) about 17 miles west of Trevose Head. In a broadcast the enemy has claimed this, sinking to have been made by a U-Boat but a search by aircraft and surface vessels failed to make contact with it.

The possibility of the enemy operating close inshore in the months to come is not being overlooked and in Section 6 of this Report will be found a questionnaire which will give some guidance to anti-submarine vessels called upon to hunt U-Boats operating in shallow waters.

General Remarks

It was indeed satisfactory that the number of U-Boat sinkings rose for the second month in succession. The low December figure of six was about doubled in January and for February the provisional figure is 18. The great triumph of the Second Support Group and the success of the Tenth Escort Group showed that a boat cannot escape its fate merely by remaining submerged for 20 hours out of the 24. Aircraft have to a large extent denied to the U-Boat its mobility; the asdic has always deprived it of some of its invisibility. The passage of Convoys O.N.224 and O.N.S.29 showed not only the weakness of the enemy's present tactics — the appearance of shadowing aircraft betrayed his intentions — but also something of our strength. Our convoys can pass through concentrations of U-Boats, inflicting loss and suffering little or none themselves.

The ascendancy which we have established over the enemy in ocean waters may perhaps be challenged in the not far distant future under very different conditions, which will test to the uttermost the training of our anti-submarine forces.

Successful use of Flares by Coastal Command Aircraft Attacking at Night

To defeat the cautious tactics of the U-Boats, which now surface for only a few hours during darkness, aircraft of Coastal Command not fitted with Leigh Lights have been supplied with flares. They are of two million candle-power and burn for 50 or 60 seconds. Released from a height of about 700 ft. when the aircraft is some 3,000 yards from its target on its A.S.V. run-in, they will give, in clear weather, a sighting range of about 1,700 yards and in haze about 800 yards.

Five attacks by aircraft using these flares in the Bay area have recently been assessed. Unfortunately, although the attacks were well carried out, it was difficult to obtain evidence of damage. At 2305 on 5th January, 1944, Halifax aircraft R/58, on anti-submarine patrol, obtained an A.S.V. contact. It had already made several contacts with trawlers but on closing this contact it sighted a wake about 4 miles distant. Visibility up moon was about 5 miles and down moon about 2 miles, but there was a slight haze and the aircraft could not see the U-Boat itself until the range was about 3,000 yards; three flares were then released. The U-Boat first tried to shoot them out but turned its guns on the aircraft as it came in to attack. After dropping six charges from 150 ft. the aircraft climbed to 800 ft. and, circling the U-Boat, which had remained on the surface, released another flare when about four points abaft the starboard beam. The U-Boat again tried to shoot it out. The aircraft then attacked with gunfire and the U-Boat dived, apparently within about five minutes of the depth-charge attack.

The next attack in which flares were used was made by Halifax aircraft S/502 at 0403 on 29th January. Visibility was bad, being not more than a mile. After making one blind attack on an A.S.V. contact, the aircraft obtained a second A.S.V. contact bearing Red 80°, range 6 miles. It homed on to it on a course of 090° and at a range of 2 miles by Radar the stop watch was started and run for 24 seconds. Two flares were then released, at an estimated range of 2,000 yards. The Radar operator continued to home the Captain and at 300 yards range a surfaced U-Boat was sighted dead ahead. Using the Mark XIV bombsight, the aircraft dropped two 600 lb. A/S bombs from a height of 1,300 ft.. They were released when the conning-tower of the U-Boat, illuminated by the flares, was seen on the graticule ('cross wires') of the bombsight. It was estimated that the bombs straddled forward of the conning-tower; they were felt to explode and immediately afterwards the U-boat's flak ceased. The aircraft crossed the position a second time and then had to set course for base.

March 1944

General Remarks

The successes which rewarded our counter-measures in February continued into March and it is estimated that again 19 or 20 U-Boats were destroyed. The Fleet Air Arm alone achieved two kills under very difficult conditions and contributed towards two others. In general, events in the first quarter of 1944 have followed a uniform pattern. Convoys have sailed more or less unmolested and the rate of exchange of merchant ships for U-Boats has continued to be on the whole very much in our favour, namely 55 U-Boats for 45 ships. It is satisfactory that a number of U-Boats have been destroyed by units operating independently of convoys.

In March, however, the pattern showed some variations in its design; the two longest hunts of the war occurred, one U-Boat resisting for 38 hours and another for 30 hours. The first U-Boat torpedoed and sank one of the hunting ships as it came up for the final encounter on the surface. However much the morale of the U-Boat arm as a whole may have deteriorated after nearly a year of adversity, it is clear that there are still some well-trained and skilfully commanded U-Boat crews to be met with at sea. This is further emphasised by an enterprising attack delivered on a transatlantic convoy and the sinking of one merchant ship in it. A year ago such attacks were commonplace bad news; today they are not only a startling reminder of past disasters but evidence of the continued need for unremitting effort to break the still great potential power of the U-Boat.

Two Very Long Hunts

The two very long hunts referred to were made by the First Escort Group on the 29th February — 1st March, (*U358 : Kptlt. Rolf Manke*) and by Group C.2 on 5th — 6th March (*U744 : Oblt.z.S. Heinz Blischke*) respectively. A total of nearly 600 depth-charges as well as eight Hedgehog salvoes, were expended; in both cases the weather, after being very favourable, deteriorated — a danger to the success of long hunts mentioned in the last Report.

The First Escort Group's Successes

Before their hunt on the 29th February — 1st March, the First Escort Group had already sunk "U91." (*Kptlt. Heinz Hungerhausen*) The U-Boat was detected by H.M.S. "Gore's" asdic at 2240 on the 25th February and was attacked and sent deep at 2302. H.M.S. "Gould" made a creeping attack at 0041/26, H.M.S. "Affleck" (Senior Officer, First Escort Group) following up at 0048. The Senior Officer then thought of waiting until dawn before attacking again but the weather showed signs of deterioration; his team was new and still very raw, but thanks to the short spell allowed with H.M.S. "Philante" and her excellent exercise programme all ships, except "Affleck," had done at least one practice creep and this, together with a very valuable forenoon's tactical exercise upon the Belfast Tactical Unit Table, gave him sufficient confidence to put the issue to the test forthwith. In difficult conditions "Gould" made another creeping attack at 0041, "Affleck" following up, but the U-Boat made a quick last-minute turn away to port and then went still deeper. "Gore" regained contact and, approaching on what was, in the prevailing weather, an easier course, dropped an accurate pattern at 0237. "Affleck" again followed up. As she did so, she could hear "very loud tank blowing noises"; turning back she obtained a short range radar contact, the U-Boat was then sighted and, after a brisk "free for all" gun action, surrendered. The hunt had lasted about four hours.

The Longest Hunt on Record

Three days later, at 0507 on the 29th February, H.M.S. "Garlies" made contact by asdic at 1,600 yards range. "Affleck" closed and holding contact down to 300 yards made a Hedgehog attack, the Senior Officer choosing this weapon because, if it failed, it would not "scare the enemy into some wild evasion." There was no result and at 0612 "Garlies" was started upon a creeping attack, which promised well. Unfortunately, at the eighteenth charge, due to a sudden defect in the frigate's main machinery, she stopped amid her own pattern, unable to do anything. "Affleck" had, of course, to delay her attack and decided to wait for an hour when it would be daylight.

In perfect asdic conditions — there was bright sunshine and a flat calm sea — "Gore" resumed the attack at 0758, "Affleck" following up. The group was able to keep continuous contact but, as soon as the range was closed to distances varying between 650 and 950 yards, the echo would fade and disappear. It was thought that the U-boat was keeping at between 900 and 1000 feet and, though the frigates attacked repeatedly throughout the day, it was with the realisation that they were doing little harm to a redoubtable opponent. At 1615 a first-class H/F D/F naval enigma was obtained within twenty miles and "Garlies" and "Gore" were sent off to investigate. "Affleck" and "Gould" continued to attack at intervals until 1742, when it was decided to cease for the night. At dark the U-Boat was steering to the northward at about 1.5 knots, with "Affleck" holding contact 1,200 yards astern and "Gould" keeping station at about the same range upon the U-Boat's starboard beam. "Affleck" had a foreboding — and in fact warned "Gould" — that the U-Boat, on surfacing, might endeavour to destroy one of the hunters, but, nevertheless, remained astern in such a position that she could at once carry out an attack.

"Garlies" and "Gore" were back by 1930 — they had found nothing — and were ordered to carry out Observant two miles away from the ships in contact on a datum course of 355°. This datum course was altered from time to time during the night as the enemy doubled round and got first under "Gould" and then under "Affleck." It was easy to detect the start of the U-Boat's manoeuvres but difficult to counter them owing to the contact disappearing at 700 yards range. Weather conditions continued to be perfect.

The moon was due to set at 0157/1 and it was hoped that the enemy would then surface and endeavour to escape but he did not and between 0200 and 0300, "Gore" and "Garlies" changed places with "Affleck" and "Gould" ; the former's asdic operators had been holding contact for over twenty hours. At dawn the attack was taken up again by "Gould" and "Affleck" but the long hunt had not impaired the enemy's cunning and he avoided the danger. A mass creep attack was then organized, the four ships each firing a full 26-charge pattern, but though well synchronized, it had no result; the U-Boat was keeping deep enough to be safe from even such a marine convulsion as this. It was then about 1000 and at this lack of success the ships, after twenty-nine hours of hunting, were tempted to despair. To add to their fatigue, the weather had deteriorated; there was a rising south-easterly wind with an accompanying sea. When, at 1606, "Gore" and "Garlies" had to leave the scene and proceed to Gibraltar, asdic conditions were extremely bad but, although contact was lost from time to time, either "Affleck" or "Gould" always managed to regain it.

The end came at 1920. "Gould" had just lost the contact on her port quarter and "Affleck" had picked it up on her port beam, when a sudden improvement in the echo was followed by "Gould" being torpedoed in the after motor room on her port side. It was thought that, as the periscope broke surface, the U-Boat fired at "Gould," who was the last ship she knew to be in asdic contact. "Affleck" sighted the conning-tower some 1,500 yards on her port beam and with depth-charges and gunfire brought the long contest to an end. Only one survivor was picked up, for "Affleck" had to rescue "Gould's" crew. The U-Boat was "U358" (*Rolf Mancke*).

This hunt had lasted from 0507 on the 29th February until 1920 on the 1st March, a period of more than thirty-eight hours. The hunt of Group C.2 was not quite so long but it was in progress for thirty hours. In both, Senior Officers overcame the temptation to disbelieve the evidence offered by the asdic and were duly rewarded.

Group C2's Thirty - hour Hunt

At about 1000 on the 5th March, H.M.C.S. "Gatineau," 8 miles on the port bow of Convoy H.X.280, obtained an asdic contact H.M.C.S. "St. Catherines" closed and the hunt began. Fifteen attacks were made with depth-charges and Hedgehog between 1028 and 2120, H.M.S. "Icarus" and H.M.C. Ships "Chaudiere," "Chilliwack" and "Fennel" taking part in them with "Gatineau" and "St. Catherines." H.M.S. "Kenilworth Castle" also attacked, using Type 147B and Squid; she achieved no success but the result has not diminished her Commanding Officer's faith in the new gear and weapon. There was a lull between 2120/5 and 0015/6 and it was then decided that the hunt was becoming too quiet from the U-Boat's point of view and three attacks were made in the next hour. The U-Boat Captain — described by "Gatineau's" Commanding Officer as a man "who knew exactly what steps to take in order to confuse hunting vessels" — then seems to have thought that the hunt was becoming too easy from the point of view of the ships, for he spent the next three hours in taking violent evasive action.

After this he settled down somewhat and two Hedgehog attacks were made between 0745 and 0830 but he was keeping deep and they were without success. At 0910 when the hunt had entered on its twenty-fourth hour, the U-Boat Captain detected "Chaudiere" increasing speed as she manoeuvred for a creeping attack and, altering course, compelled her to postpone it for an hour. Another creeping attack was made at 1100, but the U-Boat, by doubling back to port again, avoided the pattern. Shortly after noon the U-Boat settled down and the Group, being in firm contact, decided to let four hours go by before taking up the attack again; asdic conditions were extraordinarily good. It was considered that the U-Boat would try to remain submerged until about 2100 but at about 1530 she surfaced — she was "U744" — and her crew abandoned her without any attempt to reply to the ships' gunfire. It was fortunate that the Captain of this U-Boat had not quite the same determination as that displayed by "U358's," for soon afterwards the wind and sea increased and the barometer fell fast.

Two U-Boats Sunk on 10th March

On the 10th, two U-Boats were sunk, one (*U625 : Oblt.z.S. Siegfried Straub*) by a Sunderland aircraft of 422 Squadron, R.C.A.F. in a position about 400 miles west by north of Cape Clear, and somewhat further south, "U845" (*Korvkpt. Werner Weber*) was destroyed by H.M.S. "Forester" and H.M.C. Ships "St. Laurent," "Owen Sound" and "Swansea."

The Destruction of "U845" (*Korvkpt. Werner Weber*) by Group C.1

The U-boat had sighted Convoy S.C.154 and at about 1330 her signal reporting it was D/F'd by "Swansea," who was oiling in the convoy, and by "St. Laurent," who was 30 miles astern escorting the merchantman "San Francisco" with "Owen Sound." After a hunt of about three hours, "St. Laurent" sighted the U-Boat and she and "Owen Sound" made attacks. "Forester" and, later, "Swansea" joined and the two destroyers made a creeping attack at 1900, after which contact was lost for an hour. "St. Laurent" then regained it and held it until 2230 when the U-Boat surfaced 1,400 yards ahead of her and 1,200 yards on "Forester's" port beam. The enemy set off at about nineteen knots zigzagging violently, pursued by and under fire from "St. Laurent," "Forester" and "Swansea."

Weather conditions were perfect for the general chase which ensued — a bright moon and no wind or sea. "Forester" reduced to seven knots until seventeen minutes had elapsed and then increased to twenty-eight knots, by which time the U-Boat was about 8,000 yards away from her. "St. Laurent," who had asked "Forester" whether she should ram and had been told not to, maintained a range of 3,000 yards astern and at 2251, after the chase had been in progress for seventeen minutes, streamed her C.A.T. gear. To "Forester" it appeared that the U-Boat might escape and at 2309, considering that "St. Laurent's" C.A.T. gear could protect her until she was doing twenty-four knots and that it was immaterial if it came adrift or not, ordered her to increase to twenty-six knots to close and destroy the U-Boat.

The enemy, now down by the stern, was still taking evasive action, but "St. Laurent," getting her 100 yards to starboard, fired at her with every gun which would bear, and then, passing ahead of her, dropped a shallow ten-charge pattern. This brought "U845" to a standstill.

"Swansea" closed, hoping to board, but before she could send away a party, the U-Boat began to sink, finally disappearing at 2338.

The Sinking of "U575" (*Oblt.z.S. Wolfgang Boehmer*)

On the 13th March, "U575" fell a victim to attacks by aircraft and surface craft — British, Canadian and United States units combining to destroy her. All the reports have not been received, but that of Fortress aircraft J/220 states that it took off from the Azores at 0916/13 with instructions to proceed to the position of an attack which Wellington B/172 had made at 0151/13. On its way, J/220 intercepted the sighting and attack report of Fortress aircraft R/206, which was approximately in the same position, and later began to pick up its homing transmissions at a range of 150 miles. When J/220 reached the vicinity of the position the homing transmissions ceased, but, while it was waiting for them to be resumed, it sighted an oil slick and saw some markers dropped by an aircraft from U.S.S. "Bogue." The Fortress, observing that the head of the oil slick was moving past a flame which it itself had dropped, then attacked with half her depth-charge load. While circling after the attack, 3/220 saw that the oil slick had altered course about 90° to port and that its head had become noticeably blunter. The aircraft attacked again and called up H.M.C.S. "Prince Rupert," who was known to be in the vicinity, and directed her to the target. U.S. Ships "Hobson" and "Haverfield" joined the frigate, and the U-Boat was brought to the surface with depth-charges and finally destroyed by gunfire and by rocket attacks by aircraft. A number of survivors were picked up.

The Second Escort Group's Thirteenth Kill
(U653 : Oblt.z.S. Hans-Albrecht Kandlet)

On the 15th, the Second Escort Group added one more to its long list of successes. The group, which had begun this patrol with four days of exercises with H.M.S. "Philante," had H.M.S. "Vindex" in company. At 0115/15 the carrier, which with her screen was about 30 miles astern of the sloops, reported that one of her aircraft was in A.S.V. contact with the Group and that a sixth contact had also been obtained. The flares and marker which the aircraft dropped were seen at the port end of the line of ships, which were spread in line abreast two miles apart. H.M.S. "Wren," the port wing ship, closed without making contact but at 0119 "Vindex" reported that another aircraft had obtained, two miles ahead of the ships, an A.S.V. contact which had disappeared on investigation. Half an hour later, H.M.S. "Wild Goose" made contacts which H.M. Ships "Magpie" and "Starling" confirmed.

The attack which followed was in complete contrast with those described in the last Report. Using her "Q" attachment, in poor asdic conditions, "Starling" held contact down to almost "instant echoes," having lost it on the main set at 350 yards. At the very last moment the bearing appeared to move slowly right but it was too late to alter course. At 0231 the single pattern of the action was dropped. It evidently started some serious trouble inside the U-Boat, for, within a minute of its being dropped, explosions began to he heard and it is thought that the U-Boat eventually blew up at about 0305. Much wreckage and a headless torpedo were seen.

The Group's Fourteenth Kill
(*U961 : Oblt.z.S. Klaus Fischer*)

On the 29th, the Group, operating in the unfamiliar waters in Iceland — Faeroes area, sank another U-Boat during the passage of Convoy J.W.58 but no details of this success are at present available in the Admiralty.

Success of U.S.S. "Block Island's" Operations in the Area of the Cape Verde Islands

During the month U.S.S. "Block Island's" Task Group, operating in the area of the Cape Verde Islands, maintained its reputation as great killers of U-Boats, sinking one on the 17th and another on the 19th. Forty-seven survivors were picked up from the first boat and eight from the second. (*U801 : Kptlt. Hans-Joachim Brans and U1059 : Oblt.z.S. Günther Leupold*)

The Bay of Biscay

The lack of sightings in the Bay — only thirty-three were reported — caused Coastal Command to send its aircraft closer in to the French coast so as to cover the swept channels leading out of the bases. Mosquito aircraft are largely used for this work and on the 25th a U-Boat was probably sunk by them in position 46°47'N. 02°42'W. The aircraft attacked with six-pounder gunfire, obtaining hits on the conning tower, forward deck and water line. (*U976 : Oblt.z.S. Raimund Tiesler was sunk*)

April 1944

A total of 13 U-Boats were sunk or probably sunk during the month. In addition there were three promising attacks which, it is hoped, will prove to be kills when finally assessed. Of these 16 encounters, ships were responsible for six, carrier-borne aircraft for four, combined ship and carrier-borne aircraft attacks for three and shore-based aircraft for two. A submarine attack completed the total.

Two U-Boats sunk in Attacks on North Atlantic Convoys

The first attack was made on the 6th April on Convoy S.C.156, which was then about 500 miles east of Cape Race. The weather was fair and visibility about four miles, the moon, though overcast, being nearly full. There were apparently two U-Boats in the vicinity of the convoy. The first was fixed by H/F D/F sometime before midnight about 15 miles on the starboard quarter, but was not detected by a sweep carried out by H.M.S. "Swale;" though there was time for it to have worked round ahead, it is not thought that it did so. The Captain of the second U-Boat, which actually made the attack, may have been surprised to find himself in contact with a convoy, but he made good use of his chances. It is thought that he may have passed submerged between two of the escorts, as no Radar contact was made before the ships in positions 12 and 44 were hit by torpedoes. (*"South America" and "Ruth I" sunk by U302 : Herbert Sickel*) About twelve minutes after the first torpedo had struck, "Swale," who had just resumed station about two miles on the port quarter, obtained a Radar contact 4,000 yards on her starboard quarter. Altering course to the bearing she fired starshell, sighted the U-Boat stern on, and, opening fire, forced it to dive at a range of about 5,500 yards. Five minutes later she obtained asdic contact.

The U-Boat Captain, having seized his opportunity so profitably, made but feeble efforts to escape the consequences. Apparently he employed neither Gnats nor S.B.T., nor did he make a serious attempt at evasive tactics. "Swale" attacked him with her Hedgehog when he was at about 450 ft. and obtained three explosions with her second pattern. This was followed five minutes later by a single loud, deep, muffled explosion. (*U302 : Herbert Sickel was sunk.*)

Ten days later at 0806/16 "U 550" (*Kptlt. Klaus Hänert*) torpedoed a tanker ("*Pan Pennsylvania*" 11017GRT) in Convoy C.U.21 when it was about 250 miles east by south of New York. After a search in difficult asdic conditions, U.S.S. "Joyce" made contact at 0948 and attacked, bringing the U-Boat to the surface soon afterwards. U.S. Ships "Gandy" and "Peterson" joined in the gun action which then ensued and the boat was rammed by "Gandy." Twelve survivors were picked up.

Successes against U-Boats operating against North Russian Convoys

The passage of Convoy J.W.58 provided two known "kills" — and there is the possibility of a third — one of these being achieved by aircraft from the escort carriers "Tracker" and "Activity," and the other by H.M.S. "Keppel." During the night of 2nd/3rd April, H.M.S. "Keppel," when about 25 miles from the convoy, obtained contact by asdic at 2,700 yards range and attacked with Hedgehog. At least four bombs were heard to explode and five minutes later there was an extremely violent underwater explosion. Oil and wreckage, from which a tin of coffee beans was recovered, then came to the surface. (*It would seem that U360 : Kptlt. Klaus Becker was sunk*)

Early on the 3rd April, Avenger and Wildcat aircraft from H.M.S. "Tracker" and Swordfish aircraft from H.M.S. "Activity" attacked a U-boat which was found by the latter about 15 miles from the convoy. After all the aircraft had made attacks, the U-boat submerged horizontally, leaving a large patch of oil, reappeared momentarily, and then sank. The Second Escort Group closed and, in addition to the oil, found some wreckage, a fur cap and a pillow, the latter being picked up. (*U288 : Oblt.z.S. Willy Meyer*)

Comparison between Conditions in Arctic and North Atlantic Waters

This was the first occasion on which the Second Escort Group had operated in Arctic waters and the reflections of the Senior Officer are of interest. He reported that he had had the humiliating experience of getting on to three U-Boats at close range, by sighting and by Radar, and of being unable to make any asdic contact at all. He found H/F D/F conditions and asdic conditions almost equally bad. The reports received show that asdic conditions varied between "poor" and "atrocious," the weather being virtually a flat calm. The difficulty of making asdic contact is caused by the existence of a layer of icy water near the surface, below which the asdic beam will not penetrate. The cold-layer is broken up by bad weather, after which better asdic conditions may be expected. In the case of "Keppel's" Hedgehog kill, when asdic conditions were described as "average," the U-Boat was probably at less than 100 feet and had presumably not had time to dive to a greater depth and so obtain the protection of the cold layer

Carrier Operations to the Westward of the Bay of Biscay

Another of our escort carriers, H.M.S. "Biter," patrolled a probability area to the westward of the Bay of Biscay with the Seventh and Ninth Escort Groups. The weather was bad, flying was reduced to a minimum and the surface craft themselves obtained only three contacts. The most was made of these sparse opportunities. On the 8th four attacks, the results of which were regarded as promising, were made, and on the 14th H.M.S. "Pelican" and H.M.C.S. "Swansea" destroyed "U448."

The Destruction of "U448" (*Oblt.z.S. Helmut Dauter on 14 April 1944*)

"Pelican" had just completed oiling from "Biter" when "Swansea," on the starboard side of tile screen, obtained a contact. She made a successful counter-attack on the U-Boat which was closing to attack the carrier, and then dropped a pattern of depth-charges set to 350 and 550 ft. "Pelican" was ordered to join and reached the position just as "Swansea" was about to make a third attack. After both ships had been out of contact for about half an hour "Pelican" made an attack which was without result. She regained contact and, finding that the U-Boat was deep and that "Swansea" could not confirm, decided on a creeping attack. During the run-in, it became evident that the U-Boat had altered course and, when the firing range was reached, "Pelican" realized that "Swansea" was not suitably placed to fire a pattern which would have a killing effect. The sloop's Commanding Officer had a hard decision to make, especially as the contact was difficult to hold, but, being convinced that it was essential to ensure that the first pattern should be lethal, he adjusted station on the U-Boat and asked "Swansea" to make a second attempt. This decision was amply rewarded. The U-Boat again made an alteration of course as "Swansea" was making her second run in, but this was successfully countered and five minutes after the attack had been completed the U-Boat surfaced, came under fire and was abandoned. As regards the creeping attack, survivors said that they were quite unaware that anything was impending until they heard the explosion of the charges, which did great damage.

Three more U-Boats destroyed by United States C.V.E.s

The United States C.V.E.s had another very successful month, their kills being widely spread over the North Atlantic. On the 7th aircraft from U.S.S. "Croaten" destroyed a U-Boat about 250 miles south of Halifax; 28 prisoners were taken. Between the 8th and 10th U.S.S. "Guadalcanal" and her escorts, operating to the north-westward of Madeira, accounted for two U-Boats, recovering 41 survivors from the first boat (*U515 : Kptlt. Werner Henke, with 43 survivors*); only one of the crew of the second boat was rescued. Finally on the 25th/26th, aircraft from "Croaten" and U.S. Ships "Frost" and "Huse" of her escort sank a U-Boat (*U488 : Oblt.z.S. Bruno Studt was sunk on 26 April*) to the westward of Cape Verde Islands. (*These sinking are still somewhat confusing and difficult to identify. Further study is necessary before positive identifications can be made.*)

98

Few opportunities for Land-based Aircraft

Land-based aircraft had a poor month. On the 17th the Canadian-manned Canso aircraft S/162 made an almost certain kill 295 miles south-west of Reykjanes. Of the 20 other attacks made only one is considered to have shown much promise of success. This was an attack on the 28th by a Leigh-light Wellington, W/612, made by moonlight, as a result of which the U-Boat was probably sunk. (*U193 : Oblt.z.S. Ulrich Abel was sunk*)

A U-Boat destroyed by a Norwegian Submarine in Norwegian Waters

An especially gratifying success was that of H.Nor.M. Submarine "Ula," operating very close inshore in the Hangesund area. (*U974 : Oblt.z.S. Heinz Wolff was sunk*)

The submarine, which was on an anti-shipping patrol, sighted the conning-tower of an escorted U-Boat at a range of 400 yards. Despite an alteration of course by the escort after "Ula" had dived to attack, the Norwegian submarine got into an attacking position and fired four torpedoes at a range of 600 yards. It is thought that the second hit. "Ula" was depth-charged by the escort and two other vessels for nearly three hours afterwards.

Destructive Raids on Toulon

Reports of the result of the heavy daylight raid on Toulon on 11th March have now filtered through from prisoners of war. It seems certain that two U-Boats were completely destroyed and two or three others were damaged in varying degrees, while considerable havoc was wrought in the dockyard. Another raid by between 400 and 500 "heavies" was made on 29th April and it seems hardly possible that a raid on this scale can have failed to have caused further damage to U-Boats and the base.

The importance of these raids cannot be over-emphasized. Apart from the elimination of U-Boats, each one of which is sorely needed by the enemy in this theatre where his total U-Boat strength is not likely to be more than 20 boats, the effect on crews, attempting to rest between arduous patrols, must be considerable.

A total of 24 U-Boats were sunk or probably sunk during the month. Of these 24 encounters, ships were responsible for five, carrier-borne aircraft for one, combined ship and carrier-borne aircraft for two, shore-based aircraft for 14, and combined ship and shore-based aircraft for one. A submarine attack completed the total. These figures, taken with those for merchant shipping losses, set forth the measure of our success in June.

Operations in the English Channel and its Western Approaches

"Operation Neptune" — the naval side of the Normandy landings — must have made it clear to the enemy that the Allies had won the Battle of the Atlantic and, after four years, the centre of the U-Boat war shifted from that ocean to the English Channel and its Western Approaches. To those planning the liberation of Europe the potential threat of the U-Boats must have appeared a grave one. The "Schnorkel" gear would enable them to proceed submerged for the whole of the passage from the Biscay ports to the Channel traffic lanes. Other boats would be stationed in the less confined waters off the coast of Cornwall to lie in wait for the "build-up" convoys, which could be expected to come, sooner or later, from Bristol Channel and West Coast ports.

While the main weight of our counter-measures was in the English Channel and its Western Approaches, subsidiary operations of great importance were carried out to the north-eastward of the Shetlands. In both we had considerable success.

The honours must undoubtedly go to Coastal Command. Between "D-Day" (the 6th June) and the 10th June, aircraft made 18 attacks in the Western Channel - Ushant - Bay of Biscay area, sinking two U-Boats for certain and probably destroying four more. Nearly half of the other attacks are regarded as promising. On the 8th, Liberator G/224 achieved a "probably sunk" and a "known sunk" within 20 minutes, and other aircraft scoring kills were Sunderlands S/201 and R/228 on the 7th and Liberators F/120 and K/206 on the 9th and 10th respectively. (*Recent research by Innes McCartney followed by visits to the wrecks would suggest a far greater number of U-boats reached the invasion area than has previously been recorded.*)

These heavy losses forced the enemy to adopt yet more cautious tactics. Between the 10th and 20th the number of sightings and attacks in this area fell off considerably and no kills, by aircraft were recorded. Reconnaissance showed that a U-Boat had entered St. Peter Port, Guernsey, presumably to carry out the charging which, even with the "Schnorkel," it could not do at sea. The approaches to the harbour were mined and an air attack made on it, though with what result is not known.

Successful Operations by Aircraft to the North-Eastwards of the Shetlands

Though aircraft of 19 Group might find this second period unremunerative, it was very different with 18 Group, operating to the north-eastwards of the Shetlands. The record of 162 Squadron R.C.A.F. is brilliant. T/162, which had already achieved a "'probably sunk" on the 3rd June (*U477 : Oblt.z.S. Karl Joachim Jenssen was sunk*), destroyed U715 (*Kptlt. Helmut Rottger*) on the 13th; on the 11th B/162 reported seeing 35 survivors (*from U980 : Hermann Dahms*) in the water after an attack carried out in a position about 140 miles north-north-west of Stadtlandet. The Norwegian Air Force again played its part in these operations in - Norwegian waters, Catalina D/333 reporting the destruction of a U-Boat on the 17th. Forty survivors and wreckage were seen. (*U423 : Oblt.z.S. Klaus Hackländer*)

During this period the enemy lost a fourth U-Boat in this area, though somewhat further to the northward, for on the 15th H.M. Submarine "Satyr" attacked a U-Boat in a position about 160 miles west of the Lofoten Islands, scoring two hits. (*U987 : Oblt.z.S. Hilmar Schreyer was sunk on 5 June*)

In the course of the last ten days of the month extremely foul weather restricted our operations, but none the less three more U-Boats were destroyed in the area to the north-eastward of the Shetlands, two by aircraft of 86 Squadron. In sinking the third, 162 Squadron ended a month of outstanding achievement with an action of the utmost gallantry. P/162 as it ran in to attack, was met by intense flak, which set the starboard ring on fire and put the starboard engine put of action. Despite this the captain controlled the aircraft so skilfully that he defeated a last minute turn by the U-Boat and straddled it forward of the conning-tower. The starboard engine then fell off and it was decided to ditch the aircraft. This was done with great skill and without injury to the crew, the aircraft not sinking for 20 minutes. Unfortunately the crew had to spend 21 hours, most of the time in a single dinghy, before being rescued and three of them died from exposure. The captain of the aircraft, who unhappily did not survive, has, been posthumously awarded the Victoria Cross. (*U1225 : Oblt.z.S. Ernst Sauerberg was sunk*)

The 14th Escort Group destroy a U-Boat under Fire from Shore Batteries

Between the 20th and 30th June, a change came over the operations in the Channel area. More kills were made by surface craft, with or without air co-operation, than in the earlier part of the month. Between the 10th and the 20th there was only one kill by surface craft. This was achieved on the 18th by the 14th Escort Group (H.M.S. "Fame," Senior Officer, and H.M. Ships "Hotspur," "Inconstant," "Icarus" and "Havelock "). At 1005,18 a U-Boat was D/F'd by the Group and, though the signal was weak and the base narrow and estimates of distances in the Channel had already been found unreliable, the position of the enemy was about noon fixed within 10 miles of 49°10'N. 03°10'W. This position — to the westward of Le Plateau des Roches Douvres — was consistent with a U-Boat making passage along the coast and the Group proceeded to the area at full speed. At 1620 "Fame" obtained contact by asdic at 2,300 yards and attacked first with Hedgehog and then with depth-Charges. "Havelock" also dropped depth-charges. "Inconstant" was running in for a Hedgehog attack when one of the U-Boat's crew surfaced in an air bubble. He was picked up by "Fame" and it was learnt from him that the U-Boat had been hit forward by the first Hedgehog attack; he had escaped from the after compartment. Shortly afterwards, a shore battery, probably located near Paimpol (*France*), opened accurate fire and, to counter this novel intrusion into the Group's anti-U-Boat operations, "Fame" ordered "Hotspur," who was carrying out "Observant" with "Icarus," to make smoke. Under cover of this, the ships withdrew to the north-westward, having first satisfied themselves that the U-Boat, which was giving off much oil and air, was lying stone-dead on the bottom in 40 fathoms. (*U767 : Oblt.z.S. Walter Denkleff was sunk*)

The Destruction of "U971" and "U269"
(Oblt.z.S. Walter Zeplien and Oblt.z.S. Georg Uhl)

On the 24th "U971" (*Walter Zeplien*) was destroyed by H.M.C.S. "Haida" and H.M.S. "Eskimo" about 15 miles to the north-westward of Ushant. Prisoners taken from the boat stated that they were newly out from Germany on their first operational patrol.Early next day, the 25th, H.M.S. "Bickerton" (Senior Officer, 5th Escort Group), made contact with a U-Boat — "U 269" (*Georg Uhl*) — to the south-eastward of Start Point, and, after a number of depth-charge attacks, brought her to the surface. The boat was abandoned and a number of survivors picked up. During the afternoon H.M.S. "Goodson," one of the ships in the Group, was hit by a "Gnat" (*from U984 : Heinz Sieder*). The 1st Escort Group (H.M.S. "Affleck," Senior Officer, and H.M. Ships "Balfour," "Bentley," "Garlies," "Gore" and "Capel") was ordered to search. After closing two of the ships of the 5th Escort Group which were searching round the position of the attack, "Affleck" began operations somewhat further to the westward. At 2129 "Balfour" obtained contact by Asdic and "Affleck" made a Hedgehog attack, the target being at 175 ft. and the bombs detonating after nine seconds sinking time. When "Affleck" ran in 20 minutes later, "to disintegrate a smitten enemy" with depth-charges, a rapidly widening patch of very thick oil was seen. After satisfying herself that she was not in contact with the wreck of "Bickerton's" U-Boat — this was later found to be three miles away — she and "Balfour" attacked until there could be little doubt that the U-Boat had been destroyed. A thick fog made it impossible to look for wreckage. (*This was U1191 : Oblt.z.S. Peter Grau, who should not be confused with Peter-Ottmar Grau*)

Finally, on the 29th June, Liberator aircraft L/224 sighted a "Schnorkel" south of Start Point (*Devon, England*). Its attack caused a large oil slick and the Third Escort Group were ordered to close the position. Early on the following morning the ships of the group attacked and reported finding some evidence of destruction on the surface (from *U988 : Oblt.z.S. Erich Dobberstein*).

One promising attack was made during this period by a Polish-manned Wellington of 304 Squadron and another by a U.S.N. Liberator of 103 Squadron, Fortress D/206 and ships of the Ninth Escort Group.

Failure of a Diversionary Enterprise

The enemy's disappointment at his insignificant success in the Channel and its Western Approaches must have been increased by the failure of a diversionary enterprise off the north-west coast of Ireland. Early on the 26th June a U-Boat was reported in a position about 50 miles to the west-north-westward of Blacksod Bay (*County Mayo, Ireland*). A force, of which H.M.S. "Inman" was Senior Officer, was sweeping the area, when at 0755/28 H.M.C.S. "St. Thomas" obtained an H/F D/F bearing inside ground wave. H.M. Ships "Bulldog" and "Awe" were detached to search along the line of bearing and after about two and a half hours made contact by asdic in a position about 75 miles to the northward of the position in which the U-Boat had earlier been reported. "Bulldog" made three Hedgehog attacks and with the third obtained explosions 22 seconds after firing, despite the fact that the U-Boat zig-zagged violently, steaming directly away at about four knots. In the first attack the U-Boat had been at 250 ft., coming to 80 ft. at the time of the second attack. "Bulldog" attacked at 7 knots in both cases and, in the prevailing weather, found it difficult to steer an accurate course. A dummy run after the second attack showed that the U-Boat had gone down 200 ft. and speed was increased to 9 knots, making steering much easier.

No contact was obtained after the third attack, though the 147 sword was tilted to 45°, and it is thought that the U-Boat, after being hit, must have sunk to the bottom in 450 fathoms. Three hours passed before there was anything to show that the attack had been successful. Then, at 1415, a small patch of oil appeared. By 1800 the oil had covered an area of over 3 square miles and it was still welling up when the ships finally left the scene.

"Bulldog" had fitted a sound power asdic intercommunication system which was specially effective between the bridge cabinet and the plot and, in the opinion of her Commanding Officer, had much to do with the ship's success; there was a complete lack of noise and unnecessary repetition of reports during the action. (*U719 : Kptlt. Klaus-Dietrich Steffens was sunk*)

The Atlantic

Our activities in the Atlantic can be briefly recorded. The whole area was very quiet but, despite the calm which prevailed, the United States C.V.E.s found opportunities to add to their long list of successes. All the honours in the Atlantic in June fell to them. Of the three U-Boats which the enemy lost, U.S.S. "Croaten's" Group sank one (*U154 : Oblt.z.S. Gerth Gemeiner*), U.S.S. "Solomon's" Group, operating south of the Equator, sank the second (*U860 : Fregkpt. Paul Büchel*), and the third (*U543 : Kptlt. Hans-Hürgen Hellriegel*) was sent to the bottom by aircraft from U.S.S. "Bogue."

The Mediterranean

After the successes, of last month there was little to report from the Mediterranean. Air and surface sweeps were carried out south of Sardinia in the hope of intercepting two U-Boats withdrawing from the Tyrrhenian Sea but without result.

U.S.N. Blimps, fitted with M.A.D. have arrived at , Port Lyautey and are now carrying out night MA.D. patrols in the Strait of Gibraltar. It is therefore now possible to maintain a continuous patrol by M.A.D. fitted aircraft.

SUCCESSFUL ANTI-U-BOAT OPERATIONS IN THE MEDITERRANEAN

As a result of closely co-ordinated operations by surface craft and aircraft — on two occasions of different nationalities — the enemy lost five U-Boats, two of them commanded by the most experienced and successful captains operating in this area. By means of "Operation Swamp," "U616" (*Siegfried Koitschka*) was sunk on the 17th May, "U960" (*Günther Heinrich*) on the 19th and "U453" (*Dierk Lührs*) on the 21st. The operation was also put into force after the sinking of U.S. "P.C.558" off Palermo on the 9th May, (*by U230 : Paul Siegmann*) but on this occasion it was without result.

Briefly described, "Operation Swamp" aims at covering with aircraft the area in which it is anticipated that a U-Boat can move after it has disclosed its presence; immediately it has done this, strike aircraft are despatched to cover a semi-circular area round the position and surface units are detailed to act as a striking force in co-operation. To prevent the U-Boat from escaping, it is necessary that each part of the area should be swept either visually or by Radar at half-hour intervals.

The Hunting and Destruction of "U616"
(Siegfried Koitschka)

At 0408 on the 14th May, U.S.S. "Bibb," one of the escort of Convoy G.U.S.39, which was then off Cape Tenez, attacked an asdic contact. About 20 minutes later, "U616" broke surface ahead of the convoy. She was engaged by the leading ship of Column 10 and dived, torpedoing two merchant of the convoy. U.S. Ships "Vance," "Bostwick," "Bronstein" and "H.P. Jones," were detached from the escort to hunt, the last-named ship making an attack on a good contact at 1226. At the same time, "Operation Swamp" was put into force. U.S. Ships "Gleaves," "Nields" and "Macomb," who had been making an anti-submarine sweep near Alboran Island, and U.S. Ships "Ellyson," "Hambleton," "Rodman" and "Emmons," who had sailed, from Oran, relieved the ships of the convoy escort at 1400. In case "U 616" should copy "U371's" (*Oblt.z.S. Horst-Arno Fenski*) tactics and steer inshore; arrangements were made for the coastal sweeps by light craft from Algiers and Oran.

The seven destroyers hunted without result throughout the day and into the night. At 2148/14, the U-Boat surfaced to charge her batteries but within a few minutes she was sighted, attacked and forced to dive by Wellington aircraft "X" of 36 Squadron. "Ellyson," then about 25 miles to the southward, was homed to the position and made an attack at 2243, being then unable to regain contact. As a result of these attacks a fuel tank was, damaged causing the U-Boat to leave an oil track 10 miles long

"Operation Swamp" was re-centred on this position and was so effective, that "U 616" had to spend all the 15th submerged.

After dark she surfaced with her batteries very low, but was only allowed two very short charges being first forced to dive by Wellington aircraft H/36 and later, at about 0200/16, by aircraft T/36. The destroyers, operating in two groups to the eastward, reached the position by daylight and were disposed on the assumption that the U-Boat would make for the Spanish coast. Air patrols were also arranged to cover a withdrawal in this direction, The U-Boat captain was, however, so anxious to conserve what little electricity remained in his batteries that he stayed in the same area throughout the 16th.

His endeavours to charge his batteries were as unsuccessful on the third night of the hunt as they had been on the first and second. In his first attempt, at 2220, he was engaged and put down by aircraft A/36. The destroyers and the five other aircraft operating proceeded to the position, ComdesRon 10 with four destroyers, closing from the south-westward, while ComdesDiv 21 with the other three approached from the north-westward. When the U-Boat Captain made his second attempt at about midnight, he was quickly caught by "Macomb's" searchlight and engaged by gunfire. Surprised by the destroyers approaching from two directions, the U-Boat crash-dived and was attacked by "Macomb" and "Gleaves."

It was appreciated that the state of the U-Boat's batteries would probably allow her to spend the 17th submerged, provided she was unmolested, but her Captain was forced to make short bursts of speed to avoid the destroyers attacks. At 0807, an attack with 600 ft. settings by "Hambleton" forced him to surface and scuttle the boat.

Resumption of "Operation Swamp" to Destroy "U960"
(Günther Heinrich)

"Operation Swamp" thus terminated after being in force' for more than 75 hours. Four hours later, at 1250/17, -"Ellyson," on passage to Oran with survivors from "U616" was missed astern by three torpedoes and it was restarted. U.S. Ships "Woolsey," "Benson," "Madison," "Niblack" and "Ludlow" sailed from Oran and began, in poor asdic conditions, an expanding box search which was without result.

During the night the Wellington aircraft covering the most easterly area was forced to return due to instrument failure. The U-Boat found the gap and made, off to the north-eastward on the surface. She had got outside the "Swamp" area and might possibly have escaped altogether, had not a relief aircraft (M/36), on its way to one of the northern areas, chanced upon her. On the Wellington's report being received "Swamp" was re-centred on the position of the sighting.

Asdic conditions were still poor and, during the 18th, the hunting destroyers could make no contacts. As it was appreciated that the U-Boat was probably attempting to pass eastward of the Balearic Islands and so reach Toulon, the destroyers were, after dusk, disposed in two groups, one ahead and one astern of the position in which it was estimated that she would surface after dark.

The U-Boat did not; however, make so far to the Northward as was expected, being reported by Wellington U/36 at 2228/18 in a position about 28 miles south of the estimated surfacing position. Alter being put down by the aircraft, the U-Boat made some headway towards the north-east and then surfaced again at about 0130/19, only to be sighted and put down for the second time by U/36. "Niblack" and "Ludlow," who formed the nearer of the two groups, had been ordered to close after the first sighting by U/36, and, on reaching the area, began a search. The "Swamp" pattern had meanwhile been re-centred and the more distant group ("Woolsey," "Benson" and "Madison") ordered to join from the north-east.

At 0240/19 aircraft reported an A.S.V. contact 10 miles ahead of "Niblack" and dropped markers. "Ludlow" closed, obtained contact by Radar and asdic and made an attack with depth-charges. "U960" had by now been hunted for over 36 hours but it took another four hours of depth-charge attacks by "Niblack" and "Ludlow" before she was finally beaten. At 0708 she broke surface at a steep angle. She was engaged by gunfire by the destroyers and attacked by aircraft V/500 with depth-charges; men were seen in the water but the U-Boat had not apparently been abandoned and it seemed as though she was attempting to dive. "Niblack" therefore delivered another depth-charge attack which brought the action to an end. Twenty prisoners were taken and from them it was learned that the U-Boat had only recently passed through the Strait of Gibraltar.

The Conduct of the Operations

Both these operations were controlled from Area Combined Headquarters at Algiers, a. tactical plotting board in the Combined War Room being used to co-ordinate the forces engaged. When a sighting by aircraft had been reported, a forecast could be made of the time at which ships would arrive at the position and aircraft could be instructed to illuminate and carry out homing procedure accordingly. Each A.S.V. contact was assessed at Headquarters and ships informed whether it need be investigated or not. To enable aircraft to know what ships to expect in their respective areas, Senior Officers of surface forces were instructed to report, every four hours, their positions and intention to Control, which briefed air crews accordingly.

The Senior Officer of the ships hunting "U616" (*Siegfried Koitschka*) carried a Signals officer of the Royal Air Force and his services in expediting air/sea intercommunication were so valuable that it is intended in future to embark a Signals officer or N.C.O. in ships of a hunting group.

The Sinking of "U453" (Oblt.z.S. Dierk Lührs)

In the hunt of "U453," in which Italian units took part, there were not sufficient aircraft for a full "Swamp" operation. At 1755 on the 19th May, Convoy H.A.43 was attacked when off Punto Stilo and had one ship torpedoed. (*Fort Missanabi, 7147GRT by U453*) Italian Ships "Urania" and "Danaide" made contact by asdic and attacked and then searched in company with I.S. "Monzambano." Aircraft, some, of them Italian, were sent from Malta and Taranto, H.M. Ships "Termagant" and "Tenacious" were diverted from the Strait of Otranto and H.M.S. "Liddesdale" sailed from Malta. The three ships reached the area at about 1030/20 and, after about an hour's search, obtained asdic contact in a position about 12 miles from where the Italian ships were still searching. Between 1250 and 2040 the destroyers made 11 attacks, including one "creeper." After 2040 contact was held continuously until 0024/21 when the U-Boat surfaced and was destroyed by gunfire. There were 52 survivors from this boat, which was based on Pola.

H/F D/F IN "OPERATION NEPTUNE"

The operations against U-Boats in the English Channel have set a new problem in obtaining H/F D/F bearings of their transmissions.

It was appreciated that the W/T aspect of these operations would not follow the classic lines of the pack attack and that transmissions from U-Boats would be few. It was all the more important to obtain accurate "fixes" of any transmissions made.

The large number of escorts operating provided an H/F D/F system of considerable extent and great potential value, as support for the shore H/F D/F stations. The escorts were therefore instructed to report all bearings on the operational U-Boat frequency, in the hope that these would add materially to the intelligence available from shore stations.

Some of the ships' H/F D/F staffs evidently interpreted this instruction in the light of their experience in the Atlantic and confined reports to those transmissions which they estimated as originating in their vicinity. Another novel factor was introduced by the U-Boats apparently transmitting when submerged, using a small and inefficient aerial. This had two results so far as H/F D/F was concerned. The weak signal resulted in poor bearings from Shore Stations; it also caused ships to estimate that the transmitter was distant, with the result that they did not forward their own bearings.

The present situation is that ships are reporting all bearings, using a rapid communications system arranged for this purpose. The effect on the general H/F D/F situation has been appreciable.

An additional shore D/F station is being erected on Bolt Head (*Devon, England, to the south of Salcombe*) in an attempt to improve the shore station cover in the Channel.

August 1944

A total of 13 U-Boats were sunk or probably sunk during the month. In addition, there were four promising attacks, of which further information is awaited and which it is hoped will prove to be kills. Of these encounters, ships were responsible for seven, shore-based aircraft for three, combined ship and shore-based aircraft for four, and carrier-borne aircraft for three.

Patrol of the Second Escort Group — The First Squid Kill

The patrol of the Second Escort Group between the 3rd and the 13th August was in the nature of a graceful compliment to its first Senior Officer, for it made history by achieving the first destruction of a U-Boat with Squid and took part in the sinking of two others. The kill with Squid was remarkably quick. H.M.S. "Loch Killin" sighted a periscope on her starboard bow, and then heard the U-Boat pass down her starboard side. Reducing speed, she altered course under full starboard wheel and obtained asdic contact at 600 yards range. She slowed down from 7 to 6 knots, but even so there was only just enough time to obtain a clear 147B depth — 80 feet — before the pattern of six Squid charges was fired. Almost simultaneously with the detonation of the pattern, a counter-mined "Gnat" exploded 20 yards on the port side abreast the pom-pom. This prevented "Loch Killin" from altering course to avoid the pattern and the U-boat broke surface at a steep angle heading in the direction of the port beam.

"Loch Killin" went full astern and then stopped her engines, but the U-Boat continued to surface, fouling her hull abreast the bridge, and eventually came to rest apparently caught up in the port "A" bracket. A few rounds of Oerlikon were fired, but the conning-tower and armament were already a mass of wreckage and all that the U-Boat's crew seemed anxious to do was to clamber on to the frigate's quarter deck. The U-Boat then took on a steeper trim and, after hanging for about 5 minutes, sank almost vertically by the stern. "Loch Killin" hastily cleared the position in case the boat blew up, but fortunately she did not and, after she had sunk to the bottom, was finished off with 20 depth-charges from "Starling."

Survivors were under the impression that they had been rammed. At the time of the attack the U-Boat, which was apparently altering under full starboard wheel, was on a course of 090 degrees. The effect of the Squid pattern may be judged by the fact that she surfaced with her bows pointing 340 degrees. She was "U736," a 500-ton boat, (*commanded by Oblt.z.S. Reinhard Reff*).

The second U-Boat destroyed was "U608," (*Oblt.z.S. Wolfgang Reisener*) which was sunk on the 9th August. Liberator aircraft C53 reported a U-Boat on the surface 25 miles to the northward of the group, and they proceeded to the position, streaming C.A.T. gear when 5 miles from it. By the time that they reached it, the U-Boat had been attacked by the aircraft and had disappeared, leaving oil and wreckage. The ships swept the area but could not make contact and, appreciating that the U-Boat was lying on the bottom, "Starling" resumed patrol with H.M. Ships "Loch Fada" and "Dominica," leaving H.M. Ships "Wren" and "Loch Killin" to continue the search. Eventually the latter obtained an echo sounder trace and attacked an object detected on the bottom with depth-charges. This was about 2200. About six hours later, "Wren," following up a Radar contact, which had disappeared, came upon a U-Boat's crew in the water.

At 2057 on the following night, "U385" (*Hans-Guido Valentiner*) surfaced about 9,600 yards ahead of the group. The ships opened fire and closed at full speed with their C.A.T. gear streamed. The U-Boat turned away, fired a recognition signal and then dived, giving off a cloud of black smoke as she did so. The group searched the position and found nothing but "non-subs." Six hours later, at about 0300/11, Sunderland aircraft A/461, RA.A.F., reported that it was attacking a surfaced U-Boat 10 miles to the westward of them, and began to home the ships to the position. They found that the line of approach was taking them down the path of a very bright moon and therefore divided, proceeding at 18 knots and with C.A.T gear streamed 2-3 miles on either side of the aircraft's markers until they were 10 miles beyond it. They then reformed, recovered their C.A.T. gear and swept back at 7 knots. At 0600, the Sunderland reached her limit of endurance and left the scene. Half an hour later the U-Boat surfaced 3,000 yards ahead of the ships and lay stopped, bows on. She was abandoned under fire and sank five minutes later. The U-Boat Captain was among the survivors and told the Senior Officer of the group that he had given up the fight "after being chased all night." The ships had, in fact, twice swept over him, but, owing to bad conditions, none of them had obtained a genuine asdic contact. The same conditions had prevailed in the search for "U385 "on the previous day.

The ships were supplied with C.A.T. gear before starting on this patrol and found it highly satisfactory, though they did not test it with a "Gnat." It was considered that, though the gear made a great deal of noise, asdic efficiency was hardly reduced at all for the short period of approaching a definite contact.

Operations in the Mediterranean

The outstanding event of the month has been Operation "Dragoon" — the landing of the liberating armies in the South of France. It will be recalled that, during the spring of 1944, considerable U-Boat reinforcements entered the Mediterranean and it then appeared that a concentration which might be beyond our resources to combat was accumulating. In May, however, a swift run of five sinkings, followed in June and July by some effective air attacks on Toulon, seem to have occasioned a change of policy on the part of the enemy, who must have appreciated that the Allies would sooner or later land on the Riviera coast. He apparently decided to husband such U-Boats as were still effective for a final offensive effort against the liberating forces; no U-Boats seem to have operated from Toulon since the third week in June, though some may have been engaged in landing agents in Corsica.

A heavy air attack on Toulon on 6th August is known to have caused considerable damage to U-Boats and immediately before "D" Day it was estimated that not more than three boats could be assumed to be operational. (*U471 : Kptlt. Friedrich Kloevekorn, U952 : Kptlt. Oskar Curio and U969 : Oblt.z.S. Max Dobbert were destroyed.*)

In the event, however, the landings seem to have found the U-boats still out of action and, apart from a number of unsubstantiated reports, there were no U-boat incidents. U.S.S. "Ericsson" reported capturing a U-Boat crew of four officers and 46 men, who were attempting to escape in a fishing vessel to the westward of Marseilles. But for the wearing-down process of the previous three months, a landing so close to the U-boats' base might have produced a very different reaction.

September 1944

A total of nine U-Boats were sunk or probably sunk during the month. In addition there were three promising attacks of which further information is awaited and which it is hoped will prove to be kills. Of these twelve encounters, ships were responsible for four, shore-based aircraft for five, and carrier-borne aircraft and a submarine each for one. The total is completed by a joint kill by carrier-borne aircraft and surface craft in the Arctic.

The North Western Approaches

Taking advantage of their Channel experience in the use of Schnorkel, a number of U-Boats from the force which had been driven out of the Bay ports appear to have been diverted to carry out a preliminary inshore offensive round the United Kingdom. Activity flared up in the North Western Approaches early in the month when five ships, including H.M.S. "Hurst Castle," were torpedoed and sunk between 30th August and 8th September. (*Fjordheim by U482 : Hartmut Graf von Matuschka; Livingston by U541 : Kurt Petersen; Empire Heritage, Pinto and Hurst by U482*) and Intensive air and surface patrols resulted in a U-Boat* being sunk by H.M.S. "Porchester Castle" while acting in support of Convoy ONF252 about 120 miles west-north-west of Tory Island on 9th September. Two days later a promising attack was made by H.M.C.S. "Hespeler" after a Schnorkel had been sighted off Malin Head. From then onwards, thanks to a big air and surface effort, we gained the upper hand and the enemy did not succeed in making any further-attacks. (**There are still some question marks about the identification of this U-boat.*)

The North Russian Convoys

Convoy screening dispositions were employed to secure the safety of both R.A.59A and the corresponding eastbound J.W.59. No U-Boat was able to approach within striking distance of them. The dispositions adopted made provision for a reasonable strength of close anti-submarine escort and allowed for the remainder of the surface escorts and all the anti-submarine air escort to be operated from the Convoy horizon out to a maximum depth of 90 miles. In addition to providing for the safety of the convoy this policy of defence in depth produced many opportunities for attacking U-Boats.

Anti-U-Boat Operations

The follow-up on air sightings was most satisfactory. Striking forces, comprised of part of the anti-submarine escort, being stationed in suitable positions 20 to 25 miles from the convoy in the most likely direction of the enemy according to H/F D/F indications. The passage of Convoy J.W.60 adds one more to the list of successful operations in Arctic waters, and it is probable that at least one U-Boat was destroyed by a combined attack by carrier-borne aircraft and surface craft.

Operations in the Indian Ocean and in the Atlantic

On the 23rd September "U859" (*Kptlt. Johann Jebsen*) was sunk by H.M. Submarine "Trenchant" as the U-Boat was about to enter Penang at the end of her first patrol. She had left Kiel at the end of May and claimed a number of sinkings, the last of them a merchantman off Mombassa on the 5th September. On the 28th another U-Kreuzer (*U863 : Kptlt. Dietrich von der Esch*) was destroyed by United States Liberator aircraft about 700 miles west-southwest of Ascension Island. It is not yet known whether the boat was outward bound to the Indian Ocean or was returning to Europe.

There were only two other likely kills in the whole of the Atlantic. The first was the result of a hunt spread over three days by two U.S.N. Task Groups, which included U.S. Ships "Bogue" and "Core," operating in an area 300 to 400 miles south-west of Cape Race (*Newfoundland, to the south of St. John's*); the other was an attack made by Fortress J/220 to the north-westward of the Azores, which brought oil and some canisters to the surface. (*Bogue sank U1229 : Kptlt. Armin Zinke with a 'secret' agent, who was due to be landed in the United States, on board*)

"U 247" (Oblt.z.S. Gerhard Matschulat) sunk at the Entrance to the English Channel

This U-Boat was destroyed off Wolf Rock as a result of the persistence of ships of the 9th Escort Group, particularly H.M.C.S. "St. John." On the afternoon of the 31st August, a sweep produced a contact which was promising but difficult to hold. H.M.C. Ships "Swansea" and "St. John" attacked, obtained little evidence of success and then lost contact. A sweep regained it, more attacks were carried out and finally — nearly 20 hours after the first contact had been made — depth-charges dropped by "St. John" brought up satisfactory evidence of a kill in the shape of large quantities of oil, a mass of wreckage and a number of papers. It is hoped to analyse these operations at an early date.

Operations in the Mediterranean

During September two out of the three U-Boats based at Salamis were destroyed. On the 15th and 24th, U.S. Liberators bombed the harbour and, in the second attack, one U-Boat was hit and sunk. (*U596 : Oblt.z.S. Hubertus Korndorfer*) The second was destroyed while patrolling near Crete. At 1700 on the 18th September, O.R.P. "Garland," operating independently south of Milos, sighted exhaust from a Schnorkel at a range of no less than 8 miles. She was able to close to within 200 yards before the U-Boat dived, probably, it is thought, because the smoke from the Schnorkel which had betrayed its presence also blinded its periscope. "Garland" attacked with hedgehog and then lost contact. H.M.S. "Troubridge" (D.24) and H.M. Ships "Terpsichore," "Brecon" and "Zetland" joined, and depth-charge attacks were made by "Troubridge" at 1842 and 2235 and by "Terpsichore" at 2322. Contact was then held until 0438/19 when the-U-Boat surfaced and abandoned ship. She was "U407." (*Oblt.z.S. Hans Kolbus*)

The remaining U-Boat based on Salamis has shown no signs of activity.

In the western part of the Mediterranean F.S. "Forbin" and U.S.S. "Madison" had an encounter with midget U-Boats off Villefranche on the 26th. One is known to have been sunk and another probably destroyed by "Forbin."

110

The general clearance of the U-Boats and enemy aircraft from the Mediterranean has enabled the number of ships employed in convoy escort to be reduced. Groups have been reduced to two ships and their most important duty has become the shepherding of merchantmen through minefields. A large number of independent sailings has been arranged and the monthly number of ships convoyed has fallen to below 1,000.

M.A.D. Practices in the Strait of Gibraltar
(*Magnetic Airborne Detector*)

Two M.A.D. fences were established, one patrolled by Catalina aircraft and the other by Blimps. One of our submarines made passages at depths of 50, 100 and 150 ft. and at speeds varying between 2 and 5 knots and between 5 and 8 knots. Of the 12 passages at the lower speeds, the Catalinas detected 11, but they were not so successful during seven more runs when the submarine was proceeding between 5 and 8 knots.

The Blimps were extremely effective, as they detected 13 out of 14 crossings of their fence.

October 1944

Only four U-Boats were sunk during October and two probably sunk. (*A total of twelve were lost*) Of these six attacks carrier-borne aircraft were responsible for two, and H.M.C.S. "Annan" and H.Neth.M. Submarine "Zwaardvisch" for one each. "U993" (*Oblt.z.S. Karl-Heinz Steinmetz*) was sunk in the bombing raid on Bergen when a second U Boat was probably sunk. In addition there were four promising attacks, one by Bomber Command aircraft, one by U.S.S. "Mission Bay's" group and two by ships. Three U-Boats were damaged to an unknown extent by shore-based aircraft.

These were disappointing results for a month in which great efforts were made to find and kill the comparatively few U-Boats which were at sea. Aircraft patrolled the probable routes to and from the Norwegian bases and along the coast of Norway; air and surface forces consistently covered the focal areas in the waters surrounding the United Kingdom and a large scale bombing raid was carried out on Bergen, one of the main U-Boat bases in Norway.

The reasons for our difficulty in finding the enemy, apart from the extreme caution shown by him were: first the Schnorkel, the fitting of which has provided the enemy with means of avoiding our air patrols by remaining submerged for prolonged periods and lying in wait for our convoys in focal areas inshore; secondly, his bottoming tactics in inshore waters where wrecks and "non-sub" contacts abound and where the high reverberation background tends to drown weak echoes and, thirdly, the necessity for our use of anti-Gnat devices which make asdic detection more difficult. New anti-Gnat devices which lessen asdic interference are being prepared, intensive training for escorts is being undertaken and a method of marking of wrecks is being investigated.

The Destruction of "U1006" (*Oblt.z.S. Horst Voigt*)

Apart from a promising attack on the 25th by the 31st Escort Group operating about 250 miles west of the Scilly Isles, the only success achieved by ships operating in the vicinity of the United Kingdom fell to H.M.C.S. "Annan," of the 6th Escort Group (H.M.C.S. "New Waterford," Senior Officer), who destroyed "U1006" on the night of the 16th, 60 miles east-south-east of Munken Rocks, while carrying out a "Gamma" patrol. Many whales had previously been encountered and, after one deliberate attack and searching for half-an-hour, "Annan" lost contact and proceeded to the patrol line. Subsequently the U-Boat surfaced and was hunted by Radar, illuminated and engaged again by "Annan." After a brief gun and depth-charge action, the U-Boat was abandoned and sank. Forty-six survivors were picked up.

Operations in the Atlantic and Arctic

With probably not more than a dozen U-Boats operating in the Atlantic north of the Equator, little could be expected, but two U.S.N. Task Groups — U.S.S. "Tripoli's" Group on the 3rd, in a position about 600 miles south-west of Cape Verde Islands and U.S.S. "Mission Bay's" Group on the 4th, about 200 miles further north — found opportunities for attacks which are regarded as promising, the former's U-Boat being probably destroyed. One U-Boat was bold enough to attack Convoy O.N.S.33 when it was about 600 miles to the westward of Cape Clear. H.M.C.S. "Chebogue," the Senior Officer of the Escort, was torpedoed, (*By U1227 : Friedrich Altmeier*) but managed to reach harbour in tow. This attack was followed up by U.S.S. "Card" and led to a promising attack on the 12th. (*The boat escaped as none appear to have been lost.*)

As has been the case in recent months, the enemy's main effort was directed against the North Russian convoy, but though W/T traffic indicated the presence of a strong force of U-Boats, J.W.61 arrived at Murmansk without loss.

A Dutch Submarine's successful Patrol in the Java Sea

On 6th October, H.Neth.M. Submarine "Zwaardvisch," in the course of a very successful patrol in the Java Sea, torpedoed and sank a German U-Boat in a position about 90 miles north-west of Sourabaya. Twenty-seven survivors were picked up. This is by far the most easterly position in which a German U-Boat has ever been destroyed. (*U168 : Kptlt. Helmut Pich*)

OPERATION "NEPTUNE"
(*Naval Operations connected with the Normandy Landings*)

The Strength of the Enemy

It is pleasing to reflect that, if the enemy had done as we expected him to do, his achievements and our losses would probably have been much greater than they actually were. Grand Admiral Dönitz must have felt that he had a strong hand. He could guess the date of the landings fairly accurately and he had ample U-Boats in readiness. He could not ask for a better target than the dense mass of shipping in the cross-Channel area; if he failed to guess the right day and the first wave of the liberating armies got ashore, there were the almost equally important build-up convoys to attack; if he found the cross-Channel area too strongly guarded, he had the whole of the route from Trevose Head to the Start by which the convoys from the Liverpool - Bristol Channel area must come. He had a choice of routes by which to send his U-Boats — they could either go up the centre of the Channel or along the coast of Brittany, where they would be safe under the guns of the coastal batteries and the fighters of the German Air Force. Having served in the U-Boat arm in the last war, Dönitz would probably have a fair knowledge of the advantages and disadvantages of operating in the English Channel.

The German, though lacking in understanding of sea power, has a keen appreciation of air power, and he had experienced its effectiveness in the Mediterranean. In June, 1944, he had a new device in the Schnorkel which, by largely neutralizing our immense air power, made possible the U-Boat operations against "Neptune" shipping.

A curious feature of the "Neptune" operations is that they began normally with a large number of contacts and a most satisfactory number of attacks by aircraft and then, after about 10 days, the contacts by aircraft suddenly fell off, and, owing to the Schnorkel, have remained disappointingly low ever since. Possibly the U-Boat captains had not taken very kindly to the gear, with all the discomforts that it was capable of causing in inexperienced hands, and only intended to use it as a last resource, if the weight of air power against them became intolerable. It apparently took them about a week to appreciate the value of the Schnorkel —and to learn how to use it efficiently.

Our Counter-measures

Apart from walling off the cross-Channel area and guarding the convoy routes leading to it, our plan was to make the approaches to both a difficult and exhausting operation. If the enemy reacted forcefully to the landings, there would probably be heavy losses in shipping and, we hoped, a great slaughter of U-Boats, particularly if the enemy tried to force his way up the centre of the Channel. It was, however, considered that the enemy would use the safer route up the French coast. In the last week of May the 14th Escort Group made two patrols in this area and, when its presence was apparently ignored, it was hoped that we should be able to operate surface forces closer than had been at first thought practicable. In the event, the air threat to our forces after D-Day was decisively countered. The enemy in fact made only a few serious bombing attacks on our surface forces. Coastal Command had prepared for this and a force of enemy aircraft which attempted an attack was annihilated by Mosquitoes. The enemy then lost heart.

Anti-U-Boat Operations

The North Cornish coast had always been regarded as a dangerous area and from time to time had been heavily patrolled. Two months after D-Day the enemy attacked a convoy off Trevose Head and sank one merchantman (Ezra Weston sunk by U667 (*Karl-Heinz Lange*) and H.M.C.S. "Regina," (*also sunk by U667*) the first ships to be lost by U-Boat in Plymouth Command since D-Day.

In the last weeks of August the battle moved south of Ushant, but before Operation "Neptune" could be said to have ended one more kill was made — off Wolf Rock by H.M.C. Ships "Swansea" and "St. John" on the 1st September. (*U247 : Oblt.z.S. Gerhard Matschulat*)

A/S RESULTS DURING INSHORE OPERATIONS (OPERATION "NEPTUNE")

Difficulties

A/S operations since D-Day have shown that the U-Boat which operates inshore with caution is a difficult target for the asdic to detect. It is more than likely that the enemy evolved his successful Anti-asdic tactics owing to the circumstances which forced him to bottom in the Channel area the West-going tidal stream when proceeding to take up patrol positions in the dense shipping area between, the Isle of Wight and the Bay of the Seine. The interference to our asdic searches caused by the large number of wrecks inside the Fifty fathom line, and also the heavy reverberation background which increases as soundings get less, proved of great assistance to the enemy. Tidal variations layering added to our difficulties of identifying, and at times even of detecting, a bottomed U-Boat. However, in spite of all these difficulties, we succeeded in preventing the U-Boats doing us serious harm in the Channel area and its approaches during the U-Boat offensive which opened after 6th June, 1944.

Results

In the area of the English Channel, its approaches and the Bay of Biscay from 6th June to 1st September a total of 32 U-Boats were sunk or probably sunk. Surface craft and shore based aircraft in joint action against the enemy succeeded in disposing of five U-Boats, one being sunk and one probably sunk in June and two being sunk and one probably sunk in August.

Surface craft alone detected by asdic and sank a total of sixteen U-Boats, four of these being initially located on the bottom. Two U-Boats were sunk and one probably sunk by ships in June, four sunk and two probably sunk in July, and five sunk and two probably sunk in August. Shore-based aircraft, in addition to the combined action with surface craft mentioned above, disposed of eleven U-Boats, two being sunk and five probably sunk in June and one being sunk and another probably sunk in each of the two following months. It is notable that of the eleven aircraft successes seven were achieved in the first twelve days from D-Day. It was only at the end of this period that the first surface craft success occurred, when H.M.S. "Fame" sank "U767" (Oblt.z.S. Walter Dankleff) under the guns Paimpol (west of Dinard, *France*) on 18th June. These figures bear out the view that the enemy had intended to operate his U-Boats in the Channel, accepting all risks, and proceeding on the surface in order to press on and reach the vital invasion area. It was due to the initial blows dealt him by Coastal Command in the early days of the Operation that he was forced to adopt the more cautious tactics of remaining continuously submerged, which the advent of Schnorkel gave him the means of doing.

After the first two weeks of Operation "Neptune" the results in kills obtained by aircraft were meagre due, of course, to the extremely difficult and intermittent Radar target presented by the Schnorkel. However, the influence of air power remained throughout the operations and resulted in the U-Boats not daring to use their mobility by proceeding on the surface by night or in low visibility.

Analysis

The outstanding feature of the analysis of surface craft U-Boat hunts was the difficulty in the initial detection of a U-Boat which adopts anti-asdic tactics when escort vessels are heard approaching. Numerous wrecks, together with difficult water conditions and a high reverberations background which occurs in shallow waters, did, in a large number of cases, give the U-Boat immunity from the asdic, according to reports of Prisoners of War. Once, however, the asdic picked up U-Boat contact and identified it as such the chance of success proved to be very much higher than it has been in the past. The percentage chance of obtaining a kill on an asdic contact classified "submarine" during Operation "Neptune" rose to fifty-three per cent as against the figure of ten cent which was recorded in the first three months of 1943. An added complication was introduced by the threat of the Gnat, which necessitated the use of counter-measures unfavourable to the requirements of asdic detection.

Conclusion

The conclusion reached from the experience of anti-U-Boat operations in the area the English Channel and the South Western Approaches thereto from D-Day to 1st September is that if a means can be found of preventing the U-Boat from lying on the bottom, and preferably forcing it to operate comparatively near the surface, much better asdic results will be obtained. The use of deep minefields for this purpose, laid on the convoy lanes and running out to the Fifty fathom line, should prove effective in countering the cautious "Schnorkeller" which has presented us with one of the most difficult U-boat problems of the war.

December 1944

During December three German U-Boats were sunk and three probably sunk. There were in addition five promising attacks. One of the three U-Boats which the enemy lost was "U1209" (*Oblt.z.S. Ewald Hülsenbeck*) which, on the 18th, grounded on the Wolf Rock and subsequently foundered. Another was "U877" (*Kptlt. Eberhard Findeisen*) which was destroyed on the 27th in mid-Atlantic by H.M.C.S. "St. Thomas," who was escorting Convoy H.X.327. The third (*U735 : Oblt.z.S. Joachim Borner*) was sunk as the result of a bombing raid on Horten (*Norway*) on the 28th. During the passage of Convoy R.A.62 two U-Boats were probably sunk and two other attacks, made by aircraft of 813 Squadron, are regarded as promising. A report has also been received of a U-Boat being rammed and depth-charged by U.S.S.R. destroyers in the vicinity of Kola at the beginning of the month.

Operations in United Kingdom Waters

A promising attack was made on the 6th December on (*U297 : Oblt.z.S. Wolfgang Aldegarmann was sunk*) by an aircraft of Coastal Command after H.M.S. "Bullen" had been torpedoed and sunk (*by U775 : Erich Taschenmacher*) while operating with the 19th Escort Group off Cape Wrath (*Sutherland, NW Scotland*). About one-and-a-half hours after the frigate had been hit, H.M.S. "Loch Inch" made contact and she and H.M.S. "Goodall" carried out attacks which brought wood and oil to the surface. Aircraft were ordered to search the area and during the afternoon of the 6th, Sunderland Y/201 sighted a patch of white smoke and a long narrow wake. In its first attack the depth-charges hung up, but with its second the aircraft straddled the wake and afterwards observed a large patch of oil.

The phase in the U-Boat war which had begun after the close of "Neptune" lasted until the middle of December. For three months the enemy had cautiously operated round the United Kingdom, protected from attack by the Schnorkel and by the difficult asdic conditions, prevalent in inshore waters. The escort groups, though deprived of the satisfaction of destroying U-Boats, could congratulate themselves that their continuous patrols of focal areas had effectively protected our shipping.

Operations in the Western Atlantic

On the other side of the Atlantic the enemy continued his operations off the North American seaboard. On the 5th, after a merchantman (*Cornwallis, 5458GRT*) had been sunk in the Gulf of Maine (*by U1230 : Hans Hilbig on 3rd*), U.S.S. "Bogue's" Group made several attacks on a firm contact about 60 miles south-south-west of Cape Sable, but a detailed report of the operations has not yet been received. As in the English Channel, activity increased in the last ten days of the month. On the 21st a merchantman (*Samtucky, 7219GRT*) was torpedoed (*by U806 : Klaus Hornbostel*) within 20 miles of Halifax and three days later H.M.C.S. "Clayoquot" was sunk (*also by U806*) in the same area, two other ships reporting torpedo explosions astern on the same day. On the 25th December a promising attack was made by an aircraft of 11 Squadron, R.C.A.F., which attacked a periscope off Halifax and reported oil and wreckage.

Operations in Other Areas

Early on the 20th a U-Boat was attacked by an aircraft of 220 Squadron in a position about 360 miles north-east of San Miguel, Azores, apparently without inflicting any serious damage as an L.S.T. (*LST 359*) and U.S.S. "Fogg" were torpedoed (*by U870 : Ernst Hechler*) in the vicinity later that day. From later reports it is thought that this U-Boat was on its way to patrol in the Western Approaches to the Strait of Gibraltar.

In the Indian Ocean there was a fair amount of activity. On the night of the 3rd December, a Liberator aircraft sighted and attacked a surfaced U-Boat in the Bay of Bengal, but without success. H.M. Submarine "Thule" fired three torpedoes at a Japanese U-Boat thirty miles south-west of Penang on the 28th December, and one hit amidships was observed.

General Remarks

The brisk ten days with which the year ended gave the enemy the greatest success which he had enjoyed since the spring of 1943, and it will, no doubt, have an appreciable effect on the morale of the enemy captains. U-Boat war depends on individuals and, if a dozen captains thought that they could expect even half as good a rate of exchange — eight ships for no loss — as was achieved in the English Channel in the last ten days of December, the U-Boat arm might easily be restored to something of its former power.

January 1945

During January two German U-boats were sunk, one was probably sunk and a fourth encounter is regarded as extremely promising. The U-Boat probably sunk fell to U.S.S. "Otter," operating with a U.S.N. Task Group in mid-Atlantic; according to the information available, wreckage and human remains were picked up. (*U248 : Oblt.z.S. Johann Loos was sunk*) The other three incidents all took place in United Kingdom coastal waters — two of them (*U1051 : Oblt.z.S. Heinrich von Hollben and U1172 : Oblt.z.S. Jürgen Kuhlmann*) in the Irish Sea and the other (*U1199 : Kptlt. Rolf Nollmann*) off Land's End (*Cornwall*). In addition to these successes which were achieved in the latter part of the month; by overrunning East Prussia they threatened important working-up bases in the eastern Baltic and by entering Silesia they paralysed part of the elaborate organisation for the construction of the new type of U-boats.

February 1945

During February ten German U-Boats were sunk or probably sunk. In addition there were four promising attacks, which it is hoped will prove to be kills when finally assessed. All but three of these successes were achieved by ships; of the other kills H.M. Submarine "Venturer" probably destroyed a U-Boat in Norwegian waters. (*U864 : Korvkpt. Ralf-Reimar Wolfram was sunk*) A U-Boat was possibly mined in Oslo Fjord after a sortie by Bomber Command aircraft and a third boat may have sunk as a result of a promising attack by a Polish-manned aircraft of 304 Squadron in the Rockall area.

The Tenth Escort Group's Successful Patrol

These figures are the best since last August and show that the improvement in the rate of killing U-Boats which occurred in the last ten days of January was no mere flash in the pan. Operations continued to be mainly in United Kingdom waters but there was a shift of activity to the northward, the Tenth Escort Group in particular carrying out a very successful patrol in the area between the Shetlands and the Faeroes against U-Boats on passage to their operational areas. On 3rd February E.G.10, which consists of H.M. Ships "Braithwaite" (Senior Officer), "Bayntun," " Loch Eck" and "Loch Dunvegan" made an attack about 45 miles north-west of Muckle Flugga (*Shetland Isles*), which is regarded as promising; a large quantity of oil was sighted and the air bottle of a torpedo was picked up. (*U1279 : Oblt.z.S. Hans Falke was sunk*) Eleven days later the Group attacked with Squid and Hedgehog an asdic contact obtained in the same area and about 3.5 hours after the action had begun two Germans were picked up. Both died shortly after being rescued, but it was learnt that one of them was the Captain of the U-boat

— "U989." (*Kptlt. Hardo Rodler von Roithberg*) The third action, which occurred three days later about ten miles from the position in which "U989" was sunk, resulted in large quantities of oil coming to the surface as well as a rubber dinghy and an inflated rubber-ball covered with green canvas.

Two Kills in Irish Waters

Late on the 4th February, H.M.S. "Loch Scavaig," who was later joined by H.M. Ships "Nyasaland" and "Papua" (E.G.23), obtained contact by asdic with an object lying on the bottom off Lough Foyle (Ireland). (*U1014 : Oblt.z.S. Wolfgang Glaser*) Breaking into the working-up exercise period on which they were engaged, the ships attacked and eventually returned to harbour with clothing, paper and other wreckage of undoubted German origin.

All these kills were the result of asdic detection of submerged U-Boats. In the last ten days of the month there were five occasions on which a U-Boat was destroyed after it had disclosed its presence. At 1155 on the 20th February, H.M.S. "Vervain," rear escort of Convoy H.X.337, was torpedoed about 20 miles south of Waterford (*by U1276 : Karl-Heinz Wendt*). Five minutes later H.M. Ships "Amethyst" and "Peacock," of the Twenty-second Escort Group which was in support, made contact by asdic and their attacks on the U-Boat eventually produced wreckage which included its navigator's notebook and some German seaboots. (*There is still some confusion about which U-boat was actually sunk*) (H.M.S. "Vervain" shared with H.M.S. "Clematis" the record for Atlantic crossings, having made the passage 32 times in just under two years.)

Gibraltar Area

The improvement in the results of our anti-U-Boat operations extended to the Gibraltar area, where the boat on patrol in January had had things rather too much its own way. In contrast to the sinkings in United Kingdom waters which have produced very few prisoners, the majority of the crew of "U300" (*Oblt.z.S. Fritz Hein*) were picked up when she was destroyed near Cape St. Vincent on the 22nd February. On a patrol made last autumn " U300" spent 61 out of 65 days at Schnorkel depth but none the less succeeded in torpedoing off Iceland two of the four merchantmen which we lost during November. (*Godafoss, Shirvan and Empire Wold appear to have lost, but the last mentioned probably succumbed to the atrocious weather.*) She left Trondheim on her third and last, patrol on the 20th January and, proceeding at Schnorkel depth between the Faeroes and Shetlands and then westward of the Hebrides and Ireland reached the Scilly Isles, where her captain surfaced to send a signal requesting permission to make for the Strait of Gibraltar.

Control eventually agreed but not before "U300" had had to surface six times in order to pick up the signal — evidence of one of the disadvantages of the Schnorkel — and course was then shaped for Cape Finisterre. After hugging the coast, the U-Boat surfaced to take a bearing on the old convent that stands on the tip of Cape St. Vincent. Having been informed that a convoy from the United States was due to enter the Strait of Gibraltar, the U-Boat closed the route that it was likely to take and, finding it eight miles south-west of Tarifa, attacked and with four torpedoes hit two merchantmen. (*Michael J. Stone and Regent Lion*) The escort took offensive action and damaged the U-Boat, causing a leak in the bows and fracturing an oil tank. "U300" proceeded to Tangier Bay where the hole, temporarily closed with a wooden plug and bacon fat, was repaired by welding, and then crossed the Straits proceeding to the area between Cadiz and Cape St. Vincent, where she lay on the bottom.

On the 22nd February the U-Boat came to Schnorkel depth for W/T reception and sighted one of the escort of a convoy of L.S.T.s. She fired a" Gnat "torpedo which missed owing to the ship stopping. A second attack was intended but the U-Boat's captain sighted another ship of the escort and, considering the position hopeless, gave orders to surface and abandon ship. This was done under fire from H.M. Ships "Pincher" and "Recruit," who picked up 41 survivors.

North Russian Waters

The enemy found his inshore operations against North Russian convoys more profitable than those carried out in the open sea during recent months. Convoy J.W. 64 reached the approaches to Kola Inlet without loss on the 13th February — though attacked on passage by aircraft — but H.M.S. "Denbigh Castle" was then torpedoed and sunk (*by U992 : Hans Falke*). On the next day two ships in the White Sea portion of the return convoy were torpedoed off Kola Inlet but managed to reach harbour. (*Horace Grey was hit by U711 : Hans-Günther Lang; Norfjell and Thomas Scott by U968 : Otto Westphalen*) On the 17th H.M. Ships "Lark" and "Alnwick Castle," who were patrolling off Kildin Island before Convoy R.A. 64 sailed, sank a U-Boat (*U425 : Kptlt. Heinz Bentzien*) and recovered one German survivor — he was particularly welcome as the U-Boat had fired the current Russian recognition signal as it surfaced just before its final disappearance. Later "Lark" was herself torpedoed (*by U968*) but was able to reach harbour in tow. A torpedoed merchantman also got in but the third vessel hit — H.M.S. "Bluebell" — blew up and sank with heavy casualties. (*U711*) The convoy suffered no more losses by U-Boat but, becoming disorganized as a result of a series of gales, had a straggler sunk by aircraft attack. The anti-submarine dispositions of defence in depth on the lines of the Red, White and Blue scheme again proved satisfactory in frustrating air attacks as well as deterring U-Boats from getting to grips and delivering a pack attack.

Bombing Operations

Bremen, Hamburg and Horten in Oslo Fjord were attacked during February. Eight Mosquito raids were made on Bremen between the nights of 17th/18th and 27th/28th, and on the 24th 200 aircraft of the 8th U.S.A.A.F. attacked, the Deschimag Yards. As a result of these raids, a big floating dock containing one, or possibly two, Type XXI boats was sunk and damage was done to two U-Boats on the slips as well as to buildings and workshops.

The result of the attack on the Blohm and Voss yards at Hamburg, made by 166 aircraft of the 8th U.S.A.A.F., is not yet known.

The dockyard at Horten, of great importance to the enemy now that Danzig is threatened by the Red Army, was practically destroyed on the night of 23rd/24th by 83 aircraft of Bomber Command.

Both Bomber Command and the 8th U.S.A.A.F. made successful attacks on bases in Holland, where the enemy has built concrete shelters for his midget U-Boats.

Attacks on the organization for the construction of Type XXI U-Boats were continued. Factories at Duisburg and Essen making components were bombed, and canals connecting the Ruhr with the assembly yards were also successfully attacked.

Conclusion

The fact that many of the incidents referred to in this review of the month's operations were the result of detection by the asdic makes manifest its effectiveness in inshore waters now that more experience has been gained. Last month the three kills made in United Kingdom waters followed on the U-Boat being detected by asdics after it bad disclosed its presence by an attack. In February three U-Boats paid the same penalty for such boldness, but double that number were detected and killed while proceeding submerged or lying on the bottom. In view of the anticipated expansion by the enemy of what is already a considerable effort, these successes come at a crucial time to give to our forces renewed confidence in their ability to sap the still increasing boldness of German captains, who have so often seen initial success turned into failure or disaster by the essential soundness of our tactics and devices.

March - May 1945

During March ten German U-Boats were sunk or probably sunk and, in addition, there were six attacks which, it is hoped, will prove to be kills when finally assessed. Shore-based aircraft had a better month than in February, when only one promising attack was made; two Liberators of Coastal Command may have obtained kills, B/86 near the Orkneys on the 20th March (*U905 Oblt.z.S. Bernard Schwarting was lost*), and M/120 in the North Channel on the 22nd, while an aircraft of 103 Squadron, U.S.N. ensured the destruction of "U681" (*Oblt.z.S. Werner Gebauer*) and the capture of her crew to the westward of the Bishop Rock on the 11th.

A U-Boat is considered to have been destroyed in a mine-field off Beachy Head (*Sussex*), wreckage being obtained when the Tenth Escort Group investigated an oil patch and attacked a bottomed contact in this area on the 11th.

Rate of Exchange at First in the Enemy's Favour

There was a considerable increase in the number of anti-submarine attacks carried out in the Western Atlantic but the main centre of activity continued to be in United Kingdom coastal waters and off South-West Iceland. In the first ten days of the month the rate of exchange was in the enemy's favour. We had merchantmen torpedoed or sunk in the Irish Sea, in St. George's Channel and off Beachy Head (*Sussex, England*); all were in convoy and in each case the U-Boat escaped detection. As regards warships, we lost a minesweeper off Aberdeen and a trawler off Reykjavik. In the same period, apart from a promising attack by H.M.S. "Bulldog" in the Wolf Rock area, we could only claim a single but notable success. This was the probable sinking of a U-Boat off the North Pembrokeshire coast on the 7th March by ships of the Twenty-fifth Escort Group (H.M.C. Ships "Strathadam" (Senior Officer), "La Hulloise," and "Thetford Mines." "La Hulloise" obtained contact, first by asdic and then, at a range of 200 yards, by radar, and switched on her searchlight in time to sight the Schnorkel and periscope of a diving U-boat. The three ships made a number of hedgehog and depth-charge attacks producing a large quantity of diesel oil and wreckage which indicated that the boat was "U1302." (*Kptlt. Wolfgang Herwatz*)

The Concluding Episode in the U-Boat War

This concluding episode in the U-Boat war actually started with a most skilfully executed attack on the 9th April by Mosquito aircraft of 143, 235, 248 and 333 Squadrons. Making full use of the sun, they took two U-Boats completely by surprise and overwhelmed them with accurate R.P. fire before they could take effective avoiding action. The leading boat attempted to dive after attacks by aircraft of 143 and 235 Squadrons, but was so damaged that it had to surface. Attacked then by aircraft of 248 Squadron, it blew up. The second U-Boat was shattered by R.P. and cannon fire and foundered amid oil and wreckage. (*U804 : Oblt.z.S. Herbert Meyer, U1065 : Oblt.z.S. Johann Panitz and U843 : Kptlt. Oskar Herwatz.*)

The same squadrons attacked again ten days later. Sighting three U-Boats escorted by a minesweeper, they sank one (*U251 : Oblt.z.S. Franz Sack*) and severely damaged the others.

In the first week of May operations in this area came to their climax and in six days there were 13 successful or promising attacks. Coastal Command Liberators were in at the death. It was strange but pleasurable to read of aircraft from such squadrons as 86, 206 and the Czech-manned 311, which had achieved such great things in the Battle of the Atlantic, attacking in such unfamiliar positions as "18 miles south of the Skaw" (Shetland Isles) and "15 miles northeast of Arnholt Light."

THE SURRENDER OF THE GERMAN U-BOAT FLEET

On the 4th May, 1945, a short signal with time of origin 1614/4 was transmitted on all U-frequencies. It was learnt next day that by this signal Grand-Admiral Dönitz had ordered his U-Boats to cease hostilities and return to base. In an Order of the Day issued at the same time, he explained that a crushing superiority had compressed the U-Boats into a very narrow area and that the continuation of the struggle was impossible from the bases which remained. Not without justice, he paid tribute to the tenacity shown by his men who were now laying down their arms "after a heroic fight which knows no equal."

The capitulation was signed at Rheims during the night of the 6th/7th May. By a signal timed 1200B/8, the Admiralty announced that the German High Command had been directed to give surrender orders to U-Boats at sea. The U-Boats were to surface, report in plain language their position and number and proceed by fixed routes to certain designated ports or anchorages. The first U-Boat to comply was "U249," (*Oblt.z.S. Rudolf Lindschau*) which surfaced off the Lizard at 0922B/9. H.M. Ships "Magpie" and "Amethyst" escorted her in. At 1100B/10 the formalities of surrender were completed at Portland — an appropriate place as being the earliest home of the Anti-Submarine School.

Up to the 31st May, 49 U-Boats had surrendered at sea, leaving about a, dozen unaccounted for. Failure to comply with the surrender orders is likely to be due to the fact that the Allies have over-run all the German high power transmitters which alone can reach submerged U-boats.

Index

Spellings and terms have not been
standardised nor modified, but kept
as they appeared in the original text.

124

Depth charges; 10, 17, 24, 33, 38, 44, 51, 65, 86, 88, 92, 93, 101, 121
Depth predictor Type 147B; 87, 88, 93, 107
Destroyers, Home Fleet; 5
Dispersion of convoy routeing; 13
Diversionary Enterprise; 102
Dönitz, Admiral Karl; (Not always named also called Admiral U-boats); 37, 41, 42, 48, 51, 55, 113, 121
Dover Mine Barrage; 4
Dragoon, Operation; 108
Dummy starshell battle; 33
Dutch Submarines; 8, 112
Dutch West Indies; 53, 58
East Coast Barrage; 4, 8
East Coast Routes; 16
East London; 60
East Prussia; 117
Eighth Army; 54
English Channel; 100, 102, 106, 110, 114
Escort carrier(s); 60, 62, 70, 78, 97
  See also CVE
Escort Group also see Support Group
Escort Group B2; 59, 64
Escort Group:-
— B3; 73
— B6; 76, 88
— B7; 63
— C1; 88
— C2; 73, 75
—, 10th; 86, 87, 90, 117, 120
—, 14th; 101, 113
—, 19th; 116
—, 1st; 92, 102
—, 20th; 46, 48
—, 22nd; 118
—, 23rd; 118
—, 25th; 120
—, 2nd; 67, 68, 69, 78, 79, 95, 97, 107
—, 31st; 112
—, 36th; 34
—, 3rd; 62, 102
—, 40th; 78
—, 42nd; 43
—, 4th; 63, 77, 78
—, 5th; 64, 78, 92, 102
—, 6th; 83, 88, 112
—, 7th; 78, 88, 98
—, 9th; 74, 98, 110
Escort, Ocean; 64
Evacuation duties; 7
Evasive routeing; 16, 34
Evasive tactics; 97
Faeroe Islands; 49, 62, 68
FFC = Free French Corvette included with HMS
Fighter aircraft; 28
Fire from shore batteries; 101
Flares; 90, 91
Fleet Air Arm; 9, 11, 33, 91
Focke-Wulf aircraft; 15, 22, 25, 28, 33, 35, 61, 67
Foxer; 75
Freetown; 19,20, 30, 41, 48, 55, 65
French Guiana; 49
General Chase signal; 69
Genuine neutral; 37
German Air Force; 51
Gibraltar; 25, 28, 30, 31, 33, 45, 49, 53, 55, 61, 68, 72, 73, 79, 81, 85, 116, 118
Glider bombs; 78, 79
Gnat (Acoustic torpedo – T5); 80
Greek destroyers see HMS
Greenland; 28, 55, 59
Grounding of aircraft; 51
Guadalcanal; 54
Guernsey; 100
Gulf of Aden; 79

Gulf of Mexico; 48
Gulf of Oman; 77
Gulf of St. Lawrence; 45
Gunfire from U-boat; 70
Gunfire; 38, 54, 104
H/F (High Frequency); 66
H/F D/F (High Frequency Direction Finder); 40, 42, 43, 44, 45, 50, 54, 55, 57, 58, 59, 60, 63, 64, 69, 73, 76, 86, 96, 97, 102, 106, 109
Haifa; 43
Half Raspberry see Raspberry
Halifax; 20, 116
Hampton Roads; 68
Hangesund; 99
Harbour Defence Asdics; 4
Harrying effect; 9
Hedgehog; 40, 44, 62, 65, 74, 78, 83, 86, 92, 93, 94, 97, 101, 102, 110, 117, 121
HHMS (Greek) Pindos; 72
High Power transmitters; 121
Hjalfiord / Hjalfjord; 17, 19, 23
HM Submarine E54; 36
— Graph; 48
— P34; 36
— Sahib; 54
— Satyr; 101
— Seawolf; 36
— Tally-Ho; 90
— Thorn; 35
— Thule; 116
— Trenchant; 110
— Truculent; 68
— Tuna; 62
— Turbulent; 39
— Unbeaten; 35
— Upholder; 35, 36
— Venturer; 117
HM Submarines; 36
HMAS Ipswich; 89
— Launceston; 89
HMCS Algoma; 36
— Amherst; 56
— Annan; 111, 112
— Assiniboine; 42, 88
— Bactouche; 31
— Bayntun; 83
— Camrose; 83
HMCS Chambly; 28, 74
— Chaudiere; 93, 94
— Chilliwack; 93
— Clayoquot; 116
— Collingwood; 56
— Drumheller; 73
— Edmundston; 83
— Fennel; 93
— Gatineau; 73, 93
— Georgian; 45
— Haida; 102
— Hespeler; 109
— Huron; 84
— Kamloops; 73, 75
— La Hulloise; 120
— Levis; 28
— Lunenburg; 83
— Moosejaw; 28
— Morden; 74
— New Waterford; 112
— Oakville; 42
— Ottawa; 45
— Owen Sound; 94
— Port Arthur; 54
— Prince Rupert; 95
— Regina; 114
— Restigouche; 56, 57
— Sackville; 74
— Sherbrooke; 56

Any readers wishing to contribute further annotations please contact the editor. Details at the front of this book.

MILITARY PRESS
List of Publications

1 GALLAGHER CLOSE, MILTON KEYNES BUCKINGHAMSHIRE, ENGLAND MK8 0LQ
TELEPHONE 01908 265095   E-MAIL:- militarypress@btopenworld.com

BLETCHLEY ARCHIVE SERIES
Available in cased [£25.00]
and softback [£15.00] editions
Volume 1: The Secret War of Hut 3 edited by John Jackson
Volume 2: Ultra's Arctic War by John Jackson
- - - - - -
Volume 3: Official History of British Signals Intelligence 1914-1945 Volume I
(1914 – February 1942) by Frank Birch: Edited by John Jackson
Available in cased [£32.99] and softback [£19.99] editions

INDIAN ARMY AND INDIAN MILITARY HISTORY

VALOUR & GALLANTRY: H.E.I.C. & INDIAN ARMY VICTORIA CROSSES AND GEORGE CROSSES 1856-1945
by Chris Kempton -
Available in cased [£45.00] and softback [£25.00] editions

INDIAN CAMPAIGNS
Available in cased [£25.99] and softback [£12.99] editions
SITANA   by Colonel [later General Sir] John Adye RA
SIKKIM   by Colonel John Cox Gawler

THE ARMIES OF THE INDIAN PRINCELY STATES
by Richard Head and Tony McClenaghan
Available in softback edition [£19.99]
THE ARMIES OF THE INDIAN PRINCELY STATES: Volume 1
THE ARMIES OF THE INDIAN PRINCELY STATES: Volume 2: Patiala
THE ARMIES OF THE INDIAN PRINCELY STATES: Volume 3: Gwalior
THE ARMIES OF THE INDIAN PRINCELY STATES: Volume 4: Sappers & Miners:
    Part 1
THE ARMIES OF THE INDIAN PRINCELY STATES: Volume 5: Sappers & Miners
    :Part 2
THE ARMIES OF THE INDIAN PRINCELY STATES: Volume 6: Bikaner Army

BUTTONS OF THE INDIAN ARMY
by Lt.Colonel N Poulsom
Available in softback editions [£19.99]
Volume 1. Cavalry
Volume 2. Bengal Army Infantry
Volume 3. Punjab Frontier Force, Madras Army Infantry, Hyderabad Infantry
Volume 4. Bombay Army Infantry, Gurkha Infantry
Volume 5. Arms and Services
Volume 6. Comprehensive Index covering Sections 1-5, Summary of Battle Honours awarded
    to each Regiment to 1914, and summaries of the post 1922   Amalgamations.
Volume 7. Additions and amendments, also with Battle Honours 1914-1945.

THE CAMPAIGNS AND MEDALS OF THE HONOURABLE EAST INDIA COMPANY AND THE INDIAN ARMY
by A G Stone OBE :
THE VICTORIA CROSS AND GEORGE CROSS RECIPIENTS OF THE HONOURABLE EAST INDIAN COMPANY AND INDIAN ARMY
by Chris Kempton -
Available in cased [£22.99] and softback [£12.99] editions

"LOYALTY & HONOUR" THE INDIAN ARMY
September 1939 - August 1947
By Chris Kempton
Available in cased [£32.99] and softback [£19.99] editions
Volume I. Divisions
Volume II. Brigades
Volume III. Higher Formations, Deployment, Forces & Columns

UNITED STATES MILITARY HISTORY

UNITED STATES ARMY GROUND FORCES IN WORLD WAR II: TABLES OF ORGANIZATION AND EQUIPMENT IN WORLD WAR II
by J J Hays
Available in cased [£32.99] and softback [£19.99] editions
Volume 1 : The Infantry Division: Part I
Volume 1 : The Infantry Division: Part II
Volume 1 : The Infantry Division: Part III

Volume 2 : The Armored Division: Part I
Volume 2 : The Armored Division: Part II
Volume 3 : The Airborne Division : Part I
Volume 3 : The Airborne Division : Part.II

CROSSFIRE: A CIVIL WAR ANTHOLOGY.
by the American Civil War Round Table [U.K.] Branch
Available in cased [£29.99] and softback [£17..99] editions

BRITISH ARMY

THE TACTICAL EMPLOYMENT OF MACHINE GUNS AND TANKS IN
THE FIRST WORLD WAR - cased [£24.99] and softback editions [£12.99]
INSTRUCTIONS FOR THE TRAINING OF DIVISIONS FOR OFFENSIVE
ACTION 1916/INSTRUCTIONS FOR THE TRAINING OF PLATOONS FOR
OFFENSIVE ACTION 1917 - Available in cased [£24.99] and softback editions
[£12.99]
DRIVER'S HANDBOOK FOR EXCELSIOR 98cc "WELBIKE" - Available in
softback edition only [£5.99]
REGIMENTS OF THE BRITISH ARMY 1939-1945 [ARTILLERY] by M Bellis -
cased edition only [£19.99]
KAFIR WAR OF 1834-1835 by C Andrews - Available in cased edition [£19.99] -
softback edition [£9.99]
BATTLES AND BATTLEFIELDS OF THE ANGLO-BOER WAR 1899-1902 by
Anthony Baker - Available in cased edition [£35.00] - softback edition [£19.99]
A GAZETTEER OF THE SECOND-ANGLO BOER WAR 1899-1902 by H & M
Jones - Available in cased edition [£45.00] - softback edition [£25.00]
THE BOER ARMY : 1899-1902: A MILITARY HANDBOOK: The Organisation,
Experiences and Methods of the Boer Army by A D Jones
Available in cased edition [£25.99] - softback edition [£12.99]

A GENEALOGY OF THE REGIMENTS OF THE BRITISH ARMY SERIES by
Anthony Baker - Available in cased [£32.99] and softback [£19.99] editions
Volume 1: CAVALRY
Volume 2: YEOMANRY
Volume 3: INFANTRY (Part 1)
Volume 4: INFANTRY (Part 2)
Volume 5: INFANTRY (Part 3)
Volume 6: INFANTRY (Part 4)
Volume 7: INFANTRY (Part 5)
Volume 8: INFANTRY (Part 6)

FRENCH MILITARY HISTORY

FRENCH ARMY 1939-1940
ORGANISATION : ORDER OF BATTLE : OPERATIONAL HISTORY
by L Sharp
Available in cased [£32.99] and softback [£19.99] editions
Volume 1 : High Command, Military Districts, Army Group, Army, Army Detachment, Army Corps,
    Motorised & Cavalry Corps, Armoured Group &c
Volume 2 : Divisions inc Motorised, Infantry , Mountain , Foreign , Colonial , North African , Light,
    Cavalry, Light, Light Mechanised and Armoured &c
Volume 3 : Maginot Line Formations: Tables of Organisation Infantry, Cavalry & Tanks
Volume 4: [in preparation]

GERMAN MILITARY HISTORY

GERMAN WORLD WAR II ORGANIZATIONAL SERIES
by Leo W G Niehorster
Available in cased [27.99] and softback [15.99] editions
4/II - June 1942 GHQ Units & Waffen SS Formations
1/I- September 1939 Mechanized Army Formations & Waffen SS Formations (3rd Revised
    Edition) [in preparation]
1/III - October 19.39 Higher Headquarters, Mechanized GHQ Unit, Static Units [in
    preparation]
2/I- October 1940 Mechanized Army Formations and Waffen-SS Formations (2nd Revised
    Edition)[in preparation]
5/I- July 43 Mechanized Army Formations [in preparation]

NAZI COUNTER-INSURGENCY POLICY AND METHODS
by Dr P Blood Available in cased [£27.50] and softback [£17.99] editions
Volume 1 : German Security Doctrine 1814-1945   [Winter 2004]
Volume 2: Staatschutzkorps - The SS and the German Police [Winter 2004]
Volume 3 : Bandenbekämpfung-January-August 1942 [Spring 2005]

GERMAN ARMY
BLITZ ASSAULT : THROUGH FIRE AND WATER- COMBAT ENGINEERS IN ACTION -
Available in cased edition only [£16.99]
THE GERMAN ARMY 1940: AN ORDER OF BATTLE - Available in cased [£32.99] and
softback [£19.99] editions

THE GERMAN ARMY 1939-1945
Available in cased [£32.99] and softback [£19.99] editions
GERMAN ARMY 1939-1945: VOLUME II : Army Groups, Armies, Army Task Forces and
Army Detachments [revised edition in preparation]
GERMAN ARMY 1939-1945: VOLUME III : Panzer Armies & Groups, Mountain, Parachute &
SS Armies, Infantry Corps (Part 1)
GERMAN ARMY 1939-1945: VOLUME IV : Infantry Corps (Part 2), Motorised Corps,
Armoured Corps, Mountain Corps
GERMAN ARMY 1939-1945: VOLUME V : Corps - Cavalry, Named, Groups, Reserve Corps,
Higher Commands, Luftwaffe Field, Luftwaffe Flak (Mobile), Parachute, Waffen SS, and Fortresses
GERMAN ARMY 1939-1945: VOLUME VI : DIVISIONS (part 1)
GERMAN ARMY 1939-1945: VOLUME VII : DIVISIONS (part 2)
GERMAN ARMY 1939-1945: VOLUME VIII : DIVISIONS (part 3)
GERMAN ARMY 1939-1945: VOLUME IX : DIVISIONS (part 4)[in preparation]

PANZER DIVISIONS - PANZER GRENADIER DIVISIONS - PANZER BRIGADES-
by J Dugdale- Available in cased [£32.99] and softback [£19.99] editions

PANZER DIVISIONS - PANZER GRENADIER DIVISIONS - PANZER BRIGADES - of the
Army and the Waffen SS in the West -utumn 1944 - February 1945 - Ardennes and Nordwind -
Their Detailed and Precise Strengths - Volume I [Part 1] September 1944 Refitting and Re-
equipment
PANZER DIVISIONS - PANZER GRENADIER DIVISIONS - PANZER BRIGADES - of the
Army and the Waffen SS in the West-Autumn 1944 - February 1945 - Ardennes and Nordwind -
Their Detailed and Precise Strengths Volume I [Part 2] October 1944 Refitting and Re-equipment
PANZER DIVISIONS - PANZER GRENADIER DIVISIONS - PANZER BRIGADES - of the
Army and the Waffen SS in the West-Autumn 1944 - February 1945 - Ardennes and Nordwind -
Their Detailed and Precise Strengths Volume I [Part 3] November 1944 Refitting and Re-
equipment .
PANZER DIVISIONS - PANZER GRENADIER DIVISIONS - PANZER BRIGADES - of the
Army and the Waffen SS in the West-Autumn 1944 - February 1945 - Ardennes and Nordwind -
Their Detailed and Precise Strengths Volume I [Part 4 A]
PANZER DIVISIONS - PANZER GRENADIER DIVISIONS - PANZER BRIGADES - of the
Army and the Waffen SS in the West-Autumn 1944 - February 1945 - Ardennes and Nordwind -
Their Detailed and Precise Strengths Volume I [Part 4 B]

DECORATIONS OF THE THIRD REICH SERIES
by D Lyne-Gordon
Available in cased [£32.99] and softback [£19.99] editions
KNIGHT'S CROSS: GERMAN AND AXIS ARMED FORCES: Volume I
KNIGHT'S CROSS: GERMAN AND AXIS ARMED FORCES: Volume II
KNIGHT'S CROSS: GERMAN AND AXIS ARMED FORCES: Volume III
KNIGHT'S CROSS: GERMAN AND AXIS ARMED FORCES: Volume IV
KNIGHT'S CROSS: GERMAN AND AXIS ARMED FORCES: Volume V
KNIGHT'S CROSS: GERMAN AND AXIS ARMED FORCES: Volume VI
KNIGHT'S CROSS: GERMAN AND AXIS ARMED FORCES: Volume VII
KNIGHT'S CROSS: GERMAN AND AXIS ARMED FORCES: Volume VIII
KNIGHT'S CROSS: GERMAN AND AXIS ARMED FORCES: Volume IX
KNIGHT'S CROSS: GERMAN AND AXIS ARMED FORCES: Volume X

KNIGHT'S CROSS: GERMAN AND AXIS ARMED FORCES: Volume X1[in preparation]
AND YET YOU HAVE CONQUERED: Notable Recipients of the Blood Order: Volume I
AND YET YOU HAVE CONQUERED: Notable Recipients of the Blood Order: Volume II
KNIGHT'S CROSS OF THE WAR SERVICE CROSS: Volume I
KNIGHT'S CROSS OF THE WAR SERVICE CROSS: Volume II
HITLER'S POLITICAL GENERALS: THE GAULEITERS. Volume I
HITLER'S POLITICAL GENERALS: THE GAULEITERS: Volume II

INSURGENCY AND COUNTER-INSURGENCY

FRANCO'S MOROCCAN DIARY Available in cased [£27.50] and softback [£17.50
editions [publication Winter 2004]
ANTI-PARTISAN WARFARE IN THE BALKANS 1941-1945 - Available in cased
[£25.99] and softback [£12.99] editions
THE OTHER SIDE OF THE MOUNTAIN: Mujahideen Tactics in the Soviet-
Afghan War: Volume I
Available in cased [£32.99] and softback [£19.99] editions
THE OTHER SIDE OF THE MOUNTAIN: Mujahideen Tactics in the Soviet-
Afghan War: Volume II
Available in cased [£32.99] and softback [£19.99] editions
THE OTHER SIDE OF THE MOUNTAIN: Mujahideen Tactics in the Soviet-
Afghan War: Volume III
Available in cased [£32.99] and softback [£19.99] editions
**RUSSIAN & SOVIET COUNTER-INSURGENCY WARFARE IN THE
CAUCAUCUS, CENTRAL ASIA & AFGHANISTAN**
Available in cased [£32.99] and softback [£19.99] editions

WARFARE IN THE FAR EAST
Available in cased [£32.99] and softback [£19.99] editions
JAPAN'S BATTLE FOR OKINAWA

U-BOAT ARCHIVE SERIES
Available in cased [£25.00] and softback [£15.00] editions
Volume 1: WHAT BRITAIN KNEW AND WANTED TO KNOW ABOUT U-BOATS
Volume 2 : WEAPONS USED AGAINST U-BOATS
Volume 3 : THE BRITISH MONTHLY COUNTER MEASURES REVIEWS
Volume 4 : THE BRITISH MONTHLY U-BOAT OFFENSIVE REVIEWS
Volume 5 : EXTRACTS FROM THE STRATEGIC BOMBING SURVEY OF THE GERMAN
        U- BOAT INDUSTRY
Volume 6 : FROM THE EARLY U-BOAT ARCHIVE JOURNALS [publication Spring 2005]

SUBMARINE WARFARE SERIES
U-570 - H.M.S. GRAPH: THE TECHNICAL REPORT Available in cased [£27.50] and
softback [£15..00] editions [publication Winter 2004]

Manuscripts and proposals that are appropriate for publication are welcome
Summer 2004 - Details and prices subject to alteration without notice

Full details of our publications will be found on our web page militarypress.co.uk
Alternatively we will send you a catalogue of our publications on request